WEST
WITH THE
NIGHT

BERYL MARKHAM

NORTH POINT PRESS
FARRAR, STRAUS AND GIROUX
NEW YORK

For
MY FATHER

North Point Press
A division of Farrar, Straus and Giroux
18 West 18th Street, New York 10011

Copyright © 1942, 1983 by Beryl Markham
All rights reserved
Distributed in Canada by Douglas & McIntyre Ltd.
Printed in the United States of America
Reprinted by arrangement with the author
and with the Houghton Mifflin Company, Boston

Library of Congress catalog card number: 82-062789
ISBN-13: 978-0-86547-118-4
ISBN-10: 0-86547-118-5

www.fsgbooks.com

46 48 50 51 49 47

I wish to express my gratitude
to Raoul Schumacher for his constant encouragement
and his assistance in the preparations
for this book.

I speak of Africa and golden joys

HENRY IV, Act V, Sc. 3

Contents

Contents

BOOK ONE

I

Message from Nungwe

How is it possible to bring order out of memory? I should like to begin at the beginning, patiently, like a weaver at his loom. I should like to say, 'This is the place to start; there can be no other.'

But there are a hundred places to start for there are a hundred names — Mwanza, Serengetti, Nungwe, Molo, Nakuru. There are easily a hundred names, and I can begin best by choosing one of them — not because it is first nor of any importance in a wildly adventurous sense, but because here it happens to be, turned uppermost in my logbook. After all, I am no weaver. Weavers create. This is remembrance — revisitation; and names are keys that open corridors no longer fresh in the mind, but nonetheless familiar in the heart.

So the name shall be Nungwe — as good as any other — entered like this in the log, lending reality, if not order, to memory:

> DATE — 16/6/35
> TYPE AIRCRAFT — Avro Avian
> MARKINGS — VP — KAN
> JOURNEY — Nairobi to Nungwe
> TIME — 3 hrs. 40 mins.

After that comes, PILOT: Self; and REMARKS — of which there were none.

But there might have been.

3

Nungwe may be dead and forgotten now. It was barely alive when I went there in 1935. It lay west and south of Nairobi on the southernmost rim of Lake Victoria Nyanza, no more than a starveling outpost of grubby huts, and that only because a weary and discouraged prospector one day saw a speck of gold clinging to the mud on the heel of his boot. He lifted the speck with the tip of his hunting knife and stared at it until it grew in his imagination from a tiny, rusty grain to a nugget, and from a nugget to a fabulous stake.

His name eludes the memory, but he was not a secretive man. In a little while Nungwe, which had been no more than a word, was both a Mecca and a mirage, so that other adventurers like himself discounted the burning heat of the country, the malaria, the blackwater, the utter lack of communications except by foot through forest trails, and went there with shovels and picks and quinine and tinned food and high hopes, and began to dig.

I never knew what their digging got them, if it got them anything, because, when I set my small biplane down on the narrow runway they had hacked out of the bush, it was night and there were fires of oil-soaked rags burning in bent chunks of tin to guide my landing.

There's not much to be seen in light like that — some dark upturned faces impassive and patient, half-raised arms beckoning, the shadow of a dog slouching between the flares. I remember these things and the men who greeted me at Nungwe. But I took off again after dawn without learning anything about the success of their operations or the wealth of their mine.

It wasn't that they meant to keep those things concealed; it was just that they had other things to think about that night, and none of them had to do with gold.

I had been working out of Nairobi as a free-lance pilot with the Muthaiga Country Club as my headquarters. Even in nineteen-thirty-five it wasn't easy to get a plane in East Africa and it was almost impossible to get very far across country without one. There were roads, of course, leading in a dozen directions out of Nairobi. They started out boldly enough, but grew narrow and rough after a few miles and dwindled into the rock-studded hills, or lost themselves in a morass of red muram mud or black cotton soil, in the flat country and the valleys. On a map they look sturdy and incapable of deceit, but to have ventured from Nairobi south toward Machakos or Magadi in anything less formidable than a moderately powered John Deere tractor was optimistic to the point of sheer whimsey, and the road to the Anglo-Egyptian Sudan, north and west through Naivasha, called 'practicable' in the dry season, had, when I last used it after a mild rain, an adhesive quality equal to that of the most prized black treacle.

This minor defect, coupled with the fact that thousands of miles of papyrus swamp and deep desert lie between Naivasha and Khartoum, had been almost flippantly overlooked by a Government road commission which had caused the erection, near Naivasha, of an impressive and beautiful signpost reading:

To JUBA — KHARTOUM — CAIRO —

I have never known whether this questionable encouragement to the casual traveller was only the result of well-meant wishful thinking or whether some official cursed with a depraved and sadistic humour had found an outlet for it after years of repression in a muggy Nairobi office. In any case, there the sign stood, like a beacon, daring all and sundry to proceed (not even with caution) toward what was almost sure to be neither Khartoum nor Cairo, but a Slough of Despond more tangible than, but at least as hopeless as Mr. Bunyan's.

This was, of course, an exception. The more travelled roads were good and often paved for a short distance, but once the pavement ended, an aeroplane, if one were at hand, could save hours of weary toil behind the wheel of a lurching car — provided the driver were skilful enough to keep it lurching at all. My plane, though only a two-seater, was busy most of the time in spite of competition from the then barely budding East African — not to say the full-blown Wilson — Airways.

Nairobi itself was busy and growing — gateway to a still new country, a big country, an almost unknown country. In less than thirty years the town had sprung from a collection of corrugated iron shacks serving the spindly Uganda Railway to a sprawling welter of British, Boers, Indians, Somalis, Abyssinians, natives from all over Africa and a dozen other places.

Today its Indian Bazaar alone covers several acres; its hotels, its government offices, its race-course, and its churches are imposing evidence that modern times and methods have at last caught up with East Africa. But the core of it is still raw and hardly softened at all by the weighty hand of British officialdom. Business goes on, banks flourish, automobiles purr importantly up and down Government Road, and shop-girls and clerks think, act, and live about as they do in any modern settlement of thirty-odd thousand in any country anywhere.

The town lies snugly against the Athi Plains at the foot of the rolling Kikuyu Hills, looking north to Mount Kenya and south to Kilimanjaro in Tanganyika. It is a counting house in the wilderness — a place of shillings and pounds and land sales and trade, extraordinary successes and extraordinary failures. Its shops sell whatever you need to buy. Farms and coffee plantations surround it for more than a hundred miles and goods trains and lorries supply its markets with produce daily.

But what is a hundred miles in a country so big?

Beyond are villages still sleeping in the forests, on the great reservations — villages peopled with human beings only vaguely aware that the even course of their racial life may somehow be endangered by the persistent and irresistible pressure of the White man.

But white men's wars are fought on the edges of Africa — you can carry a machine gun three hundred miles inland from the sea and you are still on the edge of it. Since Carthage, and before, men have hacked and scrabbled for permanent footholds along the coasts and in the deserts and on the mountains, and where these footholds have been secured, the right to hold them has been the cause of endless dispute and bloodshed.

Competitors in conquest have overlooked the vital soul of Africa herself, from which emanates the true resistance to conquest. The soul is not dead, but silent, the wisdom not lacking, but of such simplicity as to be counted non-existent in the tinker's mind of modern civilization. Africa is of an ancient age and the blood of many of her peoples is as venerable and as chaste as truth. What upstart race, sprung from some recent, callow century to arm itself with steel and boastfulness, can match in purity the blood of a single Masai Murani whose heritage may have stemmed not far from Eden? It is not the weed that is corrupt; roots of the weed sucked first life from the genesis of earth and hold the essence of it still. Always the weed returns; the cultured plant retreats before it. Racial purity, true aristocracy, devolve not from edict, nor from rote, but from the preservation of kinship with the elemental forces and purposes of life whose understanding is not farther beyond the mind of a Native shepherd than

7

beyond the cultured fumblings of a mortar-board intelligence.

Whatever happens, armies will continue to rumble, colonies may change masters, and in the face of it all Africa lies, and will lie, like a great, wisely somnolent giant unmolested by the noisy drum-rolling of bickering empires. It is not only a land; it is an entity born of one man's hope and another man's fancy.

So there are many Africas. There are as many Africas as there are books about Africa — and as many books about it as you could read in a leisurely lifetime. Whoever writes a new one can afford a certain complacency in the knowledge that his is a new picture agreeing with no one else's, but likely to be haughtily disagreed with by all those who believe in some other Africa.

Doctor Livingstone's Africa was a pretty dark one. There have been a lot of Africas since that, some darker, some bright, most of them full of animals and pygmies, and a few mildly hysterical about the weather, the jungle, and the trials of safari.

All of these books, or at least as many of them as I have read, are accurate in their various portrayals of Africa — not my Africa, perhaps, nor that of an early settler, nor of a veteran of the Boer War, nor of an American millionaire who went there and shot zebra and lion, but of an Africa true to each writer of each book. Being thus all things to all authors, it follows, I suppose, that Africa must be all things to all readers.

Africa is mystic; it is wild; it is a sweltering inferno; it is a photographer's paradise, a hunter's Valhalla, an escapist's Utopia. It is what you will, and it withstands all interpretations. It is the last vestige of a dead world or the cradle of a shiny new one. To a lot of people, as to myself, it is just 'home.' It is all these things but one thing — it is never dull.

From the time I arrived in British East Africa at the in-

different age of four and went through the barefoot stage of
early youth hunting wild pig with the Nandi, later training
race-horses for a living, and still later scouting Tanganyika
and the waterless bush country between the Tana and Athi
Rivers, by aeroplane, for elephant, I remained so happily pro-
vincial I was unable to discuss the boredom of being alive
with any intelligence until I had gone to London and lived
there a year. Boredom, like hookworm, is endemic.

I have lifted my plane from the Nairobi airport for perhaps
a thousand flights and I have never felt her wheels glide from
the earth into the air without knowing the uncertainty and
the exhilaration of firstborn adventure.

The call that took me to Nungwe came about one o'clock in
the morning relayed from Muthaiga Country Club to my
small cottage in the eucalyptus grove near-by.

It was a brief message asking that a cylinder of oxygen be
flown to the settlement at once for the treatment of a gold
miner near death with a lung disease. The appeal was signed
with a name I had never heard, and I remember thinking that
there was a kind of pathetic optimism about its having been
sent at all, because the only way it could have reached me was
through the telegraph station at Mwanza — itself a hundred
miles by Native runner from Nungwe. During the two or
three days the message had been on its way, a man in need of
oxygen must either have died or shown a superhuman determination to live.

So far as I know I was the only professional woman pilot in
Africa at that time. I had no free-lance competition in Kenya,
man or woman, and such messages, or at least others not always so urgent or melancholy, were frequent enough to keep
me occupied most days and far too many nights.

Night flying over charted country by the aid of instruments

9

and radio guidance can still be a lonely business, but to fly in unbroken darkness without even the cold companionship of a pair of ear-phones or the knowledge that somewhere ahead are lights and life and a well-marked airport is something more than just lonely. It is at times unreal to the point where the existence of other people seems not even a reasonable probability. The hills, the forests, the rocks, and the plains are one with the darkness, and the darkness is infinite. The earth is no more your planet than is a distant star — if a star is shining; the plane is your planet and you are its sole inhabitant.

Before such a flight it was this anticipation of aloneness more than any thought of physical danger that used to haunt me a little and make me wonder sometimes if mine was the most wonderful job in the world after all. I always concluded that lonely or not it was still free from the curse of boredom.

Under ordinary circumstances I should have been at the aerodrome ready to take off for Nungwe in less than half an hour, but instead I found myself confronted with a problem much too difficult to solve while still half asleep and at one o'clock in the morning. It was one of those problems that seem incapable of solution — and are; but which, once they have fastened themselves upon you, can neither be escaped nor ignored.

A pilot, a man named Wood who flew for East African Airways, was down somewhere on the vast Serengetti Plains and had been missing for two days. To me and to all of his friends, he was just Woody — a good flier and a likeable person. He was a familiar figure in Nairobi and, though word of his disappearance had been slow in finding attention, once it was realized that he was not simply overdue, but lost, there was a good deal of excitement. Some of this, I suppose, was no more than the usual public enjoyment of suspense and melodrama, though there was seldom a scarcity of either in Nairobi.

Where Woody's misfortune was most sincerely felt, of course, was amongst those of his own profession. I do not mean pilots alone. Few people realize the agony and anxiety a conscientious ground engineer can suffer if an aeroplane he has signed out fails to return. He will not always consider the probability of bad weather or a possible error of judgement on the part of the pilot, but instead will torture himself with un-answerable questions about proper wiring, fuel lines, carbura-tion, valves, and all the hundred and one things he must think about. He will feel that on this occasion he must surely have overlooked something — some small but vital adjustment which, because of his neglect, has resulted in the crash of a plane or the death of a pilot.

All the members of a ground crew, no matter how poorly equipped or how small the aerodrome on which they work, will share equally the apprehension and the nervous strain that come with the first hint of mishap.

But whether storm, or engine trouble, or whatever the cause, Woody had disappeared, and for the past two days I had been droning my plane back and forth over the Northern Serengetti and half the Masai Reserve without having sighted so much as a plume of signal smoke or the glint of sunlight on a crumpled wing.

Anxiety was increasing, even changing to gloom, and I had expected to take off again at sunrise to continue the search; but here suddenly was the message from Nungwe.

For all professional pilots there exists a kind of guild, with-out charter and without by-laws. It demands no requirements for inclusion save an understanding of the wind, the compass, the rudder, and fair fellowship. It is a camaraderie *sans* senti-

11

ment of the kind that men who once sailed uncharted seas in wooden ships must have known and lived by.

I was my own employer, my own pilot, and as often as not my own ground engineer as well. As such I might easily, perhaps even justifiably, have refused the flight to Nungwe, arguing that the rescue of the lost pilot was more important — as, to me, it was. But there was a tinge of personal sympathy about such reasoning that weakened conviction, and Woody, whom I knew so little and yet so well that I never bothered to remember his full name any more than most of his friends did, would have been quick to reject a decision that favoured him at the expense of an unknown miner choking his lungs out in the soggy swamplands of Victoria Nyanza.

In the end I telephoned the Nairobi Hospital, made sure that the oxygen would be ready, and prepared to fly south.

Three hundred and fifty miles can be no distance in a plane, or it can be from where you are to the end of the earth. It depends on so many things. If it is night, it depends on the depth of the darkness and the height of the clouds, the speed of the wind, the stars, the fullness of the moon. It depends on you, if you fly alone — not only on your ability to steer your course or to keep your altitude, but upon the things that live in your mind while you swing suspended between the earth and the silent sky. Some of those things take root and are with you long after the flight itself is a memory, but, if your course was over any part of Africa, even the memory will remain strong.

When, much later than Nungwe or Tripoli or Zanzibar, or any of the remote and sometimes outlandish places I have flown to, I crossed the North Atlantic, east to west, there were headlines, fanfare, and, for me, many sleepless nights. A generous American press found that flight spectacular — and what is spectacular is news.

12

But to leave Nairobi and arrive at Nungwe is not spectacular. It is not news. It is only a little hop from here to there, and to one who does not know the plains of Africa, its swamps, its night sounds and its night silences, such a flight is not only unspectacular, but perhaps tedious as well. Only not to me, for Africa was the breath and life of my childhood.

It is still the host of all my darkest fears, the cradle of mysteries always intriguing, but never wholly solved. It is the remembrance of sunlight and green hills, cool water and the yellow warmth of bright mornings. It is as ruthless as any sea, more uncompromising than its own deserts. It is without temperance in its harshness or in its favours. It yields nothing, offering much to men of all races.

But the soul of Africa, its integrity, the slow inexorable pulse of its life, is its own and of such singular rhythm that no outsider, unless steeped from childhood in its endless, even beat, can ever hope to experience it, except only as a bystander might experience a Masai war dance knowing nothing of its music nor the meaning of its steps.

So I am off to Nungwe — a silly word, a silly place. A place of small hopes and small successes, buried like the inconsequential treasure of an imaginative miser, out of bounds and out of most men's wanting — below the Mau Escarpment, below the Speke Gulf, below the unsurveyed stretches of the Western Province.

Oxygen to a sick miner. But this flight is not heroic. It is not even romantic. It is a job of work, a job to be done at an uncomfortable hour with sleep in my eyes and half a grumble on my lips.

Arab Ruta calls contact and swings the propeller.

Arab Ruta is a Nandi, anthropologically a member of a Nilotic tribe, humanly a member of a smaller tribe, a more elect tribe, the tribe composed of those too few, precisely sensitive, but altogether indomitable individuals contributed sparingly by each race, exclusively by none.

He is of the tribe that observes with equal respect the soft voice and the hardened hand, the fullness of a flower, the quick finality of death. His is the laughter of a free man happy at his work, a strong man with lust for living. He is not black. His skin holds the sheen and warmth of used copper. His eyes are dark and wide-spaced, his nose full-boned and capable of arrogance.

He is arrogant now, swinging the propeller, laying his lean hands on the curved wood, feeling an exultant kinship in the coiled resistance to his thrust.

He swings hard. A splutter, a strangled cough from the engine like the premature stirring of a sleep-slugged labourer. In the cockpit I push gently on the throttle, easing it forward, rousing the motor, feeding it, soothing it.

Arab Ruta moves the wooden chocks from the wheels and steps backward away from the wing. Fitful splashes of crimson light from crude-oil torches set round the field stain the dark cloth of the African night and play upon his alert, high-boned face. He raises his hand and I nod as the propeller, whirring itself into invisibility, pulls the plane forward, past him.

I leave him no instructions, no orders. When I return he will be there. It is an understanding of many years — a wordless understanding from the days when Arab Ruta first came into my father's service on the farm at Njoro. He will be there, as a servant, as a friend — waiting.

I peer ahead along the narrow muram runway. I gather speed meeting the wind, using the wind.

A high wire fence surrounds the aerodrome — a wire fence and then a deep ditch. Where is there another aerodrome fenced against wild animals? Zebra, wildebeest, giraffe, eland — at night they lurk about the tall barrier staring with curious wild eyes into the flat field, feeling cheated.

They are well out of it, for themselves and for me. It would be a hard fate to go down in the memory of one's friends as having been tripped up by a wandering zebra. 'Tried to take off and hit a zebra!' It lacks even the dignity of crashing into an anthill.

Watch the fence. Watch the flares. I watch both and take off into the night.

Ahead of me lies a land that is unknown to the rest of the world and only vaguely known to the African — a strange mixture of grasslands, scrub, desert sand like long waves of the southern ocean. Forest, still water, and age-old mountains, stark and grim like mountains of the moon. Salt lakes, and rivers that have no water. Swamps. Badlands. Land without life. Land teeming with life — all of the dusty past, all of the future.

The air takes me into its realm. Night envelops me entirely, leaving me out of touch with the earth, leaving me within this small moving world of my own, living in space with the stars.

My plane is a light one, a two-seater with her registration letters, VP–KAN, painted boldly on her turquoise-blue fuselage in silver.

In the daytime she is a small gay complement to the airy blue of the sky, like a bright fish under the surface of a clear sea. In darkness such as this she is no more than a passing murmur, a soft, incongruous murmur above the earth.

With such registration letters as hers, it requires of my friends no great imagination or humour to speak of her always as just 'the Kan' — and the Kan she is, even to me. But this is not libel, for such nicknames are born out of love.

To me she is alive and to me she speaks. I feel through the soles of my feet on the rudder-bar the willing strain and flex of her muscles. The resonant, guttural voice of her exhausts has a timbre more articulate than wood and steel, more vibrant than wires and sparks and pounding pistons.

She speaks to me now, saying the wind is right, the night is fair, the effort asked of her well within her powers.

I fly swiftly. I fly high — south-southwest, over the Ngong Hills. I am relaxed. My right hand rests upon the stick in easy communication with the will and the way of the plane. I sit in the rear, the front cockpit filled with the heavy tank of oxygen strapped upright in the seat, its round stiff dome foolishly reminding me of the poised rigidity of a passenger on first flight.

The wind in the wires is like the tearing of soft silk under the blended drone of engine and propeller. Time and distance together slip smoothly past the tips of my wings without sound, without return, as I peer downward over the night-shadowed hollows of the Rift Valley and wonder if Woody, the lost pilot, could be there, a small human pinpoint of hope and of hopelessness listening to the low, unconcerned song of the Avian — flying elsewhere.

II

Men with Blackwater Die

THERE is a feeling of absolute finality about the end of a flight through darkness. The whole scheme of things with which you have lived acutely, during hours of roaring sound in an element altogether detached from the world, ceases abruptly. The plane noses groundward, the wings strain to the firmer cushion of earthbound air, wheels touch, and the engine sighs into silence. The dream of flight is suddenly gone before the mundane realities of growing grass and swirling dust, the slow plodding of men and the enduring patience of rooted trees. Freedom escapes you again, and wings that were a moment ago no less than an eagle's, and swifter, are metal and wood once more, inert and heavy.

The clearing at Nungwe blinked into my horizon about half an hour before dawn. At a thousand feet the wavering crude-oil torches outlined no more than a narrow runway — a thin scar on the vast sprawled body of the wilderness.

I circled once, watching the flares yield to the rising wind, gauging the direction of its flow. Shadows that were made by moving men criss-crossed the clearing, shifted, changed design, and became immobile.

A gentle pull on the throttle eased the motor to an effortless hum. I held the nose of the Avian on the beacons until the earth sped under her, and the wheels, reaching for solid ground, swept her onto the runway in a maelstrom of dust and

17

flickering orange light. I cut the engine, relaxed in the seat, and adjusted my ears to the emptiness of silence.

The air was heavy, with life gone out of it. Men's voices came from across the runway, sounding, after the deep drone of the plane, like the thin bleating of reed pipes or like the fluted whispers of a bamboo forest.

I climbed out of the cockpit and watched a band of dim figures approach before the dancing flares. By the manner of their walk and by their clothes, I could see that most of them were black — Kavirondo, bulky-thighed in their half-nakedness, following two white men who moved with quicker, more eager steps over the clearing.

Somewhere an ancient automobile engine roared into life, its worn pistons and bearings hammering like drumbeats. Hot night wind stalked through the thorn trees and leleshwa that surrounded the clearing. It bore the odour of swampland, the smell of Lake Victoria, the breath of weeds and sultry plains and tangled bush. It whipped at the oil flares and snatched at the surfaces of the Avian. But there was loneliness in it and aimlessness, as if its passing were only a sterile duty lacking even the beneficent promise of rain.

Leaning against the fuselage, I watched the face of a short, chunky man loom gradually larger until it was framed before me in the uncertain light. It was a flabby face under a patch of greying hair and it held two brown eyes that seemed trapped in a spider web of weary lines.

Its owner smiled and held out his hand and I took it.

'I am the doctor,' he said; 'I sent the message.' He jerked his head toward the other white man at his elbow. 'This is Ebert. Ask him for anything you need — tea, food, whatever you want. It won't be good, but you're welcome to it.'

Before I could answer, he turned away, mumbling as he

18

went about sickness, and the time of night, and the slowness of the box-body Ford now lurching across the runway to pick up the oxygen. In his wake followed half a dozen Kavirondo, any one of them big enough to lift the little doctor off the ground and carry him, like a small goat, under one arm. Instead they slouched dutifully behind at a distance I thought must have been kept so precisely unaltered out of simple fear and honest respect, blended to perfection.

'You're early,' Ebert said; 'you made good time.'

He was tall and angular in a grey, work-stained shirt and loose corduroy trousers patched many times. He spoke apologetically as if, as a visitor from the remote and glamorous civilization of Nairobi, I might find my reception somehow less than I had the right to expect.

'We fixed the runway,' he said, 'as well as we could.'

I nodded, looking into a lean-boned, sun-beaten face.

'It's a good job,' I assured him — 'better than I had hoped for.'

'And we rigged up a windsock.' He swung his arm in the direction of a slender pole whose base was surrounded by half a dozen flares. At the top of the pole hung a limp cylinder of cheap, white 'Americani' cloth looking a bit like an amputated pajama leg.

In such a breeze the cylinder ought to have been fully extended, but instead, and in defiance of the simplest laws of physics, it only dangled in shameless indifference to both the strength of the wind and its direction.

Moving closer, I saw the lower end had been sewn as tightly shut as needle and thread could make it, so that, as an instrument intended to indicate wind tendency, it was rather less efficient than a pair of whole pajamas might have been.

I explained this technical error of design to Ebert and, in the half-light of the oil torches, had the satisfaction of seeing his face relax into what I suspected was his first smile in a long, long time.

'It was the word "sock,"' he said, 'that confused us. We couldn't imagine a proper sock with a hole in its toe — not even a windsock!'

With the help of the little doctor who had lapsed into pre-occupied silence, we unstrapped the oxygen tank, lifted it from the front cockpit, and set it on the ground. It was not terribly heavy, but the Kavirondo who gaily picked it up and walked with it toward the Ford, bore the thick metal cylinder as if it had been no more than a light bedroll.

It is this combination of physical strength and willingness to work that has made the Kavirondo the most tractable and dependable source of labour in East Africa.

From the loose confines of their native territory, which originally stretched south from Mount Elgon along the eastern shores of Victoria Nyanza for two hundred miles or so, they have wandered in all directions, mingling and working and laughing until what was once an obscure and timid tribe is now so ubiquitous as to cause the unobservant traveller in East Africa to suspect all natives are Kavirondo. This misconception is harmless enough in itself, but is best left unrevealed in the presence of such fire-eaters as the Nandi, the Somali, or the Masai, the racial vanity of any one of whom is hardly less than that of the proudest proud Englishman.

The Kavirondo, though not racially conscious, is at least conscious of being alive and finds endless pleasure in that cheerful realization alone. He is the porter of Africa, the man-of-all-work, the happy-go-lucky buffoon. To the charge of other and sterner tribes that he is not only uncircumcised, but that he eats dead meat without much concern about the manner of its killing, he is blandly indifferent. His resistance to White infiltration is, at best, passive, but, consisting as it does

of the simple stratagem of eating heartily and breeding profusely, it may one day be found formidable enough.

My cargo of oxygen having been unloaded, I watched a
group of these massive and powerful men gather round my
plane, eyeing her trim lines with flattering curiosity. One of
the largest of the lot, having stared at her with gaping mouth
for a full minute, suddenly leaned back on his heels and roared
with laughter that must have put the nearest hyena to shame
if not to flight.

When I asked him, in Swahili, to explain the joke, he looked
profoundly hurt. There wasn't any joke, he said. It was just
that the plane was so smooth and her wings so strong that it
made him want to laugh!

I couldn't help wondering what Africa would have been like
if such physique as these Kavirondo had were coupled with
equal intelligence — or perhaps I should say with cunning
equal to that of their white brethren.

I suppose in that case the road to Nungwe would be wide
and handsome and lined with filling stations, and the shores
of Lake Victoria would be dotted with pleasure resorts linked
to Nairobi and the coast by competitive railways probably
advertising themselves as the Kavirondo or Kikuyu Lines.
The undeveloped and 'savage' country would be transformed
from a wasteland to a paradise of suburban homes and quaint
bathing cabanas and popular beaches, all redolent, on hot
days, of the subtle aroma of European culture. But the essence of progress is time, and we can only wait.

According to my still apologetic host, Ebert, the little doctor would have to drive at least an hour before reaching the
actual Nungwe mine site where his patient lay in a grass hut,
too sick to be moved.

'The doc's tried everything,' Ebert said, as we listened to
the splutter of the disappearing Ford — 'diet, medicine, even

witchcraft, I think; now the oxygen. The sick chap's a gold miner. Lungs gone. Weak heart. He's still alive, but for God knows how long. They keep coming out here and they keep dying. There's gold all right, but it'll never be a boom town — except for undertakers.'

There seemed to be no answer to this gloomy prediction, but I noticed that at least Ebert had made it with something that resembled a sour smile. I thought of Woody again and wondered if there could be even a remote hope of finding him on the way back to Nairobi. Perhaps not, but I made up my mind to leave as soon as I could gracefully get away.

I saw to it that the Avian was safe on the runway, and then, with Ebert, walked toward the settlement past the rows of oil flares, pink and impotent now in the early dawn.

Grey blades of light sliced at the darkness and within a few moments I could see the mining camp in all its bleak and somehow courageous isolation — a handful of thatched huts, a tangle of worn machinery, a storehouse of corrugated iron. Dogs, hollow-bellied and dispirited, sprawled in the dust, and behind the twisted arms of the surrounding thorn trees the country lay like an abandoned theatrical backdrop, tarnished and yellow.

I saw no women, no children. Here under the equatorial sun of Africa was a spot without human warmth, a community without even laughter.

Ebert led me through the door of one of the largest huts and promised tea, remarking hopefully that I might not find it too bad, since, only eight months ago, his store had been replenished from the stock of a Hindu shop in Kisumu.

He disappeared through an exit at the rear of the room and I leaned back in a chair and looked around me.

A hurricane lamp with a cracked, soot-smeared chimney still spluttered in the centre of a long plank that served as a table and was supported by two up-ended barrels on an earthen floor. Behind the plank were shelves sprinkled with tins of bully beef, vegetables and soup, mostly of American concoction. Several old copies of *Punch* were stacked at one end of the plank and, on the seat of the chair opposite mine, was an issue of the *Illustrated London News* dated October, 1929.

There was a radio, but it must have been voiceless for many months — tubes, wires, condenser, and dial, all bearing the marks of frequent and apparently futile renovation, lay in a hopeless mass on the top of a packing-crate marked: VIA MOMBASA.

I saw jars of black sand that must have contained gold, or hopes of it, and other jars labelled with cryptic figures that meant nothing to me, but were in any case empty. A blueprint clung to one of the walls and a spider, descending from the thatch overhead, contemplated the neatly drawn lines and figures and returned to its geometrically perfect web, unimpressed.

I stood up and walked to the window. It was no bigger than a small tea-tray and its lower half was battened with corrugated iron. In the path of the rising sun, scattered bush, and tufts of grass lay a network of shadows over the earth, and, where these were thickest, I saw a single jackal forage expectantly in a mound of filth.

I returned to the chair feeling depressed and a little apprehensive. I began to think about Woody again — or at least to wonder, since there was really nothing to think about.

The sight of the jackal had brought to mind the scarcely comforting speculation that in Africa there is never any waste. Death particularly is never wasted. What the lion leaves, the hyena feasts upon and what scraps remain are morsels for the jackal, the vulture, or even the consuming sun.

I dug in the pockets of my flying overalls for a cigarette, lit it, and tried to shake off a wave of sleepiness. It was a futile effort, but a moment later Ebert returned carrying the tea-things on a tray and I was able to keep my eyes open, watching him move. I noticed that his face had become sombre again and thoughtful as if, during the time he had been out of the room, an old worry, or perhaps a new one, had begun to brew in his mind.

He set the tray on the long plank and groped for a tin of biscuits on a shelf. Sunlight, full-bodied and strong, had begun to warm the drab colours of the hut and I reached over and blew out the flame of the hurricane lamp.

'You've heard of blackwater,' Ebert said suddenly.

I straightened in my chair and for want of an ashtray ground my cigarette out with my foot on the earthen floor. My memory shuttled backward to the days of my childhood on the farm at Njoro — days when the words malaria and blackwater had first become mingled in my consciousness with Goanese or Indian doctors who arrived too late, rumours of plague on the lips of frightened Natives, death, and hushed burial before dawn in the cedar forest that bounded our posho mill and paddocks.

They were dark days heavy-scented with gloom. All the petty joys of early youth, the games, the friendships with the Nandi totos lost their lustre. Time became a weight that would not be moved until the bodies themselves had been moved and grass roots had found the new earth of the graves, and the women had cleaned the vacant huts of the dead and you could see the sun again.

'One of our men,' Ebert said, handing me a cup of tea, 'is down with blackwater. The chap you brought the oxygen for has a bare chance, but this one hasn't. Nothing the doc can do — and you can't move a man with blackwater.'

'No.' I put the cup back on the long plank and remembered that people with blackwater always die if they are moved, and nearly always die if they are left alone.

'I'm terribly sorry,' I said.

There must have been other things to say, but I couldn't think of them. All I could think of was the time I *had* moved a blackwater patient from Masongaleni in the elephant country to the hospital at Nairobi.

I never knew afterward for how many hours of that journey I had flown with a corpse for company because, when I landed, the man was quite dead.

'If there's anything I can do . . .?' It seems impossible not to be trite on such occasions. The old useless phrases are the only dependable ones — 'terribly sorry,' and, 'if there's anything I can do . . .'

'He'd like to talk to you,' Ebert said. 'He heard the plane come in. I told him I thought you might spend the day here and take off tomorrow morning. He may not last that long, but he wants to talk to someone from the outside and none of us in Nungwe has been to Nairobi in over a year.'

I stood up, forgetting my tea. 'I'll talk to him, of course. But I can't stay. There's a pilot down somewhere in the Serengetti . . .'

'Oh.' Ebert looked disappointed, and I knew from his expression that he, as well as the sick man, was lonely for news of the 'outside' — news of Nairobi. And in Nairobi people only wanted news of London.

Wherever you are, it seems, you must have news of some other place, some bigger place, so that a man on his deathbed in the swamplands of Victoria Nyanza is more interested in what has lately happened in this life than in what may happen in the next. It is really this that makes death so hard — curiosity unsatisfied.

But if contempt for death is correctly interpreted as courage, then Ebert's dying friend was a courageous man.

He lay on a camp bed under a thin, sticky blanket and he had no recognizable face. What the Egyptians had done with chemicals to dead bodies, malaria and the subsequent blackwater had done to him.

I have seen baskets of raw animal skin stretched over sticks and left to dry in the sun, and these baskets were no more empty or fleshless than the half corpse Ebert presented to me in the darkened hut.

It was a tiny hut with the usual single window blocked with corrugated iron, the usual thatched roof, old and dropping its leaves like a rotted tree, and the usual earthen floor paved with burnt matchsticks, paper, and shreds of tobacco.

There never seems to be any reason for filth, but there are occasions, like this one, where it would be hard to find a reason for cleanliness. 'Poverty,' an old proverb says, 'is not a disgrace, but a great swinishness.' Here was poverty — poverty of women to help, poverty of hope, and even of life. For all I knew there might have been handfuls of gold buried in that hut, but if there were, it was the poorest comfort of all.

The sick man's name was Bergner — a Dutchman, perhaps, or a German. Not English, I thought, though whatever racial characteristics had once distinguished him were now lost in the almost Gothic contours of his shrunken head.

His eyes alone appeared to live. They were enormous, seeming to move in their sockets independently of the body they served. But they stared at me from the bed with something that was at least interest and might almost have been humour. They seemed to say, 'This is a hell of a way to receive a young lady just in from Nairobi — but you see how things are!'

I smiled, a little wanly, I think, and then turned to Ebert —

or at least to the spot where he had been. With dexterity that might have done credit to the most accomplished Indian fakir, Ebert had vanished, leaving me alone with Bergner.

For a moment I stood in the centre of the room experiencing, in spite of myself, some of the trepidation one might feel hearing the door of a burial vault close on one's back.

The comparison seems exaggerated now, but the truth is that all my life I have had an abhorrence of disease amounting almost to a phobia.

There is no reason in this; it is not fear of infection, because Africa has accorded me my full share of malaria and other illnesses, from time to time, along with a kind of compensating philosophy with which to endure them. My phobia is an unaccountable physical repulsion from persons who are sick rather than from sickness itself.

Certain people are repelled even by the thought of snakes and I can only compare my feeling toward the aspect of unhealthiness to this — mambas, pythons, puff-adders, and some of their brethren have frequently popped into my life either on treks through the forests or during elephant hunts, or when, as a child, I wandered in the bush seeking small adventure. But while I have learned to avoid snakes and have even, I think, developed a sixth sense for the purpose, I feel I could, if necessary, still face a mamba with greater calm than I can face a human being swathed in the sickly-sweet atmosphere of disease and impending death.

Here in this hut, at the side of a strange, bedridden man, I had to fight back an impulse to throw open the door and bolt across the runway into the protecting cockpit of my plane. Coupled with this was the realization that each moment the sun rose higher, the day grew hotter, and if Woody were by some miracle still alive, an hour or so more of delay on my part

27

could result in a tragedy that would not be less because of the comfort Bergner might find in my visit.

Somewhere, just beyond Nungwe, the little doctor must at that moment have been pouring oxygen into the lungs of another man, if that man were still alive.

Death, or at least the shadow that precedes him, seemed to have stalked far and wide that morning.

I pulled up a chair and sat in it near the head of Bergner's bed and tried to think of something to say, but he spoke first.

His voice was soft and controlled, and very tired.

'You don't mind being here, I hope,' he said. 'It's been four years since I left Nairobi, and there haven't been many letters.' He ran the tip of his tongue over his lips and attempted a smile. 'People forget,' he added. 'It's easy for a whole group of people to forget just one, but if you're very long in a place like this you remember everybody you ever met. You even worry about people you never liked; you get nostalgic about your enemies. It's all something to think about and it all helps.'

I nodded, watching little beads of sweat swell on his forehead. He was feverish, and I couldn't help wondering how long it would be before the inevitable delirium overtook him another time.

I don't know what the scientific term for blackwater is, but the name those who have lived in Africa call it by is apt enough.

A man can be riddled with malaria for years on end, with its chills and its fevers and its nightmares, but, if one day he sees that the water from his kidneys is black, he knows he will not leave that place again, wherever he is, or wherever he hoped to be. He knows that there will be days ahead, long, tedious days which have no real beginning or ending, but which run together into night and out of it without changing

28

colour, or sound, or meaning. He will lie in his bed feeling the minutes and the hours pass through his body like an endless ribbon of pain because time becomes pain then. Light and darkness become pain; all his senses exist only to receive it, to transmit to his mind again and again, with ceaseless repetition, the simple fact that now he is dying.

The man on the bed was dying like that. He wanted to talk because it is possible to forget yourself if you talk, but not if you only lie and think.

'Hastings,' he said. 'You must know Carl Hastings. He was a White Hunter for a while and then he settled down on a coffee plantation west of Ngong. I wonder if he ever married?' He used to say he never would, but nobody believed him.'

'He did, though,' I said. It was a name I had never heard, but it seemed a small enough gesture to lie about a nebulous Carl Hastings — even, if necessary, to give him a wife.

In the four years Bergner had been away, the town of Nairobi had swelled and burst like a ripe seedpod. It was no longer so comfortably small that every inhabitant was a neighbour, or every name that of a friend.

'I thought you knew him,' Bergner said; 'everybody knows Carl. And when you see him you can tell him he owes me five pounds. It's on a bet we made one Christmas in Mombasa. He bet he'd never get married — not in Africa, anyway. He said you could boast about living in a man's country, but you couldn't expect to find a marriageable woman in it!'

'I'll tell him about it,' I said; 'he can send it by way of Kisumu.'

'That's right, by way of Kisumu.'

Bergner closed his eyes and let a tremor of pain shake his body under the flimsy blanket. He was like a storm-trapped man who seeks shelter in the niche of a wall from a passing fury of wind and then hurries on until the next blast drives him to cover again.

'There's Phillips,' he said, 'and Tom Krausmeyer at the Stanley Hotel. You'll know them both — and Joe Morley. There are a number of people I want to ask you about, but there's lots of time. Ebert said you'd be staying over. When I heard your plane I almost prayed that you'd had a flat tire or whatever you have in planes — anything to see a new face and hear a new voice. It isn't considerate, but you get that way living in a hole like this — or dying in it.'

'You don't have to die in it. You'll get well and then I'll come back and fly you to Nairobi.'

'Or even to London.' Bergner smiled. 'After that we might try Paris, Berlin, Buenos Aires, and New York. My future looks brighter and brighter.'

'You forgot Hollywood.'

'No. I just thought it was too much to hope for all in one breath.'

I noticed that, in spite of his spirit and his courage, his voice had grown thin and less certain of its strength. He was holding himself together by sheer power of will and the effort made the atmosphere of the hut strained and tense.

'You *are* staying over, then?' He put the question with sudden urgency.

I didn't know how to explain that I had to leave. I had a feeling that he wouldn't have believed my reason; that with the quick suspicion of the insane and the very sick, he would have thought I was only trying to escape.

I mumbled something about how nice it would be to stay, and that I would, for a while, but that there were other things — a pilot down, the Avian to be refuelled ...

I don't suppose he heard any of it. He started to sweat again and his legs jerked under the blanket. A fleck of spittle

30

formed on his lips and he began to talk in meaningless garbled words.

I couldn't understand all of what he said, but even in delirium he was neither sobbing nor complaining very much. He mumbled only about small things, people he had known, places in Africa, and once he mentioned Carl Hastings and Nairobi together in an almost intelligible sentence. I had come closer to the bed and leaned down over it, feeling a wave of sickness in my own body. Trying to quiet him, I talked, but it was a wasted effort. He caught his hands in the loose folds of my flying clothes, tearing at the fabric pulling himself upward from the bed.

I wanted to call out for Ebert, for anyone. But I couldn't say anything and no one would have heard, so I stood there with my hands on Bergner's shoulders feeling the tremor of his muscles pass through my fingertips and hearing the rest of his life run out in a stream of little words carrying no meaning, bearing no secrets — or perhaps he had none.

I left him at last and tiptoed through the door of the hut, closing it quickly behind me.

Bergner may have lived for a while after that, and it may be that the other man for whom the little doctor ordered the oxygen is still mining gold at Nungwe. But I never went back there again and so I never knew.

Years later, I did meet a man named Carl Hastings at one of those cocktail parties where both the people and the conversation pass out of your life and memory by dinner-time.

'There was a man named Bergner,' I began, 'a friend of yours . . .'

Mr. Hastings, who was tall and swart and tailored smoothly, raised his glass and frowned over the edge of it.

'You mean Barnard,' he said, 'Ralph Barnard.'

'No.' I shook my head. 'It's Bergner all right. You must

remember — Christmas at Mombasa, some kind of bet about getting married? I saw him down at Nungwe and he told me about it.'

'Hmmm.' Mr. Hastings pursed his lips and thought hard. 'It's a funny thing about people,' he said, 'a very funny thing. You meet so many and remember so few. Now take this chap you're talking about . . . Barker did you say his name was . . .?'

There was a tray of cocktails near my elbow, so I reached over and took one.

'Cheers,' said Mr. Hastings.

I took a sip of the drink, remembering my take-off from Nungwe, seeing it once more, clearly, in all its detail.

There were Kavirondo helping with the fuel tins, there was Ebert still apologetic, and still a bit disappointed — and there was the bedraggled windsock, with its toe still sealed shut, hanging from its mast like the pathetic flag of a domain so small that nobody could ever take it seriously.

Beyond that there was wind enough and too much sun and the lusty song of the plane. In a little while there was the Speke Gulf, deep as the sky and just as blue. And, after that, the Serengetti Plains.

III

The Stamp of Wilderness

THE Serengetti Plains spread from Lake Nyaraza, in Tanganyika, northward beyond the lower boundaries of Kenya Colony. They are the great sanctuary of the Masai People and they harbour more wild game than any similar territory in all of East Africa. In the season of drought they are as dry and tawny as the coats of the lion that prowl them, and during the rains they provide the benison of soft grass to all the animals in a child's picture book.

They are endless and they are empty, but they are as warm with life as the waters of a tropic sea. They are webbed with the paths of eland and wildebeest and Thompson's gazelle and their hollows and valleys are trampled by thousands of zebra. I have seen a herd of buffalo invade the pastures under the occasional thorn tree groves and, now and then, the whimsically fashioned figure of a plodding rhino has moved along the horizon like a grey boulder come to life and adventure bound. There are no roads. There are no villages, no towns, no telegraph. There is nothing, as far as you can see, or walk, or ride, except grass and rocks and a few trees and the animals that live there.

Years ago one of the banking Rothschilds on a hunting trip led by Captain George Wood, now aide-de-camp to His Royal Highness, the Duke of Windsor, pitched his tents in the Serengetti Plains near a huge pile of these rocks where there was protection from the wind and where there was water.

33

Since then countless hunting parties on safari have stopped there, and Rothschild's Camp is still a landmark and a kind of haven for hunters who, coming so far, have for a while at least locked the comforts of the other world behind them.

There is no landing field at Rothschild's Camp, but there is a patch of ground flat enough to receive a plane if the wind is right and the pilot careful.

I have landed there often and usually I have seen lion in the path of my glide to earth. Sometimes they have moved like strolling dogs, indifferent and unhurried, or, upon occasion, they have taken time to pause and sit on their haunches, in cosy groups — males, females and cubs staring at the Avian with about the same expression one finds in the gold-framed family portraits of the Mauve Decade.

I do not suggest that the lion of the Serengetti have become so blasé about the modern explorer's motion-picture camera that their posing has already become a kind of Hollywoodian habit. But many of them have so often been bribed with fresh-killed zebra or other delicacies that it is sometimes possible to advance with photographic equipment to within thirty or forty yards of them if the approach is made in an automobile.

To venture that close on foot, however, would mean the sudden shattering of any kindly belief that the similarity of the lion and the pussy cat goes much beyond their whiskers. But then, since men still live by the sword, it is a little optimistic to expect the lion to withdraw his claws, handicapped as he is by his inability to read our better effusions about the immorality of bloodshed.

On the way from Nungwe I flew toward Rothschild's Camp because the spot was on Woody's route on his flight from Shinyaga in Western Tanganyika to Nairobi and I knew that, whether alive or dead, he would not be found far off his course.

He was flying a German Klemm monoplane equipped with a ninety-five horsepower British Pobjoy motor. If this combination had any virtue in such vast and unpredictable country, it was that the extraordinary wingspan of the plane allowed for long gliding range and slow landing speed.

Swiftness, distance, and the ability to withstand rough weather were, none of them, merits of the Klemm. Neither the plane nor the engine it carried was designed for more than casual flying over well-inhabited, carefully charted country, and its use by East African Airways for both transport and messenger service seemed to us in Kenya, who flew for a living, to indicate a somewhat reckless persistence in the pioneer tradition.

The available aviation maps of Africa in use at that time all bore the cartographer's scale mark, 'I/2,000,000' — one over two million. An inch on the map was about thirty-two miles in the air, as compared to the flying maps of Europe on which one inch represented no more than four air miles.

Moreover, it seemed that the printers of the African maps had a slightly malicious habit of including, in large letters, the names of towns, junctions, and villages which, while most of them did exist in fact, as a group of thatched huts may exist or a water hole, they were usually so inconsequential as completely to escape discovery from the cockpit.

Beyond this, it was even more disconcerting to examine your charts before a proposed flight only to find that in many cases the bulk of the terrain over which you had to fly was bluntly marked: 'UNSURVEYED.'

It was as if the mapmakers had said, 'We are aware that between this spot and that one, there are several hundred thousands of acres, but until *you* make a forced landing there, we won't know whether it is mud, desert, or jungle — and the chances are we won't know then!'

All this, together with the fact that there was no radio, nor any system designed to check planes in and out of their points of contact, made it essential for a pilot either to develop his intuitive sense to the highest degree or to adopt a fatalistic philosophy toward life. Most of the airmen I knew in Africa at that time managed to do both.

Flying up from Nungwe on my hunt for Woody, I had clear weather and unlimited visibility. I stayed at an altitude of about five thousand feet to give me the broadest possible scope of clear vision, and zigzagged on my course.

From the open cockpit I could see straight ahead, or peer backward and down, past the silver wings. The Serengetti lay beneath me like a bowl whose edges were the ends of the earth. It was a bowl full of hot vapours that rose upward in visible waves and exerted physical pressure against the Avian, lifting her, as heat from a smouldering fire lifts a flake of ash.

Time after time a rock, or a shadow, aided by my imagination, assumed the shape of a crumpled plane or a mass of twisted metal, and I would bank and swing lower and lower over the suspected object until its outlines were sharp and clear — and disappointing again. Every foreign speck in the landscape became a Klemm monoplane come to grief, and every wind-inspired movement of a branch or a clump of bush was, for an instant, the excited signalling of a stranded man.

About noon I reached Rothschild's Camp and circled over it. But there was no activity, no life — not even the compact, slow-moving silhouette of a lion. There was nothing but the distinguishing formation of high, grey rocks piled against each other, jutting from the earth like the weather-worn ruins of a desert cathedral.

I swung north and east with the sun straight above me spilling midday heat on the plain.

By two o'clock in the afternoon I had covered the district

around the Uaso Nyiro River which flows south past the soda basins of Magadi and on to Lake Natron.

The country here, except for the narrow valley of the river, is an undulating waste of stark ridges like the surface of water sketched in chalk. Not only an aeroplane, but even so small a thing as a pilot's helmet would be visible against the white crust. But there was neither aeroplane nor pilot's helmet. There was hardly a shadow, except my own.

I continued north, feeling a growing urge to sleep, but not really from exhaustion. The thing that contributes most to the loneliness of flying in such empty country for hours on end is the absence of smoke on the horizon. A spiral of smoke in the daytime is like a shaft of light at night. It may be off your course to starboard or port, it may be no more than the poor smudge of a Masai campfire whose keepers are as unaware of you as they are of tomorrow's worries, but it is a beacon nevertheless; it is a human sign, like a footprint or a matchstick found in the sand.

But, if there was no smoke to mark the site of a hearthstone or a camp, there were at least other signs of life, not human, but scarcely less welcome for that.

In a hundred places, as far as I could see and in all directions, little puffs of dust sprang suddenly into being, rolled across the plain and disappeared again. From the air they were like so many jinni, each bursting from the confines of his fabulous and bewitched jar to rush off with the wind on the urgent accomplishment of a long-plotted evil deed, or maybe a good one.

But when the dust puffs cleared, I could see that small bands of animals were running this way and that, looking everywhere but upward, trying to escape the sound of the plane.

Between Magadi and Narok I watched a yellow cloud take

shape beneath me and just ahead. The cloud clung close to the earth and grew as I approached it into a swaying billow that blunted the sunlight and obscured the grass and mimosa trees in its path.

Out of its farthest edge the forerunners of a huge herd of impala, wildebeest, and zebra plunged in flight before the shadow of my wings. I circled, throttled down and lost height until my propeller cut into the fringe of the dust, and particles of it burned in my nostrils.

As the herd moved it became a carpet of rust-brown and grey and dull red. It was not like a herd of cattle or of sheep, because it was wild, and it carried with it the stamp of wilderness and the freedom of a land still more a possession of Nature than of men. To see ten thousand animals untamed and not branded with the symbols of human commerce is like scaling an unconquered mountain for the first time, or like finding a forest without roads or footpaths, or the blemish of an axe. You know then what you had always been told — that the world once lived and grew without adding machines and newsprint and brick-walled streets and the tyranny of clocks.

In the forefront of the herd I could see impala leaping as they ran, and wildebeest flaunting their brittle horns, or flinging themselves on the ground with the abandon of mad dervishes. I do not know why they do this, but whether it is a faulty sense of balance or merely a shameless recourse to the melodramatic, the wildebeest, if frightened by a plane, will always react in the manner of the circus clown in his frantic attempts to escape the trained spotted dog around and around the sawdust arena.

With apology to clowns, if there are any left, I think the antics of the wildebeest, because they are less studied, are more amusing. This may be due to the fact that the wildebeest has two more legs to trip over — at least when he seems to need them most, they serve him least. When he wants to turn, he pirouettes, and when he wants to run, his progress is continually interrupted by a series of Keystone Comedy nose dives. How he gets from place to place with any dispatch would seem a mystery, but actually he does quite well when all is silent overhead — and there is no audience to watch him.

But on this occasion the greater part of the game I saw were zebra bucking like unbroken horses, running with tails extended and necks arched, their hooves crushing the tall grass to make a wide hard path behind them.

So far as I know, zebra are the most useless animals of any size in Africa — useless, that is, to men, because, especially on the Serengetti, lion live on them.

But to men the zebra is a complete ambiguity. He resembles a donkey, but will not be trained and cannot stand work; he runs wild like Thompson's gazelle and eland and eats the same food, but his meat lacks even the doubtful succulence of horse. His hide, while striking in appearance, is only fairly durable and has made its greatest decorative triumph as panelling for the walls of a New York night club. Ostrich and civet cat have contributed more to the requirements of civilized society, but I think it not unjust to say that the zebra clan, in spite of it all, is unaffected by its failure to join in the march of time. I base this conclusion on a very warm friendship that developed, not too long ago to remember, between myself and a young zebra.

My father, who has raised and trained some of the best Thoroughbreds to come out of Africa, once had a filly named Balmy. He chose all of the names for his horses with painstaking care, sometimes spending many evenings at his desk on our farm at Njoro jotting down possibilities by the light of a kerosene lamp. Balmy was selected for this particular filly because no other name suited her so precisely.

She was neither vicious nor stubborn, she was very fast on the track, and she responded intelligently to training. Besides her light bay colour and the distinguishing white star on her forehead, her chief peculiarity was an unorthodox point of view toward life. She lived and won races some time before the Noel Coward jargon became commonplace, but, had she made her début on Park Avenue in the middle thirties instead of on the race-course at Nairobi in the middle twenties, she would have been counted as one of those intellectually irresponsible individuals always referred to as being 'delightfully mad.' Her madness, of course, consisted simply of a penchant for doing things that, in the opinions of her stable mates, weren't being done.

No well-brought-up filly, for instance, while being exercised before the critical watchfulness of her owner, her trainer, and a half-dozen members of the Jockey Club, would come to an abrupt halt beside a mudhole left by last month's rains, buckle at the knees, and then, before anything could be done about it, roll over in the muck like a Berkshire hog. But Balmy did, as often as there was a mudhole in her path and a trusting rider on her back, though what pleasure she got out of it none of us ever knew. She was a little like the eccentric genius who, after being asked by his host why he had rubbed the broccoli in his hair at dinner, apologized with a bow from the waist and said he had thought it was spinach.

On a morning in my thirteenth year when Balmy was due for a canter, I rode her up a long slope that lay north of the farm and was called the Green Hill. All our horses, when doing slow work, were taken up the Green Hill to the place where it overlooked the Rongai Valley, which, in those years, was alive with game.

Balmy was alert as usual, but it seemed to me there was a pensive quality about the way she touched her neat hooves to the ground, and about the thoughtful tilt of her distinguished head. It was as if she had begun at last to see the error of her ways, and when we reached the crest of the hill, she was behaving as if no filly on God's earth had ever been so wantonly miscalled. Had there been no herd of zebra to come upon us as we rounded a little group of mimosa trees, Balmy's resolve to reform might never have been broken or even threatened.

The zebra were grazing in and out of the mimosa and on the slopes that fell into the valley. There were several hundred of them spread over an area of many acres, but those nearest us were an old dam and her foal of a few months.

Balmy had seen zebra before and zebra had often seen Balmy, but I had never observed that any gestures of mutual respect had been made by either side. I think Balmy was aware of the dictum, *noblesse oblige*, but, for all her mud-rolling, she never got very close to a zebra or even oxen without distending her nostrils in the manner of an eighteenth-century grande dame forced to wade through the fringes of a Paris mob. As for the zebra, they replied in kind, moving out of her path with the ponderous dignity of righteous proletariat, fortified in their contempt by the weight of their number.

The old dam we interrupted at her feeding on the Green Hill swept Balmy with a cold glance, kicked up her heels, and trotted toward the centre of the herd flinging over her shoulder at her spindly-legged foal a command to follow. But the foal never moved.

I once saw a London street urchin stand enraptured almost to the point of tears at the sight of a lovely lady swathed in sables stepping from her car to the curb. There was the same pathos and the same wistfulness in the eyes of the zebra foal as it hesitated chest deep in the long grass and stared upward at the Thoroughbred filly.

It was altogether a pretty picture even as observed from the saddle on Balmy's back, but I had left the farm with the specific warning to keep her calm at any cost. A race-horse, trained to the edge, can undo weeks of patient work merely by having a nervous tantrum at the wrong time.

Balmy was trained to the edge and this was the wrong time. She had at first ignored the young zebra, but the imperious voice of the old dam at once brought the situation to an issue. There must have been in it not only the call of a mother to its young, but also some cutting reference to Balmy as a pompous, vain creature not fit to be admired by honest folk. At least I am sure that was Balmy's interpretation.

She tilted her ears to their most indignant pitch, addressed a low and reassuring note to the renegade foal and then let fly a scream of defiance that might have been heard halfway across the Rongai Valley.

The details of what followed have never been quite clear in my memory. Balmy's challenge, clearly well spiced with insult, brought the old dam up on her heels and there ensued a battle of tongues that, in volume of sound and intensity of fury, would have put to shame all the aroused fishwives of literature. In the midst of it Balmy began to sweat, to tremble, and to buck, the old zebra dam galloped in erratic circles, bawling all the while, and the little foal, torn between filial duty and the fatal fascination of the bay filly, bounded and danced between the two like an hysterical child.

In the end, and in refutation of all the principles of justice, both animal and human, Balmy was triumphant.

I managed at last to bring her under control and head her toward the farm, but at her heels followed the little zebra foal, still a bit dazed and I think struggling against his own shame, and perhaps even against a minute twinge of remorse.

Behind us on the slope of the Green Hill, silent and trembling, stood the old dam surrounded by a few of her clan, and I suppose some of them must have been saying, 'You shouldn't take it too hard. Children are an ungrateful lot anyway, and it may be all for the best.'

Months later, after the zebra foal had got the run of the farm, not to say the domination of it, through exercising the same quality of instant decision and unswerving determination he had shown on the morning of his desertion, I went on a visit to Nairobi with my father, and when we returned, the foal was gone, nobody knew where.

Like a dog he had trotted into my bedroom each morning to nuzzle me out of sleep; he had established a reign of terror in the kitchen by threatening to attack the servants whenever tribute was withheld him. Because of his youth, I had at first pampered him with bottles of warm milk — an error of judgement which resulted in the often-repeated scene of my poor father, his evening pint of beer clutched grimly in his hand, flying through the house and into the garden with the little striped monster, to whom all bottles were now as one, in menacing pursuit.

In his adoration of Balmy, which never waned, the foal made her stall his own and invested her with such a sense of matronly responsibility that she could be handled even by the syces, and she never rolled in the mud again.

Punda, as I called him because it is the Swahili word for donkey, went away as he had come, even perhaps with less reason. He may have been received into the herd again like the prodigal son, or he may have been drummed out of it. Animals are not much given to sentiment, so I think it must have been the latter.

Since then, when I have seen a great herd like that which stampeded under my wings on the Serengetti, I have sometimes watched for an outcast zebra lingering at a distance from its edge. I have thought he would be full-sized now and getting along in years, but that, friendless or not, he would be content in his half loneliness because he could remember that as a mere child he had been a kind of jester and mascot at court.

What aimless dreaming! The drone of the plane, the steady sun, the long horizon, had all combined to make me forget for a while that time moved swifter than I, that the afternoon was almost spent, that nowhere was there any sign of Woody.

Or at least there had been a sign — an unmistakable sign which, but for such errant thoughts on an equally errant zebra foal, I might have seen a little sooner.

IV

Why Do We Fly?

IF YOU were to fly over the Russian steppes in the dead of winter after snow had fallen, and you saw beneath you a date palm green as spring against the white of the land, you might carry on for twenty miles or so before the incongruity of a tropical tree rooted in ice struck against your sense of harmony and made you swing round on your course to look again. You would find that the tree was not a date palm or, if it still persisted in being one, that insanity had claimed you for its own.

During the five or ten minutes I had watched the herd of game spread like a barbaric invasion across the plain, I had unconsciously observed, almost in their midst, a pool of water bright as a splinter from a glazier's table.

I knew that the country below, in spite of its drought-resistant grass, was dry during most of the year. I knew that whatever water holes one did find were opaque and brown, stirred by the feet of drinking game. But the water I saw was not brown; it was clear, and it received the sun and turned it back again in strong sharp gleams of light.

Like the date palm on the Russian steppes, this crystal pool in the arid roughness of the Serengetti was not only incongruous, it was impossible. And yet, without the slightest hesitation, I flew over it and beyond it until it was gone from sight and from my thoughts.

There is no twilight in East Africa. Night tramps on the

heels of Day with little gallantry and takes the place she
lately held, in severe and humourless silence. Sounds of the
things that live in the sun are quickly gone — and with them
the sounds of roving aeroplanes, if their pilots have learned
the lessons there are to learn about night weather, distances
that seem never to shrink, and the perfidy of landing fields
that look like aerodromes by day, but vanish in darkness.

I watched small shadows creep from the rocks and saw birds
in black flocks homeward bound to the scattered bush, and I
began to consider my own home and a hot bath and food.
Hope always persists beyond reason, and it seemed futile to
nurse any longer the expectation of finding Woody with so
much of the afternoon already gone. If he were not dead, he
would of course light fires by night, but already my fuel was
low, I had no emergency rations — and no sleep.

I had touched my starboard rudder, altering my course east
for Nairobi, when the thought first struck me that the shining
bit of water I had so calmly flown over was not water at all,
but the silvered wings of a Klemm monoplane bright and motionless in the path of the slanting sun.

It was not really a thought, of course, nor even one of those
blinding flashes of realization that come so providentially to
the harried heroes of fiction. It was no more than a hunch.
But where is there a pilot foolhardy enough to ignore his
hunches? I am not one. I could never tell where inspiration
begins and impulse leaves off. I suppose the answer is in the
outcome. If your hunch proves a good one, you were inspired;
if it proves bad, you are guilty of yielding to thoughtless impulse.

But before considering any of this, I had already reversed
my direction, lost altitude, and opened the throttle again. It
was a race with racing shadows, a friendly trial between the
sun and me.

As I flew, my hunch became conviction. Nothing in the

world, I thought, could have looked so much like reflecting water as the wings of Woody's plane. I remembered how bright those wings had been when last I saw them, freshly painted to shine like silver or stainless steel. Yet they were only of flimsy wood and cloth and hardened glue.

The deception had amused Woody. 'All metal,' he would say, jerking a thumb toward the Klemm; 'all metal, except just the wings and fuselage and prop and little things like that. Everything else is metal — even the engine.'

Even the engine! — as much of a joke to us as to the arrant winds of Equatorial Africa; a toy engine with bustling manner and frantic voice; an hysterical engine, guilty at last perhaps of what, in spite of Woody's jokes and our own, we all had feared.

Now almost certainly guilty, I thought, for there at last was what I hunted — not an incredible pool of water, but, unmistakable this time, the Klemm huddled to earth like a shot bird, not crushed, but lifeless and alone, beside it no fire, not even a stick with a fluttering rag.

I throttled down and banked the Avian in slow, descending circles.

I might have had a pious prayer for Woody on my lips at that moment, but I didn't have. I could only wonder if he had been hurt and taken into a manyatta by some of the Masai Murani, or if, idiotically, he had wandered into the pathless country in search of water and food. I even damned him slightly, I think, because, as I glided to within five hundred feet of the Klemm, I could see that it was unscathed.

There can be a strange confusion of emotions at such a moment. The sudden relief I felt in knowing that at least the craft had not been damaged was, at the same time, blended with a kind of angry disappointment at not finding Woody, perhaps hungry and thirsty, but anyhow alive beside it.

Rule one for forced landings ought to be, 'Don't give up the ship.' Woody of all people should have known this — did know it, of course, but where was he?

Circling again, I saw that in spite of a few pig-holes and scattered rocks, a landing would be possible. About thirty yards from the Klemm there was a natural clearing blanketed with short, tawny grass. From the air I judged the length of the space to be roughly a hundred and fifty yards — not really long enough for a plane without brakes, but long enough with such head wind as there was to check her glide.

I throttled down, allowing just enough revs to prevent the ship from stalling at the slow speed required to land in so small a space. Flattening out and swinging the tail from side to side in order to get what limited vision I could at the ground below and directly ahead, I flew in gently and brought the Avian to earth in a surprisingly smooth run. I made a mental note at the time that the take-off, especially if Woody were aboard, might be a good deal more difficult.

But there was no Woody.

I climbed out, got my dusty and dented water bottle from the locker, and walked over to the Klemm, motionless and still glittering in the late light. I stood in front of her wings and saw no sign of mishap, and heard nothing. There she rested, frail and feminine, against the rough, grey ground, her pretty wings unmarked, her propeller rakishly tilted, her cockpit empty.

There are all kinds of silences and each of them means a different thing. There is the silence that comes with morning in a forest, and this is different from the silence of a sleeping city. There is silence after a rainstorm, and before a rainstorm, and these are not the same. There is the silence of emptiness, the silence of fear, the silence of doubt. There is a certain silence that can emanate from a lifeless object as from a chair lately used, or from a piano with old dust upon its keys, or from anything that has answered to the need of a man, for pleasure or for work. This kind of silence can speak. Its voice may be melancholy, but it is not always so; for the chair may have been left by a laughing child or the last notes of the piano may have been raucous and gay. Whatever the mood or the circumstance, the essence of its quality may linger in the silence that follows. It is a soundless echo.

With the water bottle swinging from my hand on its long leather strap, like an erratic pendulum, I walked around Woody's plane. But even with shadows flooding the earth like slow-moving water and the grass whispering under the half-spent breath of the wind, there was no feeling of gloom or disaster.

The silence that belonged to the slender little craft was, I thought, filled with malice — a silence holding the spirit of wanton mischief, like the quiet smile of a vain woman exultant over a petty and vicious triumph.

I had expected little else of the Klemm, frivolous and inconstant as she was, but I knew suddenly that Woody was not dead. It was not that kind of silence.

I found a path with the grass bent down and little stones scuffed from their hollows, and I followed it past some larger stones into a tangle of thorn trees. I shouted for Woody and got nothing but my own voice for an answer, but when I turned my head to shout again, I saw two boulders leaning together, and in the cleft they made were a pair of legs clothed in grimy work slacks and, beyond the legs, the rest of Woody, face down with his head in the crook of his arm.

I went over to where he was, unscrewed the cap of the water bottle and leaned down and shook him.

'It's Beryl,' I called, and shook him harder. One of the legs moved and then the other. Life being hope, I got hold of his belt and tugged.

Woody began to back out of the cleft of the rocks with a motion irrelevantly reminiscent of the delectable crayfish of the South of France. He was mumbling, and I recalled that men dying of thirst are likely to mumble and that what they want is water. I poured a few drops on the back of his neck as it appeared and got, for my pains, a startled grunt. It was followed by a few of those exquisite words common to the vocabularies of sailors, airplane pilots, and stevedores — and then abruptly Woody was sitting upright on the ground, his face skinny beneath a dirty beard, his lips cinder-dry and split, his eyes red-rimmed and sunk in his cheeks. He was a sick man and he was grinning.

'I resent being treated like a corpse,' he said. 'It's insulting. Is there anything to eat?'

I once knew a man who, at each meeting with a friend, said, 'Well, well — it's a small world after all!' He must be very unhappy now, because, when I last saw him, friends were slipping from his orbit like bees from a jaded flower and his world was becoming lonely and large. But there was truth in his dreary platitude. I have the story of Bishon Singh to prove it and Woody to witness it.

Bishon Singh arrived in a little billow of dust when there was nothing left of the sun but its forehead, and Woody and I had made insincere adieus to the Klemm and were preparing to take off for Nairobi and a doctor — and a new magneto, if one could be had.

'There's a man on a horse,' said Woody.

But it wasn't a man on a horse.

I had helped Woody into the front cockpit of the Avian, and I stood alongside the craft ready to swing her propeller, when the little billow made its entrance into our quasi-heroic scene. Six wagging and tapered ears protruded from the crest of the billow, and they were the ears of three donkeys. Four faces appeared in four halos of prairie dust, and three of these were the faces of Kikuyu boys. The fourth was the face of Bishon Singh, dark, bearded, and sombre.

'You won't believe it,' I said to Woody, 'but that is an Indian I've known from childhood. He worked for years on my father's farm.'

'I'll believe anything you tell me,' said Woody, 'if only you get me out of here.'

'Beru! Beru!' said Bishon Singh, 'or do I dream?'

Bishon Singh is a Sikh and as such he wears his long black hair braided to his long black beard, and together they make a cowl, like a monk's.

His face is small and stern and it peers from the cowl with nimble black eyes. They can be kind, or angry, like other eyes, but I do not think they can be gay. I have never seen them gay.

'Beru!' he said again. 'I do not believe this. This is not Njoro. It is not the farm at Njoro, or the Rongai Valley. It is more than a hundred miles from there — but here you are, tall and grown up, and I am an old man on my way to my Duka with things to sell. But we meet. We meet with all these years behind us. I do not believe it! Walihie Mungu Yangu — I do not believe it. God has favoured me!'

'It's a small world,' groaned Woody from the plane.

'Na furie sana ku wanana na wewe,' I said to Bishon Singh in Swahili. 'I am very happy to see you again.'

He was dressed as I had always remembered him — thick army boots, blue puttees, khaki breeches, a ragged leather waistcoat, all of it surmounted by a great turban, wound, as I recalled it, from at least a thousand yards of the finest cotton

51

cloth. As a child, that turban had always intrigued me; there was so much of it and so little of Bishon Singh.

We stood a few yards in front of his three nodding donkeys, each with a silent Kikuyu boy in attendance, and each with an immense load on its back — pots, tin pans, bales of cheap Bombay prints, copper wire to make Masai earrings and bracelets. There was even tobacco, and oil for the Murani to use in the braiding of their hair.

There were things made of leather, things of paper, things of celluloid and rubber, all bulging, dangling, and bursting from the great pendulous packs. Here was Commerce, four-footed and halting, slow and patient, unhurried, but sure as tomorrow, beating its way to a counter in the African hinterland.

Bishon Singh raised an arm and included both the Klemm and the Avian in its sweep.

'N'dege!' he said — 'the white man's bird! You do not ride on them, Beru?'

'I fly one of them, Bishon Singh.'

I said it sadly, because the old man had pointed with his left arm and I saw that his right was withered and crippled and useless. It had not been like that when I had seen him last.

'So,' he scolded, 'now it has come to this. To walk is not enough. To ride on a horse is not enough. Now people must go from place to place through the air, like a *diki toora*. Nothing but trouble will come of it, Beru. God spits upon such blasphemy.'

'God has spat,' sighed Woody.

'My friend was stranded here,' I said to Bishon Singh, 'his n'dege — the one that shines like a new rupee — is broken. We are going back to Nairobi.'

'Walihie! Walihie! It is over a hundred miles, Beru, and

the night is near. I will unpack my donkeys and brew hot tea. It is a long way to Nairobi — even for you who go with the wind.'

'We will be there in less than an hour, Bishon Singh. It would take you as long to build a fire and make the tea.'

I put my hand out and the old Sikh grasped it and held it, for a moment very tightly, just as he had often held it some ten years ago when he was still taller than I — even without his fantastic turban. Only then he had used his right hand. He looked down at it now with a smile on his thin lips.

'What was it?' I asked.

'Simba, Beru — lion.' He shrugged. 'One day on the way to Ikoma . . . it makes us like brothers, you and me. Each has been torn by a lion. You remember that time at Kabete when you were a little child?'

'I'll never forget it.'

'Nor I,' said Bishon Singh.

I turned and went forward to the propeller of the Avian and grasped the highest blade with my right hand and nodded to Woody. He sat in the front cockpit ready to switch on.

Bishon Singh moved backward a few steps, close to his Tom Thumb cavalcade. The three donkeys left off their meagre feeding, raised their heads and tilted their ears. The Kikuyu boys stood behind the donkeys and waited. In the dead light the Klemm had lost her brilliance and was only the sad and discredited figure of an aerial Jezebel.

'God will keep you,' said Bishon Singh.

'Good-bye and good fortune!' I called.

'Contact!' roared Woody and I swung the prop.

He lay, at last, on a bed in the small neat shack of the East African Aero Club waiting for food, for a drink — and, I suspect, for sympathy.

'The Klemm is a bitch,' he said. 'No man in his right mind should ever fly a Klemm aeroplane, with a Pobjoy motor, in Africa. You treat her kindly, you nurse her engine, you put silver dope on her wings, and what happens?'

'The magneto goes wrong,' I said.

'It's like a woman with nerves,' said Woody, 'or no conscience, or even an imbecile!'

'Oh, much worse.'

'Why do we fly?' said Woody. 'We could do other things. We could work in offices, or have farms, or get into the Civil Service. We could ...'

'We could give up flying tomorrow. You could, anyhow. You could walk away from your plane and never put your feet on a rudder bar again. You could forget about weather and night flights and forced landings, and passengers who get airsick, and spare parts that you can't find, and wonderful new ships that you can't buy. You could forget all that and go off somewhere away from Africa and never look at an aerodrome again. You might be a very happy man, so why don't you?'

'I couldn't bear it,' said Woody. 'It would all be so dull.'

'It can be dull anyway.'

'Even with lions tearing you to bits at Kabete?'

'Oh, that was back in my childhood. Some day I'll write a book and you can read about it.'

'God forbid!' said Woody.

BOOK TWO

V

He Was a Good Lion

WHEN I was a child, I spent all my days with the Nandi Murani, hunting barefooted, in the Rongai Valley, or in the cedar forests of the Mau Escarpment.

At first I was not permitted to carry a spear, but the Murani depended on nothing else.

You cannot hunt an animal with such a weapon unless you know the way of his life. You must know the things he loves, the things he fears, the paths he will follow. You must be sure of the quality of his speed and the measure of his courage. He will know as much about you, and at times make better use of it.

But my Murani friends were patient with me.

'Amin yut!' one would say, 'what but a dik-dik will run like that? Your eyes are filled with clouds today, Lakweit!'

That day my eyes were filled with clouds, but they were young enough eyes and they soon cleared. There were other days and other dik-dik. There were so many things.

There were dik-dik and leopard, kongoni and warthog, buffalo, lion, and the 'hare that jumps.' There were many thousands of the hare that jumps.

And there were wildebeest and antelope. There was the snake that crawls and the snake that climbs. There were birds, and young men like whips of leather, like rainshafts in the sun, like spears before a singiri.

'Amin yut!' the young men would say, 'that is no buffalo spoor, Lakweit. Here! Bend down and look. Bend down and look at this mark. See how this leaf is crushed. Feel the wetness of this dung. Bend down and look so that you may learn!'

And so, in time, I learned. But some things I learned alone.

There was a place called Elkington's Farm by Kabete Station. It was near Nairobi on the edge of the Kikuyu Reserve, and my father and I used to ride there from town on horses or in a buggy, and along the way my father would tell me things about Africa.

Sometimes he would tell me stories about the tribal wars — wars between the Masai and the Kikuyu (which the Masai always won), or between the Masai and the Nandi (which neither of them ever won), and about their great leaders and their wild way of life which, to me, seemed much greater fun than our own. He would tell me of Lenana, the brilliant Masai ol-oiboni, who prophesied the coming of the White Man, and of Lenana's tricks and stratagems and victories, and about how his people were unconquerable and unconquered — until, in retaliation against the refusal of the Masai warriors to join the King's African Rifles, the British marched upon the Native villages; how, inadvertently, a Masai woman was killed, and how two Hindu shopkeepers were murdered in reprisal by the Murani. And thus, why it was that the thin, red line of Empire had grown slightly redder.

He would tell me old legends sometimes about Mount Kenya, or about the Menegai Crater, called the Mountain of God, or about Kilimanjaro. He would tell me these things and I would ride alongside and ask endless questions, or we would sit together in the jolting buggy and just think about what he had said.

One day, when we were riding to Elkington's, my father spoke about lions.

'Lions are more intelligent than some men,' he said, 'and more courageous than most. A lion will fight for what he has and for what he needs; he is contemptuous of cowards and wary of his equals. But he is not afraid. You can always trust a lion to be exactly what he is — and never anything else.'

'Except,' he added, looking more paternally concerned than usual, 'that damned lion of Elkington's!'

The Elkington lion was famous within a radius of twelve miles in all directions from the farm, because, if you happened to be anywhere inside that circle, you could hear him roar when he was hungry, when he was sad, or when he just felt like roaring. If, in the night, you lay sleepless on your bed and listened to an intermittent sound that began like the bellow of a banshee trapped in the bowels of Kilimanjaro and ended like the sound of that same banshee suddenly at large and arrived at the foot of your bed, you knew (because you had been told) that this was the song of Paddy.

Two or three of the settlers in East Africa at that time had caught lion cubs and raised them in cages. But Paddy, the Elkington lion, had never seen a cage.

He had grown to full size, tawny, black-maned and muscular, without a worry or a care. He lived on fresh meat, not of his own killing. He spent his waking hours (which coincided with everybody else's sleeping hours) wandering through Elkington's fields and pastures like an affable, if apostrophic, emperor, a-stroll in the gardens of his court.

He thrived in solitude. He had no mate, but pretended indifference and walked alone, not toying too much with imaginings of the unattainable. There were no physical barriers to his freedom, but the lions of the plains do not accept

into their respected fraternity an individual bearing in his
coat the smell of men. So Paddy ate, slept, and roared, and
perhaps he sometimes dreamed, but he never left Elkington's.
He was a tame lion, Paddy was. He was deaf to the call of the
wild.

'I'm always careful of that lion,' I told my father, 'but he's
really harmless. I have seen Mrs. Elkington stroke him.'

'Which proves nothing,' said my father. 'A domesticated
lion is only an unnatural lion — and whatever is unnatural is
untrustworthy.'

Whenever my father made an observation as deeply philo-
sophical as that one, and as inclusive, I knew there was nothing more to be said.

I nudged my horse and we broke into a canter covering the
remaining distance to Elkington's.

It wasn't a big farm as farms went in Africa before the First
World War, but it had a very nice house with a large veranda
on which my father, Jim Elkington, Mrs. Elkington, and one
or two other settlers sat and talked with what to my mind was
always unreasonable solemnity.

There were drinks, but beyond that there was a tea-table
lavishly spread, as only the English can spread them. I have
sometimes thought since of the Elkingtons' tea-table —
round, capacious, and white, standing with sturdy legs against
the green vines of the garden, a thousand miles of Africa
receding from its edge.

It was a mark of sanity, I suppose, less than of luxury. It
was evidence of the double debt England still owes to ancient
China for her two gifts that made expansion possible — tea
and gunpowder.

But cakes and muffins were no fit bribery for me. I had
pleasures of my own then, or constant expectations. I made
what niggardly salutations I could bring forth from a disinter-

ested memory and left the house at a gait rather faster than a
trot.

As I scampered past the square hay shed a hundred yards
or so behind the Elkington house, I caught sight of Bishon
Singh whom my father had sent ahead to tend our horses.

I think the Sikh must have been less than forty years old
then, but his face was never any indication of his age. On some
days he looked thirty and on others he looked fifty, depending
on the weather, the time of day, his mood, or the tilt of his
turban. If he had ever disengaged his beard from his hair and
shaved the one and clipped the other, he might have aston-
ished us all by looking like one of Kipling's elephant boys, but
he never did either, and so, to me at least, he remained a man
of mystery, without age or youth, but burdened with experience, like the wandering Jew.

He raised his arm and greeted me in Swahili as I ran through
the Elkington farmyard and out toward the open country.

Why I ran at all or with what purpose in mind is beyond
my answering, but when I had no specific destination I always
ran as fast as I could in the hope of finding one — and I always
found it.

I was within twenty yards of the Elkington lion before I
saw him. He lay sprawled in the morning sun, huge, black-
maned, and gleaming with life. His tail moved slowly, strok-
ing the rough grass like a knotted rope end. His body was
sleek and easy, making a mould where he lay, a cool mould,
that would be there when he had gone. He was not asleep; he
was only idle. He was rusty-red, and soft, like a strokable cat.

I stopped and he lifted his head with magnificent ease and
stared at me out of yellow eyes.

I stood there staring back, scuffling my bare toes in the
dust, pursing my lips to make a noiseless whistle — a very
small girl who knew about lions.

Paddy raised himself then, emitting a little sigh, and began to contemplate me with a kind of quiet premeditation, like that of a slow-witted man fondling an unaccustomed thought.

I cannot say that there was any menace in his eyes, because there wasn't, or that his 'frightful jowls' were drooling, because they were handsome jowls and very tidy. He did sniff the air, though, with what impressed me as being close to audible satisfaction. And he did not lie down again.

I remembered the rules that one remembers. I did not run. I walked very slowly, and I began to sing a defiant song.

'Kali coma Simba sisi,' I sang, 'Asikari yoti ni udari! — Fierce like the lion are we, Askari all are brave!'

I went in a straight line past Paddy when I sang it, seeing his eyes shine in the thick grass, watching his tail beat time to the metre of my ditty.

'Twendi, twendi — ku pigana — piga aduoi — piga sana! — Let us go, let us go — to fight — beat down the enemy! Beat hard, beat hard!'

What lion would be unimpressed with the marching song of the King's African Rifles?

Singing it still, I took up my trot toward the rim of the low hill which might, if I were lucky, have Cape gooseberry bushes on its slopes.

The country was grey-green and dry, and the sun lay on it closely, making the ground hot under my bare feet. There was no sound and no wind.

Even Paddy made no sound, coming swiftly behind me.

What I remember most clearly of the moment that followed are three things — a scream that was barely a whisper, a blow that struck me to the ground, and, as I buried my face in my arms and felt Paddy's teeth close on the flesh of my leg, a fantastically bobbing turban, that was Bishon Singh's turban, appear over the edge of the hill.

I remained conscious, but I closed my eyes and tried not to be. It was not so much the pain as it was the sound.

The sound of Paddy's roar in my ears will only be duplicated, I think, when the doors of hell slip their wobbly hinges, one day, and give voice and authenticity to the whole panorama of Dante's poetic nightmares. It was an immense roar that encompassed the world and dissolved me in it.

I shut my eyes very tight and lay still under the weight of Paddy's paws.

Bishon Singh said afterward that he did nothing. He said he had remained by the hay shed for a few minutes after I ran past him, and then, for no explainable reason, had begun to follow me. He admitted, though, that, a little while before, he had seen Paddy go in the direction I had taken.

The Sikh called for help, of course, when he saw the lion meant to attack, and a half-dozen of Elkington's syces had come running from the house. Along with them had come Jim Elkington with a rawhide whip.

Jim Elkington, even without a rawhide whip, was very impressive. He was one of those enormous men whose girths alone seem to preclude any possibility of normal movement, much less of speed. But Jim had speed — not to be loosely compared with lightning, but rather like the speed of something spherical and smooth and relatively irresistible, like the cannon balls of the Napoleonic Wars. Jim was, without question, a man of considerable courage, but in the case of my Rescue From the Lion, it was, I am told, his momentum rather than his bravery for which I must forever be grateful.

It happened like this — as Bishon Singh told it;

'I am resting against the walls of the place where hay is kept and first the large lion and then you, Beru, pass me going toward the open field, and a thought comes to me that a lion

63

and a young girl are strange company, so I follow. I follow to the place where the hill that goes up becomes the hill that goes down, and where it goes down deepest I see that you are running without much thought in your head and the lion is running behind you with many thoughts in his head, and I scream for everybody to come very fast.

'Everybody comes very fast, but the large lion is faster than anybody, and he jumps on your back and I see you scream but I hear no scream. I only hear the lion, and I begin to run with everybody, and this includes Bwana Elkington, who is saying a great many words I do not know and is carrying a long kiboko which he holds in his hand and is meant for beating the large lion.

'Bwana Elkington goes past me the way a man with lighter legs and fewer inches around his stomach might go past me, and he is waving the long kiboko so that it whistles over all of our heads like a very sharp wind, but when we get close to the lion it comes to my mind that that lion is not of the mood to accept a kiboko.

'He is standing with the front of himself on your back, Beru, and you are bleeding in three or five places, and he is roaring. I do not believe Bwana Elkington could have thought that that lion at that moment would consent to being beaten, because the lion was not looking the way he had ever looked before when it was necessary for him to be beaten. He was looking as if he did not wish to be disturbed by a kiboko, or the Bwana, or the syces, or Bishon Singh, and he was saying so in a very large voice.

'I believe that Bwana Elkington understood this voice when he was still more than several feet from the lion, and I believe the Bwana considered in his mind that it would be the best thing not to beat the lion just then, but the Bwana when he runs very fast is like the trunk of a great baobob tree rolling down a slope, and it seems that because of this it was not possible for him to explain the thought of his mind to the soles of his feet in a sufficient quickness of time to prevent him from rushing much closer to the lion than in his heart he wished to be.

'And it was this circumstance, as I am telling it,' said Bishon Singh, 'which in my considered opinion made it possible for you to be alive, Beru.'

'Bwana Elkington rushed at the lion then, Bishon Singh?'

'The lion, as of the contrary, rushed at Bwana Elkington,' said Bishon Singh. 'The lion deserted you for the Bwana, Beru. The lion was of the opinion that his master was not in any honest way deserving of a portion of what he, the lion, had accomplished in the matter of fresh meat through no effort by anybody except himself.'

Bishon Singh offered this extremely reasonable interpretation with impressive gravity, as if he were expounding the Case For the Lion to a chosen jury of Paddy's peers.

'Fresh meat'...I repeated dreamily, and crossed my fingers.

'So then what happened...?'

The Sikh lifted his shoulders and let them drop again 'What could happen, Beru? The lion rushed for Bwana Elkington, who in his turn rushed from the lion, and in so rushing did not keep in his hand the long kiboko, but allowed it to fall upon the ground, and in accomplishing this the Bwana was free to ascend a very fortunate tree, which he did.'

'And you picked me up, Bishon Singh?'

He made a little dip with his massive turban. 'I was happy with the duty of carrying you back to this very bed, Beru, and of advising your father, who had gone to observe some of Bwana Elkington's horses, that you had been moderately eaten by the large lion. Your father returned very fast, and

Bwana Elkington some time later returned very fast, but the large lion has not returned at all.'

The large lion had not returned at all. That night he killed a horse, and the next night he killed a yearling bullock, and after that a cow fresh for milking.

In the end he was caught and finally caged, but brought to no rendezvous with the firing squad at sunrise. He remained for years in his cage, which, had he managed to live in freedom with his inhibitions, he might never have seen at all.

It seems characteristic of the mind of man that the repression of what is natural to humans must be abhorred, but that what is natural to an infinitely more natural animal must be confined within the bounds of a reason peculiar only to men — more peculiar sometimes than seems reasonable at all.

Paddy lived, people stared at him and he stared back, and this went on until he was an old, old lion. Jim Elkington died, and Mrs. Elkington, who really loved Paddy, was forced, because of circumstances beyond her control or Paddy's, to have him shot by Boy Long, the manager of Lord Delamere's estates.

This choice of executioners was, in itself, a tribute to Paddy, for no one loved animals more or understood them better, or could shoot more cleanly than Boy Long.

But the result was the same to Paddy. He had lived and died in ways not of his choosing. He was a good lion. He had done what he could about being a tame lion. Who thinks it just to be judged by a single error?

I still have the scars of his teeth and claws, but they are very small now and almost forgotten, and I cannot begrudge him his moment.

VI

Still is the Land

THE farm at Njoro was end-
less, but it was no farm at all until my father made it. He
made it out of nothing and out of everything — the things of
which all farms are made. He made it out of forest and bush,
rocks, new earth, sun, and torrents of warm rain. He made it
out of labour and out of patience.

He was no farmer. He bought the land because it was cheap
and fertile, and because East Africa was new and you could
feel the future of it under your feet.

It looked like this at first: It was a broad stretch of land,
part of it open valley, but most of it roofed with the heads of
high trees — cedar, ebony, mahogo, teak, and bamboo —
and their trunks were snared in miles of creeping plants. The
creeping plants rose to heights of twelve and fifteen feet and,
from the ground, you never saw the tops of the trees until they
fell from the blows of axes and were dragged away by teams
of oxen handled by Dutchmen with whips that cracked all
day.

People called Wanderobo lived in the forests and hunted in
them with bows and poisoned arrows and poisoned spears, but
they were never a threat to any of my father's men or to us.
They were not quarrelsome people. They hid in the creeping
vines, in the trees, and the underbrush, and watched the work
of the axes and the teams of oxen and moved deeper into the
growth.

67

When the farm began to acquire an atmosphere of permanence and the yard in front of the first few huts was trampled hard and dogs sprawled on it in the sun, some of these Wanderobo would come out of the forest bringing the black and white skins of Colobus monkeys to trade for salt and oil and sugar. The skins were sewn together to make soft rugs for the beds, and I remembered them long after they were worn out and forgotten and Colobus monkeys were no longer easy to find — and the farm had become almost an industry.

By then there were a thousand Kavirondo and Kikuyu working on it instead of ten or twenty, and hundreds of oxen instead of just a few. The forest had fallen back, giving ground with the grim dignity of a respected enemy, and fields were cleaned of the rocks and bush that had lent them the character of wilderness for centuries. Huts had become houses, sheds had become stables, cattle had cut paths in the prairie.

My father bought two old steam engines and anchored them to make power for a grist mill. It was as if there had never before been a grist mill anywhere, as if all the maize in the world waited to be ground and all the wheat ever grown needed only to be made into flour.

You could stand on a hill and look down on the dirt-track road that went to Kampi ya Moto, where the maize was so tall that the tallest man seemed like a child when he walked in it, and you could see a ribbon of wagons, each drawn by sixteen oxen, coming loaded with grain to the farm. Sometimes the wagons followed so close upon one another that the ribbon seemed motionless. But at the entrance to the mill, you could see that it almost never stopped.

The mill never stopped, and the crew of Kavirondo who unloaded the heavy bags and reloaded them again, the coarse grain ground smooth and yellow, moved from dawn until dark, and sometimes after dark, like the lesser members of a great ballet set to the music of steam and turning millstones.

Nearly all the produce of the mill, the flour, and the posho, went to the Government to feed the labourers of the Uganda Railway.

This was a good enough railway as far as it went (from Mombasa to Kisumu), but it had an unhappy youth. As late as 1900 its trains were afraid to go out in the dark — and with reason. Lion infested the country it traversed, and a passenger or an engineer was either a brave man or one with a suicidal phobia to disembark at any of the outlying stations unarmed.

A telegraph line followed the rails to Kisumu about 1902 — or it was intended that one should. The posts were there, and the wire too, but rhino take sensual and sadistic pleasure in scratching their great hulks against telegraph posts, and any baboon worthy of his salt cannot resist swinging from suspended wires. Often a herd of giraffe found it expedient to cross the railroad tracks, but would not condescend to bow to the elevated metal strands that proclaimed the White Man's mandate over their feeding grounds. As a result, many telegrams en route from Mombasa to Kisumu, or the other way around, were intercepted, their cryptic dots and dashes frozen in a festoon of golden wire dangling from one or another of the longest necks in Africa.

With the money my father made out of the posho and flour, he bought two more old railway engines, fitted them with pulleys, and started the first important sawmill in British East Africa.

In time settlers who had lived in mud and daub huts built cedar houses and slabwood barns with shingled roofs, and the horizon took new shape and new colour. Thousands of cords of wood went from our farm into the fire boxes of the arrogant little engines of the Uganda Railway, and on dark nights the immense piles of sawdust slowly burning by the mill were like mountains with volcanic summits, dwarfed by distance.

Our stables grew from a few stalls to long rows of loose-boxes, and our Thoroughbred horses grew from two to a dozen, and then to a hundred, until my father had recovered his old love again, which had always been horses, and I gained my first love which has never left me.

Nor has my memory of the farm at Njoro ever left me.

I would stand in the little yard before the first of our few huts, and the deep Mau Forest would be behind me at my shoulder, and the Rongai Valley would be sloping downward from the tips of my toes. On clear days I could touch, almost, the high, charred rim of the Menegai Crater and see, by shading my eyes, the crown of Kenya studded in ice. I could see the peak of Sattima behind the Liakipia Escarpment that got purple when the sun rose, and smell the cedar wood and fresh-cut mahogo and hear the cracks of the Dutchmen's whips over the heads of their oxen. Sometimes the syces would sing at their work, and all day long the mares and their foals would romp and feed in the pastures or make the soothing sounds that horses make with their nostrils and with their hooves rustling the deep grass bedding in the stables. At a little distance, their imperious lords, the stallions, fretted amiably in more luxurious boxes and grew sleek and steel-muscled under constant care.

But ours was not the only farm at Njoro. Lord Delamere, whose brilliant, if vibratory, character helped so much to shape the mould in which the Kenya of today is cast, was our nearest neighbour.

His place, called 'Equator Ranch' because the Equator crossed a corner of it, had its headquarters in a little cluster of thatched huts snuggled against the foothills of the Mau Escarpment.

Those huts were the nucleus of what later became, through Delamere's courage and persistence, his vile temper and his soft charm, his vision and peculiar blindness to other points of view, not only an exemplary farm for all of British East Africa to profit by, but almost a small feudal state as well.

Delamere had two great loves — East Africa and the Masai People. To the country he gave his genius, most of his substance, and all of his energy. To the Masai he gave the help and understanding of a mind unhampered by the smug belief that the white man's civilization has nothing to learn from the black man's preferred lack of it. He respected the spirit of the Masai, their traditions, their physical magnificence, and their knowledge of cattle which, excepting war, was their only concern.

He spoke to their ol-oiboni with the same respect he employed in addressing his equals, or he turned his fury loose upon them with the same lack of respect he occasionally employed in addressing certain of his associates, members of the Government, and on at least one occasion the Governor himself.

Delamere's character had as many facets as a cut stone, but each facet shone with individual brightness. His generosity is legendary, but so is his sometimes wholly unjustified anger. He was profligate with money — his own and what he could borrow; but he spent nothing on himself and was scrupulously honest. He withstood physical hardships with stoical indifference, but he was a sick man most of his life. To him nothing in the world was more important than the agricultural and political future of British East Africa — and so, he was a serious man. Yet his gaiety and occasional abandonment to the spirit of fun, which I have often witnessed, could hardly be

equalled except by an ebullient schoolboy. Delamere looked
and sometimes acted like Puck, but those who had the temerity to scratch him found a nature more Draconian than whim-
sical underneath.

Although in later years I managed his Stud at Soysambu
before I learned to fly, and before I thought it possible that I
should ever want to do anything except handle horses, my
understanding of him, or at least of his work in the Protectorate, grew largely out of my association with the first Lady
Delamere while I was still a child.

She was, in a sense, my adopted mother, since I lived alone
with my father on the farm at Njoro, and over a period of
several years there were few days when I did not visit 'Lady
D.' at Equator Ranch. I cannot remember a time when her
understanding of my youthful problems was lacking or her
advice withheld.

Delamere is revered and remembered as a man who faced
hard tasks with irresistible will — and accomplished them all.
Lady Delamere, in the memory of those who knew her, faced
what to her must have been even harder tasks with perhaps
less will than patience, less aptitude than loyalty to her husband's ambitions; and if Delamere was the champion of the
East African settler (as indeed he was), then the devotion and
comradeship of his wife were as responsible for his many victories as his own genius.

So the two homesteads at Njoro — Delamere's and my
father's — while their huts were not within sight of each
other, stood shoulder to shoulder under the dark brow of the
Escarpment and waited for East Africa to grow.

Wainina, the head syce, tolled the stable bell each morning
and its rusty voice brought wakefulness to the farm. The

Dutchmen inspanned their oxen, syces reached for their saddles, the engines at the mills got up steam. Milkers, herdsmen, poultry boys, swineherds, gardeners, and house boys rubbed their eyes, smelled the weather, and trotted to their jobs.

On ordinary days Buller and I were a part of this, but on hunting days we escaped before the bell had struck a note and before the cocks had stretched their wings on the fences. I had lessons to do, and therefore lessons to avoid.

I remember one such day.

It began with the stirring of Buller asleep, as always, at the foot of my reimpie bed in the mud and daub hut we shared together — and with the hustle and hum of a million small insects.

I moved, I stretched, I opened my eyes on the far tableland of the Liakipia Escarpment outlined in the frame of my unglazed window, and I stepped on the earthen floor.

The water in the stable bucket was cold on my face, because nights in the East African Highlands are cold. The rawhide thong I tied around my waist was stiff and the blade of my 'bushman's friend' was unfriendly. Even the shaft of my Masai spear, which surely had life of its own, was rigid and unyielding, and its steel point, sunk in a sheath of black ostrich feather, emerged from it like a dull stone. The morning was still part of the night and its colour was grey.

I patted Buller and he wagged his lump of a tail to say he understood the need for silence. Buller was my accomplice in everything. He was a past-master at stealth and at more other things than any dog I ever owned or knew.

His loyalty to me was undeviating, but I could never think of him as being a sentimental dog, a dog fit for a pretty story of the kind that tears the heartstrings off their pegs; he was too rough, too tough, and too aggressive.

73

He was bull terrier and English sheep dog, thoroughly mixed, and turned out to look not very much like either. His jaw protruded, though, and his muscles were hard and ropy like the ones on the fantastic coursing dogs in the stone friezes of ancient Persia.

He was cynical toward life, and his black-and-white hide bore, in a cryptology of long, short, and semicircular scars, the history of his fighting career. He fought anything that needed to be fought, and when there was nothing immediately available in this category, he killed cats.

It was my father's complaint that when Buller was beaten for this, as he often was, he considered the punishment only as part of the inevitable hazard that went with cat-killing; and when the corrective treatment had been administered, it was always my father who looked chastened, and never Buller.

One night, a leopard, no doubt the chosen avenger of his species, crept through the open door of my hut and abducted Buller from the foot of my bed. Buller weighed something over sixty-five pounds and most of it was nicely coordinated offensive equipment. The sound and the fury of the first round of that battle sometimes still ring in my ears. But the advantage was with the attacker. Before I could do much more than scramble out of bed, dog and leopard disappeared in the moonless night.

My father and I followed a trail of blood through the bush, by the light of a hurricane lamp, until the trail dwindled and led to nothing. But at dawn I set out again and found Buller, barely breathing, his hard skull and his lower jaw pierced as if they had been skewered. I ran for help and carried him back on a stretcher made of sacking. He recovered, after ten months' tedious nursing, and became the same Buller again — except that his head had lost what little symmetry it ever had and cat-killing developed from a sport to a vocation.

As for the leopard, we caught him the next night in a trap, but he was beyond all caring anyway. He had no ears, only part of a throat, and great disillusionment in his handsome eyes. To my knowledge, and I think to his, it was the first time any dog of any size had been caught by a leopard and lived to dream about it.

Together, Buller and I slipped out into the little yard that separated my hut from the dining quarters. There was still no real dawn, but the sun was awake and the sky was changing colour.

Peering round the corner of my father's hut, which was close to my own, I could see that one or two of the more conscientious syces were already opening their stable doors.

Gay Warrior's box had even got a heap of manure outside it. That meant his syce had been there for some time. It also meant that my father would be out any minute to send his first string of race-horses to their morning work. If he were to see me with my spear, my dog, and the 'bushman's friend' strapped to my waist, he would hardly conclude that my mind was wrapped in ardent thoughts of 'The Fundamentals of English Grammar' or 'Exercises in Practical Arithmetic.' He would conclude, and rightly, that Buller and I were on our way to the nearest Nandi singiri to hunt with the Murani.

But we were adepts at our game. We scampered quickly through the cluster of domestic buildings, got behind the foaling boxes, and, when the moment was ripe, we hurried along the twisted path that, except to ourselves and the Natives whose feet had made it, was completely hidden by the high dry weather grass. It was wet grass so early in the day, heavy with morning dew, and the wetness clung to my bare legs and soaked into Buller's wiry coat.

I swung into the hop-and-carry-one gait — a kind of bound-ing lope used by the Nandi and Masai Murani — and ap-proached the singiri.

It was surrounded by a lattice and thorn boma, high as the withers of a cow. Inside the fence, the low thatched huts, looking as if they had grown from the earth and not been built upon it, extended in a haphazard circle. Their walls were made of logs cut from the forests, placed upright and caulked with mud. Each hut had a single door, a low door that could only be entered by crouching, and there were no windows. Smoke curled upward through the leaves of the thatch and on a still day made the singiri seem, from a dis-tance, like a patch in the prairie wreathed in the last wisps of a burned-out fire.

The ground in front of the doors and all that encircling the boma was flat and beaten hard with the feet of men, cattle, and goats.

A pack of dogs, half-bred, fawning, some of them snarling, rushed at Buller and me the moment we entered the boma. Buller greeted them as he always did — with arrogant indif-ference. He knew them too well. In packs they were good hunters; individually they were as cowardly as the hyena. I spoke to them by name to silence their foolish yapping.

We were at the door of the hut of the head Murani, and the beginning of a Nandi hunt, even so small as this would be, did not take place in the midst of noise or too much levity.

I drove the blunt end of my spear into the ground and stood beside it, waiting for the door to open.

VII

Praise God for the Blood of the Bull

ARAB MAINA clasped the
gourd of blood and curdled milk in both hands and looked
toward the sun. He chanted in a low voice:

'Praise God for the blood of the bull which brings strength
to our loins, and for the milk of the cow which gives warmth
to the breasts of our lovers.'

He drank deeply of the gourd then, let his belch roll upward
from his belly and resound against the morning silence. It
was a silence that we who stood there preserved until Arab
Maina had finished, because this was religion; it was the ritual
that came before the hunt. It was the Nandi custom.

'Praise God for the blood of the bull,' we said, and stood
before the singiri, and waited.

Jebbta had brought the gourds for Arab Maina, for Arab
Kosky, and for me. But she looked only at me.

'The heart of a Murani is like unto stone,' she whispered,
'and his limbs have the speed of an antelope. Where do you
find the strength and the daring to hunt with them, my sister?'

We were as young as each other, Jebbta and I, but she was
a Nandi, and if the men of the Nandi were like unto stone,
their women were like unto leaves of grass. They were shy
and they were feminine and they did the things that women
are meant to do, and they never hunted.

I looked down at the ankle-length skins Jebbta wore, which

77

rustled like taffeta when she moved, and she looked at my khaki shorts and lanky, naked legs.

'Your body is like mine,' she said; 'it is the same and it is no stronger.' She turned, avoiding the men with her eyes, because that too was law, and went quickly away tittering like a small bird.

'The blood of the bull...' said Arab Maina.

'We are ready.' Arab Kosky drew his sword from its scabbard and tested its blade. The scabbard was of leather, dyed red, and it hung on a beaded belt that encircled narrow and supple hips. He tested the blade and put it back into the red scabbard.

'By the sacred womb of my mother, we will kill the wild boar today!'

He moved forward behind Arab Maina with his broad shield and his straight spear, and I followed Arab Kosky with my own spear that was still new and very clean, and lighter than theirs. Behind me came Buller with no spear and no shield, but with the heart of a hunter and jaws that were weapons enough. There were the other dogs, but there was no dog like Buller.

We left the singiri with the first light of the sun warming the roofs of the huts, with cattle, goats, and sheep moving along the trails that led to open pastures — fat cattle, pampered cattle, attended as always by the young, uncircumcised boys.

There were cows, steers, and heifers — liquid brown eyes, wet, friendly nostrils, slobbery mouths that covered our legs with sticky fluid as Arab Maina pushed the stupid heads aside with his shield.

There were the pungent stench of goat's urine and a hot, comforting odour seeping through the hides of the cattle, and light on the long muscles of Arab Maina and Arab Kosky.

There was the whole of the day ahead — and the world to hunt in.

His little ritual forgotten now, Arab Maina was no longer stern. He laughed when Arab Kosky or I slipped in the cattle dung that littered our path, and shook his spear at a big black bull busy tearing up the earth with his hooves. 'Take care of your people and dare not insult me with a barren cow this year!'

But, for the most part, we ran silently in single file skirting the edge of the dense Mau Forest, wheeling north to descend into the Rongai Valley, its bottom a thousand feet below us.

Eight weeks had passed since the end of the heavy rains and the grass in the valley had already reached the height of a man's knee. The ears had begun to ripen in patches. Looking down upon it, the whole was like a broad counterpane dyed in rust and yellow and golden brown.

We filed along our path, almost invisible now, through the fresh-smelling leleshwa bush, avoiding with quick turns and careful leaps the stinging nettle and the shrubs that were armed with thorns. Buller ran at my heels with the native dogs spread fanwise behind.

Halfway down the slope of the valley a bevy of partridges rose from the grass and wheeled noisily into the sky. Arab Maina lifted his spear almost imperceptibly; Arab Kosky's long muscles were suddenly rigid. Watching him, I froze in my tracks and held my breath. It was the natural reaction of all hunters — that moment of listening after any alarm.

But there was nothing. The spear of Arab Maina dipped gently, the long muscles of Arab Kosky sprang again to life, Buller flicked his stubby tail, and we were off again, one behind another, with the warm sunlight weaving a pattern of our shadows in the thicket.

The heat of the valley rose to meet us. Singing cicadas,

79

butterflies like flowers before a wind fluttered against our
bodies or hovered over the low bush. Only small things that
were safe in the daylight moved.

We had run another mile before the cold nose of Buller
nudged against my leg and the dog slipped quickly past me,
past the two Murani, to plant himself, alert and motionless, in
the centre of our path.

'Stop.' I whispered the word, putting my hand on Arab
Kosky's shoulder. 'Buller has scented something.'

'I believe you are right, Lakweit!' With a wave of his hand
Arab Kosky ordered the pack of native dogs to crouch. In
that they were well trained. They pressed their lean bellies
on the ground, cocked their ears, but scarcely seemed to
breathe.

Arab Maina, sensing the need for free action, began laying
down his shield. The fingers of his left hand still touched the
worn leather of its handle, his legs were still bent at the knee,
when a male reed-buck bounded high into the air more than
fifty yards away.

I saw Arab Kosky's body bend like a bow and watched his
spear fly to his shoulder, but he was too late. The spear of
Arab Maina flashed in a quick arc of silver light and the reed-
buck fell with the hard point sunk deep under his heart. Not
even his first frantic bound had been completed before Arab
Maina's arm had brought him down.

'Karara-ni! The hand of our leader is swifter than the
flight of an arrow and stronger than the stroke of a leopard.'

Heaping praise on Arab Maina, Arab Kosky ran toward the
fallen reed-buck, the sword from his red leather sheath drawn
for the kill.

I looked at Arab Maina's slender arms with their even, flat
muscles and saw no visible sign of such immense strength
Arab Maina, like Arab Kosky, was tall and lithe as a young

bamboo, and his skin glowed like an ember under a whisper of wind. His face was young and hard, but there was soft humour in it. There was love of life in it — love for the hunt, love for the sureness of his strength, love for the beauty and usefulness of his spear.

The spear was made of pliant steel tempered and forged by the metallist of his own tribe. But it was also more than that.

To each Murani his spear is a symbol of his manhood, and as much a part of himself as the sinews of his body. His spear is a manifestation of his faith; without it he can achieve nothing — no land, no cattle, no wives. Not even honour can be his until that day comes, after his circumcision, when he stands before the gathered members of his tribe — men and women of all ages, from manyattas as scattered as the seeds of wild grass — and swears allegiance to them and to their common heritage.

He takes the spear from the hands of the ol-oiboni and holds it, as he will always hold it while there is strength in his arms and no cloud of age before his eyes. It is the emblem of his blood and his breeding, and possessing it, he is suddenly a man.

Possessing it, it is never afterward beyond his reach.

Arab Maina placed his left foot on the reed-buck and carefully drew out his spear.

'I do not know, it may have struck a bone,' he said.

He ran bloody fingers along the sharp edges of the weapon and let a little smile twist his lips. 'By the will of God, the metal is not chipped! My spear is unhurt.' He stooped to pluck a handful of grass and wiped the blood from the bright, warm steel.

Arab Kosky and I had already begun to skin the animal, using our 'bushman's friends.' There was not much time to waste, because our real hunt for the wild boar had not yet begun. But still the meat of the reed-buck would provide food for the dogs.

'The sun has hit the valley,' said Arab Maina; 'if we do not hurry the pigs will have gone in all directions like rolling weeds in a wind.'

Arab Kosky buried his fingers along the walls of the reed-buck's stomach, tearing it from the animal's frame.

'Hold this, Lakwani,' he said, 'and help me separate the intestines for the dogs.'

I took the slippery, jelly-like stomach in my hands and held it while I kneeled over the reed-buck.

'Maina, I still don't know how you managed to throw in time from the position you were in!'

Arab Kosky smiled.

'He is a Murani, Lakwani — and a Murani must always throw in time. Otherwise, some day a dangerous animal might charge swifter than the spear. Then, instead of mourning his death, our girls would laugh and say he should have stayed at home with the old men!'

Arab Maina leaned down and cut a chunk of meat from the cleanly skinned buck. He handed it to me for Buller. The rest, he and Arab Kosky left to the native mongrels.

Buller trotted a short distance away from the kill, dropped his reward in a little pool of shade, and regarded his snarling cousins with exquisite disdain. In the language that he spoke, and only I understood, he said quite clearly (with just a tinge of Swahili accent), 'By the noble ancestry of my bull terrier father, those animals behave like the wild dog!'

'And now,' said Arab Maina, moving away from the carnage, 'we must make ready for the hunt.'

The two Murani wore ochre-coloured shukas, each falling loosely from a single knot on the left shoulder, and each looking somewhat like a scanty Roman toga. They untied the knots now, wrapped the shukas prudently around their waists, and stood in the sun, the muscles in their backs rippling under their oiled skins like fretted water over a stony bed.

'Who can move freely with clothes on his body?' Arab Kosky said as he helped Arab Maina with the leather thong that bound his braided headdress in place. 'Who has seen the antelope run with rags upon his back to hinder his speed!'

'Who indeed?' said Arab Maina, smiling. 'I think sometimes you babble like a demented goat, Kosky. The sun is high and the valley still lies below us — and you speak to Lakwani of antelope wearing shukas! Take up your spears, my friends, and let us go.'

Single file again, with Arab Maina in the lead, then Arab Kosky, then myself, and Buller just behind, we ran on down into the valley.

There were no clouds and the sun stared down on the plain making heat waves rise from it like flames without colour.

The Equator runs close to the Rongai Valley, and, even at so high an altitude as this we hunted in, the belly of the earth was hot as live ash under our feet. Except for an occasional gust of fretful wind that flattened the high, corn-like grass, nothing uttered — nothing in the valley stirred. The chirrup-like drone of grasshoppers was dead, birds left the sky unmarked. The sun reigned and there were no aspirants to his place.

We stopped by the red salt-lick that cropped out of the ground in the path of our trail. I did not remember a time when the salt-lick was as deserted as this. Always before it had been crowded with grantii, impala, kongoni, eland, waterbuck, and a dozen kinds of smaller animals. But it was empty

today. It was like a marketplace whose flow and bustle of life
you had witnessed ninety-nine times, but, on your hundredth
visit, was vacant and still without even an urchin to tell you
why.

I put my hand on Arab Maina's arm. 'What are you thinking, Maina? Why is there no game today?'

'Be quiet, Lakweit, and do not move.'

I dropped the butt of my spear on the earth and watched
the two Murani stand still as trees, their nostrils distended,
their ears alert to all things. Arab Kosky's hand was tight on
his spear like the claw of an eagle clasping a branch.

'It is an odd sign,' murmured Arab Maina, 'when the salt-
lick is without company!'

I had forgotten Buller, but the dog had not forgotten us.
He had not forgotten that, with all the knowledge of the two
Murani, he still knew better about such things. He thrust his
body roughly between Arab Maina and myself, holding his
black wet nose close to the ground. And the hairs along his
spine stiffened. His hackles rose and he trembled.

We might have spoken, but we didn't. In his way Buller
was more eloquent. Without a sound, he said, as clearly as it
could be said — 'Lion.'

'Do not move, Lakweit.' Arab Kosky stepped closer to me.

'Steady, Buller,' I whispered to the dog, trying to soothe
his rising belligerence.

Our eyes followed the direction of Arab Maina's eyes. He
was staring into a small grass-curtained donga a few yards
from the edge of the salt-lick.

The lion that stood in the donga was not intimidated by
Arab Maina's stare. He was not concerned with our number.
He swung his tail in easy arcs, stared back through the wispy
grass, and his manner said, 'I am within my rights. If you
seek a battle, what are we waiting for?'

He moved slowly forward, increasing the momentum of his tail, flaunting his thick black mane.

'Ach! This is bad! He is angry — he wants to attack!' Arab Maina spoke in an undertone.

No animal, however fast, has greater speed than a charging lion over a distance of a few yards. It is a speed faster than thought — faster always than escape.

Under my restraining hand I felt the muscles of Buller knot and relax, in a surging flow of mounting fury. Buller's mind had reached its blind spot. Uncontrolled, he would throw himself in gallant suicide straight at the lion. I dug my fingers into the dog's coat and held tight.

Arab Maina's appearance was transformed. His face had taken on a sullen, arrogant expression, his square, bold jaw jutted forward. His eyes dimmed almost dreamily and sank behind high, shiny cheekbones. I watched the muscles on his neck swell like those on the neck of an angry snake, and saw flecks of white froth appear in the corners of his mouth Passive and rigid he stared back at the lion.

He raised his shield at last, as if to make sure it was still in his hand, and let his spear arm drop to his side to preserve all of its power for whatever might come.

He knew that if the lion attacked, his own skill and Arab Kosky's would, in the end, prove sufficient — but not before at least one of us had been killed or badly mauled. Arab Maina was more than a Murani; he was a leader of Murani, and as such he must be able to think as well as to fight. He must be capable of strategy.

Watching him still, as he in turn watched the lion, I knew that he had a plan of action.

'Observe his eyes,' he said; 'he thinks very hard of many things. He believes that we also think of those same things. We must show him that we are fearless as he himself is fearless, but that his desires are not our desires. We must walk straight past him firmly and with courage, and we must shame his anger by laughter and loud talk.'

Arab Kosky's brow was dotted with small bubbles of sweat. A slight flicker of a smile crept over his face.

'Yes, true enough! The lion thinks of many things. I too think of many things, and so does Lakweit. But your plan is a good one. We will try it.'

Arab Maina lifted his head a little higher, turning it only enough to keep the lion within the scope of his vision. He placed one sinewy leg in front of the other, and stiffly, like a man walking the trunk of a tree that bridges a chasm, he began to move. One after another, we followed. My hand still lay upon Buller's neck, but Arab Kosky let the dog and me slip past him to walk between the two Murani.

'Stay close to me, Lakweit' — Arab Maina's voice was anxious. 'I fear for you when it is not possible to see you.'

Arab Kosky burst suddenly into forced laughter.

'There is a tale about a rhino who needed a needle to do her husband's sewing...' he began.

'So she borrowed one from the porcupine...' said Arab Kosky.

'And swallowed it,' I contributed. 'I have heard that tale before, Kosky!'

The Murani laughed louder. 'But perhaps our friend the lion has not. Look at him. He is listening!'

'But not laughing,' said Arab Maina. 'He moves as we move. He comes closer!'

The lion had stalked out of the donga. Now, as we walked, we could see that he guarded the slain body of a large kongoni. Smears of blood were fresh on his forelegs, his jowls, and his chest. He was a lone hunter — an individualist — a solitary

marauder. His tail had stopped swinging. His great head
turned exactly in ratio to the speed of our stride. The full
force of the lion-smell, meaty, pungent, almost indescribable,
struck against our nostrils.

'Having swallowed the needle...' said Arab Kosky.

'Silence — he attacks!'

I do not know who moved with greater speed — Arab
Maina or the lion. I believe it must have been Arab Maina. I
think the Murani anticipated the charge even before the lion
moved, and because of that, it was a battle of wills instead of
weapons.

The lion rushed from the fringe of the donga like a rock
from a catapult. He stopped like the same rock striking the
walls of a battlement.

Arab Maina was down on his left knee. Beside him was
Arab Kosky. Each man, with his shield, his spear, and his
body, was a fighting machine no longer human, but only motionless and precise and coldly ready. Buller and I crouched
behind them, my own spear as ready as I could make it in
hands that were less hot from the sun than from excitement
and the pounding of my heart.

'Steady, Buller.'

'Do not move, Lakweit.'

The lion had stopped. He stood a few strides from Arab
Maina's buffalo-hide shield, stared into Arab Maina's eyes
challenging him over the top of it, and swung his tail like the
weight of a clock. At that moment I think the ants in the
grass paused in their work.

And then Arab Maina stood up.

I do not know how he knew that that particular instant
was the right instant or how he knew that the lion would accept a truce. It may have been accomplished by the sheer
arrogance of Arab Maina's decision to lower his shield, even

if slightly, and to rise, no longer warlike, and to beckon us on with superb and sudden indifference. But however it was, the lion never moved.

We left him slicing the tall grass with his heavy tail, the blood of the kongoni drying on his coat. He was thinking many things.

And I was disappointed. Long after we had continued our trot toward the place where we knew there would be warthog, I thought how wonderful it would have been if the lion had attacked and I had been able to use my spear on him while he clawed at the shields of the two Murani, and how later they might have said, 'If it hadn't been for you, Lakweit...!'

But then, I was very young.

We ran until we reached the Molo River.

The river took its life from the Mau Escarpment and twisted down into the valley and gave life, in turn, to mimosa trees with crowns as broad as clouds, and long creepers and liana that strangled the sunlight and left the riverbank soothing and dark.

The earth on the bank was damp and pitted with footprints of the game that followed a web-work of thin trails to drink at dawn, leaving the racy smell of their droppings and their bodies in the air. The river forest was narrow and cool and vibrant with the songs of multi-coloured birds, and clotted with bright flowers that scorned the sun.

We laid down our weapons and rested under the trees and drank the chilled water, making cups with our hands.

Arab Maina lifted his face from the edge of the river and smiled gently. 'My mouth was like unto ashes, Lakweit,' he said, 'but truly this water is even sweeter than Jebbta's carefully brewed tembo!'

'It is sweeter,' said Arab Kosky, 'and at this moment it is

more welcome. I promise you, my stomach had turned almost sour with thirst!'

Looking at me, Arab Maina laughed.

'Sour with thirst, he says, Lakweit! Sour, I think, with the sight of the lion at the salt-lick. Courage lives in a man's stomach, but there are times when it is not at home — and then the stomach is sour!'

Arab Kosky stretched his lithe, straight limbs on the tangled grass and smiled, showing teeth white as sun-cured bone. 'Talk lives in a man's head,' he answered, 'but sometimes it is very lonely because in the heads of some men there is nothing to keep it company — and so talk goes out through the lips.'

I laughed with both of them and pressed my shoulders comfortably against the tree I leaned upon and looked through a chink in the ceiling of the forest at a vulture flying low.

'Maina, you know, I hate those birds. Their wings are separated like a lot of small snakes.'

'As you say, Lakwani, they are creatures of evil omen — messengers of the dead. Too cowardly to slay for themselves, they are satisfied with the stinking flesh from another man's kill.' Arab Maina spat, as if to clean his mouth after talking of unpleasant things.

Buller and the native dogs had gone into the river and wallowed in the cool black muck along its banks. Buller returned now, sleek with slime, dripping and happy. He waited until he had the two Murani and me easily within range and then shook himself with a kind of devilish impudence and stood wagging his stump tail as we wiped water and mud from our faces.

'It is his way of making a joke,' said Arab Kosky, looking at his spattered shuka.

'It is also his way of telling us to move,' said Arab Maina. 'The hunter who lies on his back in the forest has little food and no sport. We have spent much time today at other things, but the warthog still waits.'

'What you say is true.' Arab Kosky rose from the grass. 'The warthog still waits, and who is so without manners as to keep another waiting? Surely Buller is not. We must take his advice and go.'

We went up the riverbank, falling into single file again, and threaded our way through a labyrinth of silver-grey boulders and rust-red anthills, shaped variously like witches caps or like the figures of kneeling giants or like trees without branches. Some of the anthills were enormous, higher than the huts we lived in, and some were no higher than our knees. They were scattered everywhere.

'Seek 'em out, Buller!'

But the dog needed no urging from me. He knew warthog country when he saw it and he knew what to do about it. He rushed on ahead followed by the native mongrels running in a little storm of their own dust.

I know animals more gallant than the African warthog, but none more courageous. He is the peasant of the plains — the drab and dowdy digger in the earth. He is the uncomely but intrepid defender of family, home, and bourgeois convention, and he will fight anything of any size that intrudes upon his smug existence. Even his weapons are plebeian — curved tusks, sharp, deadly, but not beautiful, used inelegantly for rooting as well as for fighting.

He stands higher than a domestic pig when he is full grown, and his hide is dust-coloured and tough and clothed in bristles. His eyes are small and lightless and capable of but one expression — suspicion. What he does not understand, he suspects, and what he suspects, he fights. He can leap into the air and gut a horse while its rider still ponders a strategy of attack, and his speed in emerging from his hole to demonstrate the advantage of surprise is almost phenomenal.

He is not lacking in guile. He enters his snug little den (which is borrowed, not to say commandeered, from its builder, the ant-bear) tail foremost so that he is never caught off guard. While he lies thus in wait for the curiosity or indiscretion of his enemy to bring him within range, he uses his snout to pile a heap of fine dust inside the hole. The dust serves as a smoke screen, bursting into a great, enshrouding billow the moment the warthog emerges to battle. He understands the tactical retreat, but is incapable of surrender, and if a dog is less than a veteran, or a man no more than an intrepid novice, not the only blood spilled will be the warthog's.

These facts were always in my mind when Buller hunted with us, as he always did. But there was never any question of leaving him. It would have been like preventing a born soldier from marching with his regiment or like denying a champion fighter the right to compete in the ring on the grounds that he might be hurt. So Buller always came, and often I worried.

He ran ahead now, flanked by native dogs. The two Murani and I spread out fanwise, running behind.

Our first sign of warthog was the squeal of a baby surprised in a patch of grass by one of the mongrels. The squeal was followed by what seemed to be the squeals of all the baby warthogs in Africa, blended, magnified, and ear-splitting. Panic-stricken, the little pigs ran in all directions, like mice in the dream of a tabby cat. Their tails, held straight and erect, whisked through the grass as if so many bulrushes had come to life to join in a frantic dance — a mad and somewhat gay dance, but hardly as abandoned as it appeared, because the squeals were not without intent or meaning. They were

91

meant for the small, alert ears of their father, who, when he came, would come with murder aforethought.

And come he did. None of us quite knew from where, but in the midst of the bedlam the grass in front of Arab Maina parted as if cleaved by a scythe, and a large boar, blind with rage, plunged from it straight at the Murani.

If Buller had not run ahead after his own quarry, things might have happened differently. As it was, there was more amusement than tragedy in what did happen.

The boar was larger than average, and the bigger they are the tougher they are. Their hides are tough as boot-leather and nothing less than a spear thrust in a vital part will stop them.

Arab Maina was ready and waiting. The boar lunged, the Murani sidestepped, the spear flashed — and the boar was gone. But not alone. Behind him, spitting the flying dust, swearing in Nandi and in Swahili, ran Arab Maina assisted by two of his mongrels — all of them following, with their eyes and their legs, the drunkenly swaying shaft of Arab Maina's spear, its point lodged fast and solid between the shoulders of the boar.

Arab Kosky and I began to follow, but we couldn't laugh and run at the same time, so we stopped running and watched. In less than a minute the dogs, the man, and the warthog had found the horizon and disappeared behind it like four fabulous characters in search of Æsop.

We turned and trotted in the direction Buller had taken, listening to his deep, excited barks which came at regular intervals. After covering about three miles, we found him at the side of a large hole where he had run his warthog to ground.

Buller stood gazing at the dusty opening in silence, as if hoping the warthog would be such a fool as to think that since there were no more barks, there was no more dog. But the warthog was not taken in. He would emerge in his own good time, and he knew as well as Buller did that no dog would enter an occupied pig-hole and expect to come out alive.

'That's a good boy, Buller!' As usual, I was relieved to find him still unhurt, but the moment I spoke, he broke his strategic silence and demanded, with much tail-wagging and a series of whining barks, that the warthog be roused from his den and be brought to battle.

More than once every inch of Buller's body had been ripped open in deep, ugly gashes on such pig-hunts, but at least he had lately learned not to go for the boar's head which, in the end, is fatal for any dog. Until now I had always managed to reach the scene of conflict in time to spear the warthog. But I might not always be so lucky.

I moved carefully to the back of the opening while Arab Kosky stood far to one side.

'If only we had some paper to rustle down the hole, Kosky . . .'

The Murani shrugged. 'We will have to try other tricks, Lakweit.'

It seems silly, and perhaps it is, but very often, after every other method had failed, we had enticed warthogs into the open, long before they were quite ready to attack, simply by rustling a scrap of paper over the entrance of their holes. It was not always easy to get so limited an article as paper in East Africa at that time, but when we had it, it always worked. I haven't any idea of why it worked. Poking a stick through the hole never did, nor shouting into it, nor even using smoke. To the warthog, I think, the paper made a sound that was clearly insulting — comparable perhaps to what is known here and there nowadays as a Bronx cheer.

But we had no paper. We tried everything else without the least success, and decided finally, in the face of Buller's contempt, to give it up and find out what had happened to Arab Maina on his quest for the vanished spear.

We were leaving the scene of our mutual discouragement when Arab Kosky's curiosity overcame his natural caution. He bent down in front of the dark hole and the warthog came out.

It was more like an explosion than an attack by a wild pig. I could see nothing through the thick burst of dust except extremities — the tail of the boar, the feet of Arab Kosky, the ears of Buller, and the end of a spear.

My own spear was useless in my hands. I might thrust at the warthog only to strike the dog or the Murani. It was an unholy tangle with no end, no beginning, and no opening. It lasted five seconds. Then the warthog shot from the tumbling mass like a clod from a whirlwind and disappeared through a corridor of anthills with Buller just behind slashing at the fleeing grey rump.

I turned to Arab Kosky. He sat on the ground in a puddle of his own blood, his right thigh cut through as if it had been hacked with a sword. He pressed a fold of his shuka against the wound and stood up. Buller's bark grew fainter, echoing through the forest of anthills. The boar had won the first battle — and might win the second, unless I hurried.

'Can you walk, Kosky? I must follow Buller. He may get killed.'

The Murani smiled without mirth. 'Of course, Lakweit! This is nothing — except reward for my foolishness. I will go back to the singiri slowly and have it attended to. It is best that you lose no time and follow Buller. Already the sun is sinking. Go now, and run quickly!'

I clasped the round shaft of the spear tight in my hand and ran with all my strength. For me — because I was still a child — this was a heart-sinking experience. So many thoughts flashed through my mind. Would my strength hold out long enough to save Buller from the tusks of the boar? What had become of Arab Maina, and why had I ever left him? How would poor Kosky get home? Would he bleed too badly on the way?

I ran on and on, following the barely audible bark of Buller, and the few drops of blood clinging at intervals to the stalks of grass or soaking into the absorbent earth. It was either Buller's blood or the warthog's. Most likely it was both.

'Ah-yey, if I could only run a little faster!'

I must not stop for a minute. My muscles begin to ache, my legs bleed from the 'wait-a-bit' thorns and the blades of elephant grass. My hand, wet with perspiration, slips on the handle of my spear. I stumble, recover, and run on as the sound of Buller's bark grows louder, closer, then fades again.

The sun is going and shadows lay like broad hurdles across my path. Nothing is of any importance to me except my dog. The boar is not retreating; he is leading Buller away from me, away from my help.

The blood spoor grows thicker and there is more of it. Buller's bark is weak and irregular, but a little nearer. There are trees now jutting from the plain, large, solitary, and silent.

The barking stops and there is nothing but the blood to follow. How can there be so much blood? Breathless and running still, I peer ahead into the changing light and see something move in a patch of turf under a flat-topped thorn tree.

I stop and wait. It moves again and takes colour — black and white and splattered with red. It is silent, but it moves. It is Buller.

I need neither breath nor muscles to cover the few hundred yards to the thorn tree. I am suddenly there, under its branches, standing in a welter of blood. The warthog, as large as any I have ever seen, six times as large as Buller, sits exhausted on his haunches while the dog rips at its belly.

The old boar sees me, another enemy, and charges once more with magnificent courage, and I sidestep and plunge my spear to his heart. He falls forward, scraping the earth with his great tusks, and lies still. I leave the spear in his body, turn to Buller, and feel tears starting to my eyes.

The dog is torn open like a slaughtered sheep. His right side is a valley of exposed flesh from the root of his tail to his head, and his ribs show almost white, like the fingers of a hand smeared with blood. He looks at the warthog, then at me beside him on my knees, and lets his head fall into my arms. He needs water, but there is no water anywhere, not within miles.

'Ah-yey! Buller, my poor, foolish Buller!'

He licks my hand, and I think he knows I can do nothing, but forgives me for it. I cannot leave him because the light is almost gone now and there are leopards that prowl at night, and hyenas that attack only the wounded and helpless.

'If only he lives through the night! If only he lives through the night!'

There is a hyena on a near hill who laughs at that, but it is a coward's laugh. I sit with Buller and the dead boar under the thorn tree and watch the dark come closer.

The world grows bigger as the light leaves it. There are no boundaries and no landmarks. The trees and the rocks and the anthills begin to disappear, one by one, whisked away under the magical cloak of evening, I stroke the dog's head and try to close my eyes, but of course I cannot. Something moves in the tall grass, making a sound like the swish of a woman's skirt. The dog stirs feebly and the hyena on the hill laughs again.

I let Buller's head rest on the turf, stand up, and pull my

spear from the body of the boar. Somewhere to the left there is a sound, but I do not recognize it and I can see only dim shapes that are motionless.

I lean for a moment on my spear peering outward at what is nothing, and then turn toward my thorn tree.

'Are you here, Lakwani?'

Arab Maina's voice is cool as water on shaded rocks.

'I am here, Maina.'

He is tall and naked and very dark beside me. His shuka is tied around his left forearm to allow his body freedom to run.

'You are alone, and you have suffered, my child.'

'I am all right, Maina, but I fear for Buller. I think he may die.'

Arab Maina kneels on the earth and runs his hands over Buller's body. 'He is badly hurt, Lakwani — very badly hurt — but do not grieve too much. I think your spear has saved him from death, and God will reward you for that. When the moon shines at midnight, we will carry him home.'

'I am so happy that you have come, Maina.'

'How is it Kosky dared to leave you alone? He has betrayed the trust I had in him!'

'Do not be angry with Kosky. He is badly hurt. His thigh was ripped by the warthog.'

'He is no child, Lakweit. He is a Murani, and he should have been more careful, knowing I was not there. After I recovered my spear, I turned back to find you. I followed the blood on the grass for miles — and then I followed Buller's barking. If the direction of the wind had been wrong, you would still be alone. Kosky has the brains of the one-eyed hare!'

'Ah-yey! What does it matter now, Maina? You are here, and I am not alone. But I am very cold.'

'Lakwani, lie down and rest. I will keep watch until it is

97

light enough for us to go. You are very tired. Your face has become thin.'

He cuts handfuls of grass with his sword and makes a pillow, and I lie down, clasping Buller in my arms. The dog is unconscious now and bleeding badly. His blood trickles over my khaki shorts and my thighs.

The distant roar of a waking lion rolls against the stillness of the night, and we listen. It is the voice of Africa bringing memories that do not exist in our minds or in our hearts — perhaps not even in our blood. It is out of time, but it is there, and it spans a chasm whose other side we cannot see.

A ripple of lightning plays across the horizon.

'I think there will be a storm tonight, Maina.'

Arab Maina reaches out in the darkness and puts his hand on my forehead. 'Relax, Lakwani, and I will tell you an amusing fable about the cunning little Hare.'

He begins very slowly and softly, 'The Hare was a thief... In the night he came to the manyatta... He lied to the Cow, and told her that her Calf would die if she moved... Then he stood up on his hind legs and began sucking the milk from the Cow's milk bag... The other...'

But I am asleep.

VIII

And We be Playmates, Thou and I

BULLER was brought home by moonlight. For a long time he lay still, seeing nothing but the earthen floor in front of his paws, until at last he could lift his head a little, and then he could walk. One day he sniffed at my spear, dipped in its sheath of black ostrich feathers, and waggled his forever expectant tail. But that was after the world had changed, and there was no more boar-hunting.

The world had changed without any reason that I could see. My father's face had become more grave than it had ever been before, and the voices of the men he spoke with were sombre. There was a lot of head-shaking and talk about gloomy, schoolbookish places that had nothing to do with Africa.

A man of importance had been shot at a place I could not pronounce in Swahili or in English, and, because of this shooting, whole countries were at war. It seemed a laborious method of retribution, but that was the way it was being done. So, by nineteen-fifteen, the lights had not only gone out 'all over Europe,' but many of what few windows there were had begun darkening in East Africa.

War was different in the hinterland. It was a war of men rather than of weapons; tanks, planes, gas masks, and guns that threw shells twenty miles remained things of the future even after they were elsewhere blended with the past.

The Protectorate fought a frontier war with frontier weapons; it was still dressed in frontier clothes.

Boers, Somalis, Nandi, Kikuyu, Kavirondo, and settlers of all nationalities went to battle, when the Empire called, in what they had on their backs when they left the plough, the singiri, or the forest. They rode mules or they walked. They carried guns if they had guns — some brought nothing more lethal than bush knives. They converged on Nairobi and stood in the streets or gathered before Nairobi House, looking at best like revolutionists, but not like soldiers of the Crown.

They wore hats, bandannas, jackets of home-cured hide, shukas, shorts, boots or no boots, and it didn't matter. Altogether it made a uniform — not for a man, but for a body of men. Each contributed to the distinguished style and colour of a regiment that had had its predecessors once in America, but had not, in this war, a counterpart.

They had come to fight, and they stayed and fought — some because they could read and understand what they read, some because they had listened to other men, and some because they were told that this, in the name of civilization — a White Man's God more tangible than most — was their new duty.

I never heard the ruffle of drums in those days or saw many flags dragging precise platoons behind them. I saw men leave their work at the mills, and there were teams of oxen on the farm without their masters.

The farm lived, but its voice was a whisper. It produced, but not with the lusty ease it had before. There was less gusto, but Kibii and I did what children do when there are things abroad too big to understand; we stayed close to each other and played games that made no noise.

Kibii was a little Nandi boy, younger than I, but we had

many things in common. We gained a bond that was forged in the war and which we would have done without; but for me, years later in another hemisphere, it exists yet, as it must for him — still in Africa.

A messenger came to the farm with a story to tell. It was not a story that meant much as stories went in those days. It was about how the war progressed in German East Africa and about a tall young man who was killed in it.

I suppose he was no taller than most who were killed there and no better. It was an ordinary story, but Kibii and I, who knew him well, thought there was no story like it, or one as sad, and we think so now.

The young man tied his shuka on his shoulder one day and took his shield and his spear and went to war. He thought war was made of spears and shields and courage, and he brought them all.

But they gave him a gun, so he left the spear and the shield behind him and took the courage, and went where they sent him because they said this was his duty and he believed in duty. He believed in duty and in the kind of justice that he knew, and in all the things that were of the earth — like the voice of the forest, the right of a lion to kill a buck, the right of a buck to eat grass, and the right of a man to fight. He believed in many wives, young as he was, and in the telling of stories by the shade of the singiri.

He took the gun and held it the way they had told him to hold it, and walked where they told him to walk, smiling a little and looking for another man to fight.

He was shot and killed by the other man, who also believed in duty, and he was buried where he fell. It was so simple and so unimportant.

But of course it meant something to Kibii and me, because the tall young man was Kibii's father and my most special

101

friend. Arab Maina died on the field of action in the service
of the King. But some said it was because he had forsaken his
spear.

'When I am circumcised and become a Murani,' Kibii said,
'and drink blood and curdled milk like a man, instead of ugali
and nettles, like a woman, I will find whoever it was that
killed my father and put my spear in his heart.'

'You are very selfish, Kibii,' I said. 'I can jump as high as
you can, and play all our games just as well. I can throw a
spear almost as far. We will find him together and put both
our spears in his heart.'

The days that marked the war went on like the ticking of a
clock that had no face and showed no time. After a while it
was difficult to remember what it had been like before, or the
remembrance had been brought to mind so often that it was
tarnished and dull, like a trinket not worth looking at. Kibii
and I began living again, from hour to hour.

He still spoke of his forthcoming circumcision as one might
speak of the prospect of being born again — better born and
with brand-new hopes. 'When I am a Murani ...' he would
boast. But when he said it he always looked smaller than he
really was, closer still to a little boy than to a man.

So, while he waited for his new birth and I, being only a
girl, just waited to grow up, we played our old games and took
increasing interest in the work with the horses my father had
assigned to us.

The games we played were Nandi games because I knew no
others and there was no white child, except myself, anywhere
near Njoro, though there may have been some Boer children
in the small colony about two hundred miles away on the
Uasin Gishu Plateau.

And We be Playmates, Thou and I

One of the games was jumping, because the Nandi said that a boy or a man must be able to jump as high as himself to be any good at all, and Kibii and I were determined to be good. When I left Njoro, at last, I could still jump higher than my head. I could wrestle too, the Nandi way, because Kibii taught me all the holds and the various tricks and how to pick another toto up over my head and throw him to the ground.

Among my galaxy of scars is one which an ungallant Nandi boy, whom I had bested in a wrestling bout, made with his father's sword. He waited until he caught me walking alone one day about two miles from the farm, and then he rushed from behind a thorn tree swinging the weapon like a demented Turk. I had a knobkerrie in my hand at the time and I caught him behind the ear with it in the fight that followed, but not before he had slashed my leg above the knee as deeply as his sword would go.

There were quiet days when Kibii and I played, all during the long afternoons, a game that took me months to learn and, having forgotten it, I could never learn again. I remember only that we used the little poisonous yellow sodom apples for counters and a series of round holes in the ground for our board, and that the mental arithmetic required was more than I have since used in twenty years. We would play it in the shade of the wattle trees, or, after finishing our work with the horses, down behind the walls of the stables, sitting cross-legged over the smooth yellow balls like diminutive practitioners of black magic, waiting for a Sign. I had a small allowance of rupees from my father and Kibii had a salary of sorts. We gambled like fiends with this largesse, but neither of us established the roots of a fortune with our winnings, though a few of the coins of the realm were worn thinner.

You couldn't live in Africa and not hunt. Kibii taught me

103

how to shoot with a bow and arrow, and when we found we
could shoot wood-pigeons and blue starlings and waxbills, by
way of practice, we decided on bigger things. Kibii had a
daring plan, but it didn't work. We invaded the Mau Forest
one day and haunted its church-like aisles and recesses until
we found a Wandorobo huntsman, a wizened little man barely
taller than a bush-buck, and begged him for poison for our
arrows. Kibii was furious when the Wandorobo wisely refused
on the grounds that we were too young to tamper with such
things, and we crept out of the forest again just before dark —
as non-poisonous as we had entered it.

'When I am a Murani...!' Kibii said with impotent feroc-
ity. 'Just wait until I am a Murani...!'

On nights when there was a full moon we would sometimes
go to the Kikuyu ingomas, which were tribal dances held usually behind a tall ridge on Delamere's Equator Ranch. As a
Nandi, Kibii had only a generous tolerance for the Kikuyu
dances, though, when pressed, he admitted that the singing
was good.

The Kikuyu are more like the Kavirondo in their way of
living than like the Masai or the Nandi. But physically they
are the least impressive of all. It may be because they are
primarily agriculturists, and generations of looking to the
earth for their livelihood have dulled what fire there might
once have been in their eyes and what will to excel might have
been in their hearts. They have lost inspiration for beauty.
They are a hard-working people; from the viewpoint of Empire, a docile and therefore a useful people. Their character is
constant, even strong, but it is lustreless.

The flippancy of the Kikuyu dances always shocked Kibii.
The emotional ones, he thought, seemed carnal — and the
purely spiritual ones lacked dignity. But I think his impatience was touched with tribal vanity.

At any rate, there were few Kikuyu ingomas whose audiences did not include Kibii, the critic, and myself.

When the edge of the moon cut into the night and the flat, grassy meadow behind the ridge on Equator Ranch was light enough to receive the shadows of moving bodies, the dancers formed in a ring. The heads of the girls were shaved smooth and the heads of the young men were resplendent in long plaits of hair decorated with coloured feathers. The young men wore rattles of metal on their legs, shaped like cowrie shells, and the skins of serval-cats swayed and dangled from their buttocks. They wore the black-and-white tails of Colobus monkeys and made them writhe like snakes when the dance was on. They sang in voices that were so much a part of Africa, so quick to blend with the night and the tranquil veldt and the labyrinths of forest that made their background, that the music seemed without sound. It was like a voice upon another voice, each of the same timbre.

The young men and the girls together stood in a wide circle with their arms on each other's shoulders. The white light of the moon bathed their black bodies, making them blacker. A leader stood alone in the centre of the ring and began the chant; he struck the spark of their song and it caught on the tinder of their youth and ran around the ring like a flame. It was a song of love — of this man's love and of that one's. It was a song that changed as many times as there were young men to proclaim their manhood, and lasted as long as there were young girls to trill their applause.

The leader swayed in the centre of the ring. The chorus took volume, the feet of the dancers began their rhythmic stomp, the tempo of the song grew faster. Chanting, the leader jumped into the air, holding his heels together, giving the song its beat. His head jerked back and forth on a rigid neck; the breasts of the young girls rose and fell with the vigour of the dance as the chorus snatched the last line of each verse and rolled it again and again from a hundred throats.

When the leader was exhausted, there was another to take his place, and after that another, and another, but the one who stayed the longest and leapt the highest was the hero of the night, and his crown was forged from the smiles of the girls.

Almost always it was dawn when the dance was over, but at times Kibii and I left when it was still dark. We liked walking in the dark, past the edge of the forest, listening to the shrill cry of the hyrax and the noise of the crickets that sounded like the snipping of a million shears.

'When the world began,' Kibii said, 'each animal, even the Chameleon, had a task to do. I learned it from my father and my grandfather, and all our people know this fact.'

'The world began too long ago,' I said — 'longer than anybody could remember. Who could remember what the Chameleon did when the world began?'

'Our people remember,' said Kibii, 'because God told it to our first ol-oiboni, and this one told it to the next. Each ol-oiboni, before he died, repeated to the new ol-oiboni what God had said — and so we know these things. We know that the Chameleon is accursed above all other animals because, if it had not been for him, there would be no Death.

'It was like this,' said Kibii:

'When the first man was made, he wandered alone in the great forest and on the plains, and he worried very much because he could not remember yesterday and so he could not imagine tomorrow. God saw this, so he sent the Chameleon to the first man (who was a Nandi) with a message, saying that there would never be such a thing as death and that tomorrow would be like today, and that the days would never stop.

'Long after the Chameleon had started,' said Kibii, 'God

106

sent an Egret with a different message, saying that there would be a thing called Death and that, sometime, tomorrow would not come. "Whichever message comes first to the ears of man," God warned, "will be the true one."

'Now the Chameleon is a lazy animal. He thinks of nothing but food, and he moves only his tongue to get that. He lagged so much along the way that he arrived at the feet of the first man only a moment before the Egret.

'The Chameleon began to talk, but he could not. In the excitement of trying to deliver his tidings of eternal life, before the Egret could speak, the Chameleon could only stutter and change, stupidly, from one colour to another. So the Egret, in a calm voice, gave the message of Death.

'Since then,' said Kibii, 'all men have died. Our people know this fact.'

At that time I was naïve enough to ponder the verity of such fables.

In the years that have passed, I have read and heard more scholarly expositions upon similar subjects; God has changed from God to an Unknown Quantity, the Chameleon has become x and the Egret y. Life goes on until Death stops it. The questions are the same, but the symbols are different.

Still, the Chameleon is a gay if sluggish fellow, and the Egret is a pretty bird. There are doubtless better answers, but somehow, nowadays, I prefer Kibii's.

IX

Royal Exile

To an eagle or to an owl or to a rabbit, man must seem a masterful and yet a forlorn animal; he has but two friends. In his almost universal unpopularity he points out, with pride, that these two are the dog and the horse. He believes, with an innocence peculiar to himself, that they are equally proud of this alleged confraternity. He says, 'Look at my two noble friends — they are dumb, but they are loyal.' I have for years suspected that they are only tolerant.

Suspecting it, I have nevertheless depended on this tolerance all my life, and if I were, even now, without either a dog or a horse in my keeping, I should feel I had lost contact with the earth. I should be as concerned as a Buddhist monk having lost contact with Nirvana.

Horses in particular have been as much a part of my life as past birthdays. I remember them more clearly. There is no phase of my childhood I cannot recall by remembering a horse I owned then, or one my father owned, or one I knew. They were not all gentle and kind. They were not all alike. With some my father won races and with some he lost. His black-and-yellow colours have swept past the post from Nairobi to Peru, to Durban. Some horses he brought thousands of miles from England just for breeding.

Camciscan was one of these.

When he came to Njoro, I was a straw-haired girl with

108

lanky legs and he was a stallion bred out of a stud book thick as a tome — and partly out of fire. The impression of his coming and of the first weeks that followed are clear in my mind.

But sometimes I wonder how it seemed to him.

He arrived in the early morning, descending the ramp from the noisy little train with the slow step of a royal exile. He held his head above the heads of those who led him, and smelled the alien earth and the thin air of the Highlands. It was not a smell that he knew.

There was a star of white on his forehead; his nostrils were wide and showed crimson like the lacquered nostrils of a Chinese dragon. He was tall, deep in girth, slender-chested, on strong legs clean as marble.

He was not chestnut; he was neither brown nor sorrel. He stood uncertainly against the foreign background — a rangy bay stallion swathed in sunlight and in a sheen of reddish gold.

He knew that this was freedom again. He knew that the darkness and the terrifying movement of the ship that strained his legs and bruised his body against walls too close together were gone now.

The net of leather rested on his head in those same places, and the long lines that he had learned to follow hung from the thing in his mouth that could not be bitten. But these he was used to. He could breathe, and he could feel the spring of the earth under his hooves. He could shake his body, and he could see that there was distance here, and a breadth of land into which he fitted. He opened his nostrils and smelled the heat and the emptiness of Africa and filled his lungs and let the rush of air go out of them again in a low, undulant murmur.

He knew men. In the three quick years of his life he had seen more of them than of his own kind. He understood that men were to serve him and that, in exchange, he was to concede them the indulgence of minor whims. They got upon his back and most often he let them stay. They rubbed his body and did things to his hooves, none of which was really unpleasant. He judged them by their smells and by the way they touched him. He did not like a hand with a tremor, or a hand that was hard, or one that moved too quickly. He did not trust the smell of a man that had nothing of the earth in it nor any sweat in it. Men's voices were bad, but there were some not too loud that came to his ears slowly, without insistence, and these he could bear.

A white man came up to him now and walked around him. Other men, all of them very black — as black as his own mane — stood in a circle and watched the first man. The stallion was used to this. It was always the same, and it made him impatient. It made him bend the sleek bow of his neck and jab at the earth with his hooves.

The white man put a hand on the stallion's shoulder and said a word that he knew because it was an old word and almost all men said it when they touched him or when they saw him.

The white man said, 'So you are Camciscan,' and the black men repeated, more slowly, 'Camciscan,' one after another. And a girl, who was white too, with straw-coloured hair and legs like a colt's, said 'Camciscan' several times.

The girl seemed foolishly happy saying it. She came close to him and said it again and he thought her smell was good enough, but he saw that she was familiar in her manner and he blew a little snort into her straw-coloured hair to warn her, but she only laughed. She was attended by a dog, ugly with scars, who never left her heels.

After a little while the girl tugged gently on the lines Cam-ciscan had learned to follow, and so he followed.

The black men, the white girl, the scarred dog, and the bay stallion walked along a dirt road while the white man rode far ahead in a buggy.

Camciscan looked neither to one side nor another. He saw nothing but the road before him. He walked as if he were completely alone, like an abdicated king. He felt alone. The country smelled unused and clean, and the smells of the black men and the white girl were not outside of his understanding. But still he was alone and he felt some pride in that, as he always had.

He found the farm large and to his liking. It harboured many other horses in long rows of stables, but his box was separate from theirs.

He remembered the old routine of food and saddle and workout and rest, but he did not remember ever being attended before by a girl with straw-coloured hair and legs that were too long, like a colt's. He did not mind, but the girl was too familiar. She walked into his stall as if they had been old friends, and he had no need of friends.

He depended upon her for certain things, but, in turn, she got on his back in the morning and they went to a valley bigger than any he had ever seen, or sometimes up the side of a certain hill that was very high, and then they came back again.

In time he found himself getting used to the girl, but he would not let it be more than that. He could feel that she was trying to break through the loneliness that he lived by, and he remembered the reasons there were to mistrust men. He could not see that she was any different, but he felt that she was, and that disturbed him.

In the early morning she would come to his stable, slip his

111

head-collar on and remove his heavy rug. She would smooth him down with a cloth and brush his black mane and his tail. She would clean the urine from his floor, and separate the good bedding from that spoiled with manure. She did these things with care. She did them with a kind of intimate knowledge of his needs and with a scarcely hidden sense of possession which he felt — and resented.

He was by Spearmint out of Camlarge, and the blood flowed arrogantly in arrogant veins.

Mornings came when Camciscan waited for the girl with his ears and with his eyes, because he had learned the sound of her bare feet on the ground that was still unsoftened by any sun, and he could distinguish the tangle of straw-coloured hair among other things. But when she was in his stable, he retreated to a far corner and stood watching her work.

He sometimes felt the urge to move closer to her, but the loneliness of which he was so proud never permitted this. Instead, the urge turned often to anger which was, to himself, as unreasonable as the unprovoked anger of another might have been. He did not understand this anger; when it had passed, he would tremble as if he had caught the scent of something evil.

The girl vaulted to his back one morning, as she always did when they went to the hill or the valley, and the anger surged suddenly through his body like a quick pain. He threw her from him so that she fell against the root of a tree and lay there with blood running through the straw-coloured hair. Her legs that were too long, like a colt's, did not move even when the white man and the black men carried her away.

Afterward, Camciscan trembled and sweated in his box and let his mistrust of the men who tried to feed him boil into hate. For seven mornings the girl did not return.

When she did return, he moved again to the farthest corner

112

and watched her work, or stood still as death while she lifted his feet, one by one, and cleaned them with a hard tool that never hurt. He was a Thoroughbred stallion and he knew nothing of remorse. He knew that there were things that made him tremble and things that filled him with anger. He did not know, always, what these things were.

He did not know what the thing was that made him tremble on the morning he saw the chestnut filly, or how it happened that there was suddenly a voice in his throat that came to his own ears unfamiliar and distant, startling him. He saw his dignity slip away like a blanket fallen from his back, and pride that had never before deserted him was in an instant shamefully vanished.

He saw the filly, smooth, young, and with a saunter in her pose, standing in an open field, under the care of four black men. Unaccountably, he had been led to this field, and unaccountably he strained against restraint toward this filly.

Camciscan called to her in a tone as unfamiliar to him as it was to her, but there must have been danger in it. It was a new sound that he did not know himself. He went toward her, holding his head high, lifting his clean legs, and the filly broke from the kicking-straps that held her and fled, screaming, in a voice as urgent as his own.

For the first time in his life he would have exchanged the loneliness he lived by for something else, but his willingness had gained him only the humility of rejection and disdain. He could understand this, but not more than this. He returned to his stable, not trembling. He returned walking with careful steps, each as even as another.

When the girl came as she always did and kneaded the new dead hairs from his bright coat with supple fingers and ran the soft body-brush over him, he turned his head and watched her, accepting the soothing stroke of her hand, but he knew that the old anger was in him again. It had welled up in his heart until now it burst and made him whirl round and catch her slender back with his teeth, biting until the brush dropped from her hand, flinging her bodily against the far wall of the box. She lay there huddled in the trampled bedding for a long time, and he stood over her, trembling, not touching her with any of his feet. He would not touch her. He would have killed any living creature that touched her then, but he did not know why this was so.

After a while the girl moved and then crawled out of the box and he pawed through the bedding to the earthen floor, tossing his head up and down, letting the anger run out of him.

But the girl was there again, in the stable, the next day. She cleaned it as she had cleaned it each other day and her touch on his body was the same, except there was a new firmness in it, and Camciscan knew, without knowing, that his strength, his anger, and his loneliness at last were challenged.

Nothing about the morning ride was different. The black men worked with the other horses and about the stables in their usual positions, with their usual movements. The large tree against which he had thrown the girl was still there making the same little pond of shade, bees criss-crossed the unresisting air like golden bullets, birds sang or just dipped in and out of the sky. Camciscan knew that the morning was slow with peacefulness. But he also knew that this thing would happen; he knew that his anger would come and would be met by the girl's anger.

By then he understood, in his own way, that the girl loved him. Also he understood now why it was that when she had lain hurt in his box, he could not trample her with his hooves, nor allow any other living thing to touch her — and the reason for this frightened him.

They came to a level spot on the green hill and he stopped

suddenly with sweat stinging his blood-bay neck and his blood-bay flanks. He stopped because this was the place.

The girl on his back spoke to him, but he did not move. He felt the anger again, and he did not move. For the first time her heels struck against his ribs, sharply, and he was motionless. He felt her hand relax the lines that held his head so that he was almost free. But she did not speak; she rapped him again with her heels, roughly, so that it hurt, and he whirled, baring his teeth, and tried to sink them into her leg.

The girl struck his muzzle with a whip, hard and without mercy, but he was startled by the act more than by the pain. The alchemy of his pride transformed the pain to anger that blinded him. He bit at her again and she struck again making the whip burn against his flesh. He whirled until their world was a cone of yellow dust, but she clung to his back, weightless, and lashed at him in tireless rhythm.

He reared upward, cutting the dust cloud with his hooves. Plunging, he kicked at her legs and felt the thin whip bite at his quarters, time after time, until they glowed with pain.

He knew that his bulk could crush her. He knew that if he reared high enough, he would fall backward, and this terrified him. But he was neither mastered by the girl nor by his terror. He reared until the ground fell away before him, and he saw only the sky, through bulging eyes, and inch by inch he went over, feeling the whip on his head, between his ears, against his neck. He began to fall, and the terror returned, and he fell.

When he knew that the girl was not caught under his weight, his anger left him as quickly as the wind had whisked the dust away. This was not reason, but it was so.

He got up, churning the air awkwardly, and the girl stood, watching him, still holding the lines and the whip, her straw-coloured hair matted with dust.

She came to him and touched the hurt places on his body and stroked his neck and his throat and the place between his eyes.

In a little time she vaulted again to his back and they went on along the familiar road, slowly, with no sound but the sound of his hooves.

Camciscan remained Camciscan. In relation to himself, nothing changed, nothing was different. If there were horses on the farm that whinnied at the approach of certain men or forsook their peculiar nobility for the common gifts of common creatures, he was not one.

He held a heritage of arrogance, and he cherished it. If he had yielded once to a will as stubborn as his own, even this had left no bruise upon his spirit. The girl had triumphed — but in so small a thing.

He still stood in the far corner of his stable each morning while she worked. Sometimes he still trembled, and once in the late evening when there was a storm outside and a nervous wind, she came and lay down in the clean bedding under his manger. He watched her while there was light, but when that failed, and she must surely have been asleep, he stepped closer, lowering his head a little, breathing warmly through widened nostrils, and sniffed at her.

She did not move, and he did not. For a moment he ruffled her hair with his soft muzzle. And then he lifted his head as high as he had ever held it and stood, with the girl at his feet, all through the storm. It did not seem a strong storm.

When morning came, she got up and looked at him and spoke to him. But he was in the farthest corner, where he always was, staring, not at her, but at the dawn, and at the warm clouds of his breath against the cold.

X

Was There a Horse with Wings?

THE black book lies on my father's desk, thick and important. Its covers are a little bent; the weight of his fingers and mine have curled back its pages, but they are not yellow. The handwriting is bold — in places it is even proud as when he has inscribed such names as these: 'Little Miller — Ormolu — Véronique.' They are all Thoroughbred mares out of stock old as boulders on an English hill.

The name 'Coquette' is inscribed more soberly, with no flourish — almost with doubt. It is as if here is a girl, pretty as any, but brought by marriage into a family of respectability beyond her birth or farthest hopes.

The brief career of Coquette is, in fact, ever so slightly chequered; her background, while not obscure, suggests something less than the dazzling gentility of her stable-mates. Still, not to be English is hardly regarded as a fatal deficiency even by the English, though grave enough to warrant sympathy. Coquette is Abyssinian. She is small and golden yellow with a pure white mane and tail.

Coquette was smuggled out of Abyssinia because Abyssinians do not permit good native mares to leave their country. I do not remember who did the smuggling, but I suppose my father condoned it, in effect, when he bought her. He must have done it with one eye shut and the other on the sweet, tidy lines of her vigorous body.

117

My father was, and is, a law-abiding citizen of the realm, but if ever he wanders off the path of righteousness, it will not be gold or silver that enticed him, but, more likely, I think, the irresistible contours of a fine but elusive horse.

A lovely horse is always an experience to him. It is an emotional experience of the kind that is spoiled by words. He has always talked about horses, but he has never unravelled his love of them in a skein of commonplace adjectives. At seventy, in competition with the crack trainers of South Africa, his name heads the list of winners in the high-stake racing centre of Durban. In view of this and other things, I demand forgiveness for being so obviously impressed with my own parent.

He came out of Sandhurst with such a ponderous knowledge of Greek and Latin that it would have submerged a lesser man. He might have gone down like a swimmer in the sea struggling with an Alexandrian tablet under each arm, but he never let his education get the better of him. He won what prizes there were translating Ovid and Æschylus, and then took up steeplechasing until he became one of the finest amateur riders in England. He took chances on horses and on Africa; he never regretted the losses, nor boasted about the wins.

He sometimes dreamed over the thick black book — almost as I am dreaming now, now that the names are just names, and the great-grandchildren of those elegant dams and sterling sires are dispersed, like a broken family.

But all great characters come back to life if you call them — even great horses.

Coquette, in her way, was great. She won races, though she never set the world agog, but she gave me my first foal.

It all goes back to the thick black book. And that is a long way back.

It lies there, dustless, because it is too much touched, and I am grown a little now and charged with duties inflexible as a drill sergeant's, but more pleasant. I have a corporal in Kibii, but he is often away from the farm these days, engaged in new and enigmatic offices.

My personal staff still numbers two — lean Otieno and fat, fat Toombo.

It is a morning in November. Some places in the world are grey as a northern sea in November, and colder. Some are silver with ice. But not Njoro. In November, Njoro and all the Highlands await their ration of warm soft rain tendered regularly by one or another of the Native Gods — Kikuyu, Masai, Kavirondo — or by the White Man's God, or perhaps by all known Gods, working amiably together. November is a month of benison and birth.

I open the black book and run my finger down one of its freshest pages. I come to Coquette.

The book says:

COQUETTE

Date of Service	Stallion
20/1/1917	Referee

Eleven months for a mare. Bred to Referee — small, perfect, gallant as a warrior, smooth as a coin — Coquette is due to foal in a matter of days. I close the book and call for Toombo.

He comes — rather, he appears; he is a visitation in ebony. Nothing in this world of extremes is blacker than Toombo, nothing is rounder than his belly, nothing is broader than his smile. Toombo is the good jinn — the one that never got locked in the pot. He suddenly fills the doorway as if he had been set into it like a polished stone into a trinket.

'Do you want me, Beru — or is it Otieno?'

No matter how many times the name Beryl goes in the Native or Indian ear, it emerges from the lips — Beru. No English word is so smooth that the tongue trained to Swahili cannot make it smoother.

'I want both of you, Toombo. The day for Coquette is very near. We must begin the watch.'

Toombo's grin spreads over his wide face like a ripple in a pond. To him, birth and success are synonymous; the hatching of a hen's egg is a triumph, or even the bursting of a seed. Toombo's own birth is the major success of his life. He grins until there is no more room for both the grin and his eyes, so his eyes disappear. He turns and shuffles through the doorway and I hear his deep voice bawling for Otieno.

The missionaries have already pitched their tents in the Kavirondo country, which is Otieno's home. They have jousted with the old black gods and even unhorsed a few They have traded a tangible Bible for a handful of intangible superstitions — the Kavirondo mind is fertile ground.

Otieno's Bible (translated into Jaluo, which he reads) has made him both a Christian and a night-owl. Night after night he sits in the yellow circle of his hurricane lamp and squints over the pages. He is indefatigable, sleepless, dependable as daylight — and half a mystic. I let him undertake, with Toombo, the night-watch in Coquette's box, knowing that he never nods.

He accepts the duty with pious gravity — as indeed he should. Tall and sombre-eyed, he stands where Toombo stood. If it were not morning, and if there were no work to be done, and if it were not my father's study, Otieno would sheepishly stroke the calf of his black leg with the sole of his black foot and tell me the story of Lot's wife.

'I have been reading in the Book,' he would begin, 'about a strange happening . . .'

But something more common, though perhaps as strange, is near its happening, and Otieno leaves and I close the black book and follow him down to the stables.

Ah, Coquette! How could a creature deserving such a gay name have become so dowdy? Once she was small and pert and golden, but now she is plain and shapeless with the weight of her foal. Her thin pasterns are bent with it until her fetlocks seem ready to touch the ground; her hooves are of lead. She has seen so much — the savage hills and plains of Abyssinia, all that wild and deep country on the way to Njoro, all those different people, those different races, those different rocks and trees. Coquette has seen the world, but the bright, wise eyes are not now so bright. Soon they will be wiser.

Her foaling-box is ready. Her body-brush, her dandy-brush, and her kitamba are there. Her coat is still no other colour than gold, her mane and her tail are still white silk. The gold is tarnished; the silk lacks lustre. Coquette looks at me as she enters the box — to wait, and wait.

All of us there — Toombo, Otieno, and myself — know the secret. We know what Coquette is waiting for, but she does not. None of us can tell her.

Toombo and Otieno begin their nightly watch. And the time goes slowly.

But there are other things. Everything else goes on as it always has. Nothing is more common than birth; a million creatures are born in the time it takes to turn this page, and another million die. The symbolism is commonplace; countless dreamers have played countless tunes upon the mystery, but horse-breeders are realists and every farmer is a midwife. There is no time for mystery. There is only time for patience and care, and hope that what is born is worthy and good.

I do not know why most foals are born at night, but most of them are. This one is.

121

Nineteen long days pass, and on the evening of the twentieth, I make the rounds of the stables, as usual, ending at Coquette's foaling-box. Buller is at my heels. Otieno The Vigilant is there — and Toombo The Rotund.

The hurricane lamp has already been lighted inside the foaling-box. It is a large box, large as a room, with walls of cedar planking milled on the farm. The floor is earthen, covered with deep grass bedding gathered fresh from the pastures; the smell of a mowed field is gathered with it.

Coquette stands heavily under the gentle glow of the lamp, her evening feed not finished. Creating new life within her, she is herself almost lifeless. She lowers her head as if it were not the exquisitely fashioned head that it is, but an ugly and tiresome burden. She nibbles at a single leaf of lucerne, too small to be tasted, then shambles on sluggish feet across the box. To her all things are poignantly lacking — but she is incapable of desiring anything.

Otieno sighs. Toombo's face beams back at the hurricane lamp, matching its glow with his glow. Outside the box, Buller challenges the oncoming night with a softly warning growl.

I bend down and lay my head against the smooth, warm belly of the mare. The new life is there. I hear and feel it, struggling already — demanding the right to freedom and growth. I hope it is perfect; I hope it is strong. It will not, at first, be beautiful.

I turn from Coquette to Otieno. 'Watch carefully. It is near.'

The tall, thin Kavirondo looks into the face of the fat one. Toombo's face is receptive — it cannot be looked at, it can only be looked into. It is a jovial and capacious bowl, often empty, but not now. Now it is filled to the brim with expectation. 'This is a good night,' he says, 'this is a good night.' Well, perhaps he is optimistic, but it proves a busy night.

Was There a Horse with Wings?

I return to my hut — my new, proud hut which my father has built for me out of cedar, with real shingles instead of thatch. In it I have my first glass window, my first wood floor — and my first mirror. I have always known what I looked like — but at fifteen-odd, I become curious to know what can be done about it. Nothing, I suppose — and who would there be to know the difference? Still, at that age, few things can provoke more wonderment than a mirror.

At eight-thirty Otieno knocks.

'Come quickly. She is lying.'

Knives, twine, disinfectant — even anæsthetic — are all ready in my foaling-kit, but the last is precaution. As an Abyssinian, Coquette should have few of the difficulties that so often attend a Thoroughbred mare. Still, this is Coquette's first. First things are not always easy. I snatch the kit and hurry through the cluster of huts, some dark and asleep, some wakeful with square, yellow eyes. Otieno at my heels, I reach the stable.

Coquette is down. She is flat on her side, breathing in spasmodic jerks. Horses are not voiceless in pain. A mare in the throes of birth is almost helpless, but she is able to cry out her agony. Coquette's groans, deep, tired, and a little frightened, are not really violent. They are not hysterical, but they are infinitely expressive of suffering, because they are unanswerable.

I kneel in the grass bedding and feel her soft ears. They are limp and moist in the palm of my hand, but there is no temperature. She labours heavily, looking at nothing out of staring eyes. Or perhaps she is seeing her own pain dance before them.

The time is not yet. We cannot help, but we can watch. We three can sit cross-legged — Toombo near the manger, Otieno against the cedar planking, myself near the heavy head of Coquette — and we can talk, almost tranquilly, about other things while the little brush of flame in the hurricane lamp paints experimental pictures on the wall.

'Wa-li-hie!' says Toombo.

It is as solemn as he ever gets. At the dawning of doomsday he will say no more. A single 'Walihie!' and he has shot his philosophic bolt. Having shot it, he relaxes and grins, genially, into himself.

The labouring of Coquette ebbs and flows in methodical tides of torment. There are minutes of peace and minutes of anguish, which we all feel together, but smother, for ourselves, with words.

Otieno sighs. 'The Book talks of many strange lands,' he says. 'There is one that is filled with milk and with honey. Do you think this land would be good for a man, Beru?'

Toombo lifts his shoulders. 'For which man?' he says. 'Milk is not bad food for one man, meat is better for another, *ooji* is good for all. Myself, I do not like honey.'

Otieno's scowl is mildly withering. 'Whatever you like, you like too much, Toombo. Look at the roundness of your belly. Look at the heaviness of your legs!'

Toombo looks. 'God makes fat birds and small birds, trees that are wide and trees that are thin, like wattle. He makes big kernels and little kernels. I am a big kernel. One does not argue with God.'

The theosophism defeats Otieno; he ignores the globular Jesuit slouching unperturbed under the manger, and turns again to me.

'Perhaps you have seen this land, Beru?'

'No.' I shake my head.

But then I am not sure. My father has told me that I was four when I left England. Leicestershire. Conceivably it could be the land of milk and honey, but I do not remember it as such. I remember a ship that sailed interminably up the hill of the sea and never, never reached the top. I remember a place I was later taught to think of as Mombasa, but the name has not explained the memory. It is a simple memory made only of colours and shapes, of heat and trudging people and broad-leaved trees that looked cooler than they were. All the country I know is this country — these hills, familiar as an old wish, this veldt, this forest. Otieno knows as much.

'I have never seen such a land, Otieno. Like you, I have read about it. I do not know where it is or what it means.'

'That is a sad thing,' says Otieno; 'it sounds like a good land.'

Toombo rouses himself from the stable floor and shrugs. 'Who would walk far for a kibuyu of milk and a hive of honey? Bees live in every tenth tree, and every cow has four teats. Let us talk of better things!'

But Coquette talks first of better things. She groans suddenly from the depth of her womb, and trembles. Otieno reaches at once for the hurricane lamp and swells the flame with a twist of his black fingers. Toombo opens the foaling-kit.

'Now.' Coquette says it with her eyes and with her wordless voice. 'Now — perhaps now ——'

This is the moment, and the Promised Land is the forgotten one.

I kneel over the mare waiting for her foal to make its exit from oblivion. I wait for the first glimpse of the tiny hooves, the first sight of the sheath — the cloak it will wear for its great début.

It appears, and Coquette and I work together. Otieno at one of my shoulders, Toombo at the other. No one speaks because there is nothing to say.

But there are things to wonder.

Will this be a colt or a filly? Will it be sound and well-formed? Will its new heart be strong and stubborn enough to snap the tethers of nothingness that break so grudgingly? Will it breathe when it is meant to breathe? Will it have the anger to feed and to grow and to demand its needs?

I have my hands at last on the tiny legs, on the bag encasing them. It is a strong bag, transparent and sleek. Through it I see the diminutive hooves, pointed, soft as the flesh of sprouted seeds — impotent hooves, insolent in their urgency to tread the tough earth.

Gently, gently, but strong and steady, I coax the new life into the glow of the stable lamp, and the mare strains with all she has. I renew my grip, hand over hand, waiting for her muscles to surge with my pull. The nose — the head, the whole head — at last the foal itself, slips into my arms, and the silence that follows is sharp as the crack of a Dutchman's whip — and as short.

'Walihie!' says Toombo.

Otieno smears sweat from under his eyes; Coquette sighs the last pain out of her.

I let the shining bag rest on the pad of trampled grass less than an instant, then break it, giving full freedom to the wobbly little head.

I watch the soft, mouse-coloured nostrils suck at their first taste of air. With care, I slip the whole bag away, tie the cord and cut it with the knife Otieno hands me. The old life of the mare and the new life of the foal for the last time run together in a quick christening of blood, and as I bathe the wound with disinfectant, I see that he is a colt.

He is a strong colt, hot in my hands and full of the tremor of living.

Coquette stirs. She knows now what birth is; she can cope with what she knows. She lurches to her feet without graceful-

126

ness or balance, and whinnies once — so this is mine! So this is what I have borne! Together we dry the babe.

When it is done, I stand up and turn to smile at Otieno. But it is not Otieno; it is not Toombo. My father stands beside me with the air of a man who has observed more than anyone suspected. This is a scene he has witnessed more times than he can remember; yet there is bright interest in his eyes — as if, after all these years, he has at last seen the birth of a foal!

He is not a short man nor a tall one; he is lean and tough as a riem. His eyes are dark and kind in a rugged face that can be gentle.

'So there you are,' he says — 'a fine job of work and a fine colt. Shall I reward you or Coquette — or both?'

Toombo grins and Otieno respectfully scuffs the floor with his toes. I slip my arm through my father's and together we look down on the awkward, angry little bundle, fighting already to gain his feet.

'Render unto Cæsar,' says my father; 'you brought him to life. He shall be yours.'

A bank clerk handles pounds of gold — none of it his own — but if, one day, that fabulous faery everyone expects, but nobody ever meets, were to give him all this gold for himself — or even a part of it — he would be no less overjoyed because he had looked at it daily for years. He would know at once (if he hadn't known it before) that this was what he had always wanted.

For years I had handled my father's horses, fed them, ridden them, groomed them, and loved them. But I had never owned one.

Now I owned one. Without even the benefit of the good faery, but only because my father said so, I owned one for myself. The colt was to be mine, and no one could ever touch him, or ride him, or feed him, or nurse him — no one except myself.

I do not remember thanking my father; I suppose I did, for whatever words are worth. I remember that when the foaling-box was cleaned, the light turned down again, and Otieno left to watch over the newly born, I went out and walked with Buller beyond the stables and a little way down the path that used to lead to Arab Maina's.

I thought about the new colt, Otieno's Promised Land, how big the world must be, and then about the colt again. What shall I name him?

Who doesn't look upward when searching for a name? Looking upward, what is there but the sky to see? And seeing it, how can the name or the hope be earthbound? Was there a horse named Pegasus that flew? Was there a horse with wings?

Yes, once there was — once, long ago, there was. And now there is again.

BOOK THREE

XI

My Trail is North

SOMEBODY with a flair for small cynicism once said, 'We live and do not learn.' But I have learned some things.

I have learned that if you must leave a place that you have lived in and loved and where all your yesterdays are buried deep — leave it any way except a slow way, leave it the fastest way you can. Never turn back and never believe that an hour you remember is a better hour because it is dead. Passed years seem safe ones, vanquished ones, while the future lives in a cloud, formidable from a distance. The cloud clears as you enter it. I have learned this, but like everyone, I learned it late.

I left the farm at Njoro almost the slowest way, and I never saw it again.

I would have turned back — Pegasus who carried me would have turned back, because even he had woven three years of memory to hold him there. But our world was gone like a scrap in the wind, and there wasn't any turning.

It all happened because those amiable gods who most times walked together, or at least agreed on larger things, fell out and neglected to send any rain.

What does a fall of rain, a single fall of rain, mean in anybody's life? What does it matter if this month there is none, if the sky is as clear as the song of a boy, and the sun shines and people walk in it and the world is yellow with it? What does a week matter, and who is so dour as to welcome a storm?

Look at a seed in the palm of a farmer's hand. It can be blown away with a puff of breath and that is the end of it. But it holds three lives — its own, that of the man who may feed on its increase, and that of the man who lives by its culture. If the seed die, these men will not, but they may not live as they always had. They may be affected because the seed is dead; they may change, they-may put their faith in other things.

All the seeds died one year at Njoro and on all the farms around Njoro, on the low fields, on the slopes of the hills, on the square plots carved out of the forests, on the great farms and on the farms built with no more than a plough and a hope. The seeds died because they were not nourished; they were starved for rain.

The sky was as clear as a window one morning. It was so the next morning, and the next, and on every morning that followed until it was hard to remember how rain felt, or how a field looked, green, and moist with life so that a naked foot sank into it. All the things that grew paused in their growing, leaves curled, and each creature turned his back on the sun.

Perhaps somewhere — in London, in Bombay, in Boston — a newspaper carried a single line (on a lesser page); 'Drought Threatens British East Africa.' Perhaps someone read it and looked upward, hoping his own skies, that day, were as clear as ours, or considered that drought on the farthest rim of Africa was hardly news.

It may not have been. It is hardly news when a man you have never seen and never will loses a year's labour, or ten years' labour, or even a life's labour in a patch of ground too far away to imagine.

But when I left Njoro, it was all too close to be easily forgotten. The rain feeds the seed, and the seed the mill. When
the rain stops, the mill wheels stop — or, if they continue to
turn, they grind despair for the man who owns them.

My father owned them. In the time that preceded the
drought he had signed contracts with the Government and
with individuals, committing himself to the delivery of hundreds of tons of flour and meal — at a fixed price and at a fixed
date. If the essence of successful business is not to receive
three times what you give, then it is at least not to receive less
than you give. I learned the tyranny of figures before I knew
the value of a pound. I learned why my father sat so long and
so late and so fruitlessly over the scribbled pages, the open
inkpot, and the sniggering lampwicks; you could not buy
maize at twenty rupees a bag, grind it to meal, then sell the
meal at ten rupees. Or at least you could (if you honoured
your own word), but you saw your substance run out of the
hoppers with every cupful of the stuff you milled.

For many months the same long chain of loaded wagons
dragged over the road from Kampi ya Moto to the farm at
Njoro. They were filled with the same grain they had brought
for years, but it was not new grain. It was not fresh grain
prodigally harvested, gleaned from the fields with shouts and
sweat. It was hoarded grain or grain combed from niggard
patches; it brought the highest price the oldest settlers with
the oldest stories could remember.

My father bought it, bringing it from wherever it could be
found, and where he spent a rupee, he lost two. The mill
wheels turned, the flour spouted into yawning bags and each
was sewn shut with a part of the farm sealed within it.

There were men who thought my father a little mad. Contracts had been evaded before, hadn't they? Wasn't God
responsible for drought?

Yes, and for a number of other things, my father thought, including lack of drought. But he held that God was reasonably innocent in the matter of a signed contract.

One day, a string of freight cars left the mill siding behind a triumphant little engine. The last of the flour had been milled; all the contracts had been honoured from the first word to the last solemn scratch of ink. The engine made the farthest turn. It hooted once, cast a smudge on the immaculate horizon, and disappeared. It carried with it most of my youth — my father's title to the farm, the buildings, the stables, and all the horses, except just one — the one with wings.

'Now,' said my father, 'we have to think.' And so we thought.

We sat for an hour in his little study and he spoke to me more seriously than he ever had done before. His arm lay across the big black book that was closed now and he told me many things I had never known — and some that I had known. He was going to Peru — an untrammelled country like this one, yet a country that loved horses and needed men who understood them. He wanted me to come, but the choice was mine; at seventeen years and several months, I was not a child. I could think; I could act with reason.

Did he consider me expert enough to train Thoroughbreds professionally?

He did, but there was much to learn.

Could I ever hope for a trainer's licence under English Jockey Club rules?

I could — but nothing succeeded like success.

I knew too little of Africa to leave it, and what I knew I loved too much. Peru was a name — a smudge of purple on a schoolbook map. I could put my finger on Peru, but my feet were on the earth of Africa. There were trains in Africa, there were some roads, there were towns like Nairobi, there were schools and bright lights and telegraph. There were men who said they had explored Africa; they had written books about it. But I knew the truth. I knew that, for myself, the country had not yet been found; it was unknown. It had just barely been dreamed.

'Go to Molo,' said my father. 'There are stables at Molo that you could use. Remember that you are still just a girl and do not expect too much — there are a few owners here and there who will give you horses to train. After that, work and hope. But never hope more than you work.'

A Spartan thread held through my father's counsel, then as now.

The trail ran north to Molo; at night it ran straight to the stars. It ran up the side of the Mau Escarpment until at ten thousand feet it found the plateau and rested there, and some of the stars burned beneath its edge. In the morning the plateau was higher than the sun. Even the day climbed the trail to Molo. I climbed it with all that I owned.

I had two saddlebags, and Pegasus. The saddlebags held the pony's rug, his brush, a blacksmith's knife, six pounds of crushed oats, and a thermometer as a precaution against Horse Sickness. For me the bags held pajamas, slacks, a shirt, toothbrush, and comb. I never owned less, nor can I be sure that I ever needed more.

We left before dawn, so that when the hills again took shape Njoro was gone, disappeared with the last impotent scowl of night. The farm was gone — its whirling mills, its fields and paddocks, its wagons and its roaring Dutchmen. Otieno and Toombo were gone, my new mirror, my new hut with the cedar shingles — all these were behind me, not like part of a life, but like a whole life lived and ended.

How completely ended! — for Buller too, bearing the scars of all his battles, holding still in his great dead heart the sealed memory of his own joys and mine, the smells he knew, the paths, the little games, those vanquished warthogs, the soundless stalking of a leopard's paws — he too had lived a life and it was ended. He lay behind me, buried deep by the path to the valley where we hunted. There were rocks over him that I had lifted and carried there and piled in a clumsy pyramid and left without a name or epitaph.

For what can be said of a dog? What can be said of Buller — a dog like any other, except only to me? Can one repeat again those self-soothing and pompous phrases: this noble beast? — this paragon of comrades? — this friend of man?

How would the shade of Buller, eager, arrogant, swaggering still under the cool light of some propitious moon, regard such sighing sentiments except to tilt once more his forever insatiable nose, open a bit wider the eye that always drooped a little, and say: 'In the name of my father, and my father's father, and of every good dog that ever killed a cat, or stole a haunch, or bit a farm boy! — could *this* be me?'

Rest you, Buller. No hyena that ever howled the hills nor any jackal cringing in the night will paw the rocks that mark you. There is respect for a heart like yours, and if its beating stop, the spirit lives to guard the ways you wandered.

My trail is north. It is thin and it curls against the slopes of the Mau like the thong of a whip. The new sun falls across it in a jumble of golden bars that lie on the earth or lean against the trees that edge the forest. The trees are tall juniper and strong cedars straining to the sky on straight shafts, thick, and rough with greying bark. Grey lichen clings in clotted mops from their high crests, defeating the day, and olive trees and wayward vines and lesser things that grow huddle safe from the hard hot light under the barrier of their stalwart brothers.

I ride my father's gift, my horse with wings, my Pegasus with the dark bold eyes, the brown coat that shines, the long mane that flows like a black silk banner on the lance of a knight.

But I am no knight. I am no knight that would earn the greeting of any other save perhaps of that fabulous and pathetic one who quested the by-paths of a distant and more ancient Spain. I am clothed in work slacks, a coloured shirt, leather moccasins, and an old felt hat, broad-brimmed and weather-weary. I ride long-stirruped, my idle hand deep in a pocket.

Giant bush-pigs bolt across my way, disturbed at their morning forage; monkeys shriek and gibber in the twisting branches; butterflies, bright, fantastic, homeless as chips on a wave, dart and soar from every leaf. A bongo, rarest of all antelope, flees through the forest, leaping high, plunging his red and white-striped coat deep in a thicket — away from my curious eyes.

The path is steep and never straight, but the clean, firm legs of Pegasus measure it with easy contempt. If his wings are fantasy, his worth is not. He never trudges, he never jolts; he is as smooth as silence.

This is silence. This ride through the boisterous birth of a forest day is silent for me. The birds sing, but they have no song that I can hear; the scamper of a bush-buck at my elbow is the whisking of a ghost through a phantom wood.

I think, I ponder, I recall a hundred things — little things, foolish things that come to me without reason and fade again ——

Kima the baboon, the big baboon that loved my father but hated me; Kima's grimaces, his threats, his chain in the court-yard; the morning he escaped to trap me against the wall of a hut, digging his teeth into my arm, clawing at my eyes, screaming his jealous hatred until, with childish courage born of terror, I killed him dead, using a knobkerrie and frantic hands and sobbing fury — and ever afterward denied the guilt.

Leopard nights — lion nights. The day the elephant trekked from the Mau to Laikipia, hundreds of them in a great irresistible phalanx, crushing the young grain, the fences, crumbling huts and barns while our horses trembled in their stables; the aftermath — the path of the elephants, broad and levelled like a route of conquest through the heart of the farm.

Lion in the paddocks — the bawling of a steer, a cow, a heifer; the rush for hurricane lamps, rifles, the whispering of one man to another; the stillness; the tawny shape, burdened with its kill, flowing through the tall grass; bullets whining away against the wind; the lion leaping, bullock and all, over the cedar fence; the lowered rifles.

And leopard nights — moonlit nights; my father and I crouched by the bulk of a Dutchman's wagon on the edge of the water tank; the smooth snick of cartridges in long guns; the wait, the tightened muscles; the gliding prowler sleek as a shadow on still water; eyes along the black barrels, the pressure of a finger.

All things to remember; some dark, some light. I nudge Pegasus into a gentle canter where the trail flattens through an open glade. The reins are threaded between the fingers of my right hand, the whip rests between my palm and the reins in the same hand. I have slipped into a thin, buckskin jacket, for, as the sun climbs, the forest deepens, the upward path finds thinner, colder air, and the green aisles are fresh with the smell of it.

I smile to myself, remembering Bombafu. What brings him to mind, I do not know, but suddenly there he is. Bom-

138

bafu means fool in Swahili; at Njoro it meant my father's parrot.

Poor Bombafu! — one day he whistled for destruction, and it came. How sad, how naked, how disillusioned he was after the moment of his greatest triumph had shone upon him like a gleam of light, then abandoned him to the darkness of despair!

They were proud feathers Bombafu gave to the Cause of his Learning, pretty feathers, long and rich and stained with jungle colour. How proudly he wore them!

How proudly he clasped the perch in the square room outside my father's study, day after day, looking with truculent, or bemused, or falsely philosophic eyes, on all who entered — on all the dogs of the motley pack my father fancied then!

And these were the undoing of Bombafu. Dogs were simple things, he saw, controlled by a single sound. A man would stand in the doorway of the house and make that sound with his lips — and the pack would come.

But who could make sounds if not Bombafu? Was he to remain a bird on a stick the whole of his long, long life? Was there to be nothing but seeds and water and water and seeds for a being as elegant as he? Who had such feathers? Who had such a beak? Who could not call a dog? Bombafu could. He did.

He practised week upon week, but so cleverly that we seldom heard him; he practised the abracadabra of calling dogs until he knew, as well as he knew the shape of the bar he clung to, that no dog that ever sought a flea could resist his summons. And he was not wrong. They came.

One morning when the house was empty, Bombafu slipped his perch and called the dogs. I heard it too. I heard the quick, urgent whistle that was my father's whistle, though my father was a mile away. I looked across the courtyard and

139

saw Bombafu, resplendent, confident, almost masterful as he
trod the doorsill on hooked, impatient toes, his brilliant breast
puffed and swelling, his green, and all too empty head cocked
with insolence. 'Come one, come all,' his whistle said — 'it is
I, Bombafu, calling!'

And so they came — long dogs, short dogs, swift dogs, hungry
dogs, running from the stables, from the huts, from the
shade of the trees where they had dozed, while Bombafu
danced under the portal of his doom and whistled louder.

I could run too in those days, but not so fast as that. Not
fast enough to prevent the frustration of an anticipant dog
from curdling to fury at the sight of this vain mop of gaudy
feathers committing forgery of the master's voice — insulting
all of dogdom with the cheek of it, holding to ridicule the
canine clan, promising even (what could be worse?) a scrap, or
a bone, yet giving nothing! That was the rub; that was the
injury heaped on insult.

Bombafu went down; he went under; he disappeared only
to rise again, feather by feather. His blaze of glory was no
abstract one. It floated on the air in crimson and chrome
yellow, in green and blue and subtler shades — a burst, a
galaxy, a comet's tail of scraps and pieces.

Sad bird! Unhappy bird! He lived, he sat again upon his
perch, his eyes half-closed and dull, a single tattered wing to
hide his nakedness, a single moment to remember.

And the immortal line so rightly his, the only word he
might have uttered, was stolen too. Surely this was tragedy
— this was irony — that not Bombafu, but a dour and morbid
raven, a creature of the printed page, a nightly nobody, had
discovered first the dramatic power of those haunting tones,
those significant syllables, that ultimate utterance — Never —
Nevermore!

So suffered Bombafu — and suffers still for all I know.

Parrots are ageless — though blessed, I suspect, with memories too short to be fatal.

While I think of him, the trail I ride finds the verge of the plateau, curls over it, and Pegasus and I move in a place no longer Africa.

A country laved with icy streams, its valleys choked with bracken, its hills clothed in the green heather that wandered Scotsmen sing about, seems hardly Africa. Not a stone has a familiar cast; the sky and the earth meet like strangers, and the touch of the sun is as dispassionate as the hand of a man who greets you with his mind on other things.

Such is Molo. Its first glance presages the character I later learn — a stern country, high and cold, demanding from those who live upon it a tithe of toil, a recompense of labour fuller than full measure and a vigour of heart against the stubborn virginity of its earth.

Sheep run here, but they are native sheep with the weather in their blood. Cattle graze, mulling the sweet grass to rhythmic cuds, staring into the full-grown day with calm eyes. There is game — scattered reed-buck, impalla, smaller things that rustle the bracken but never part it; a buffalo now and then emerges from a copse to scan the fresh hills with dubious approval, then turns, shouldering a path to less austere and more familiar levels.

There are farms — and farmers scattered like the builders of a new land, each hugging to himself all that spreads from the door of his hut to the horizon he marks with a sweep of his arm.

Yes, this too is Africa.

I dismount, slip the bit out of Pegasus' mouth and let him drink from a stream that rolls from nowhere, washing rocks immaculate for ages — rounded rocks, sleek with the wear of water. He paws at them, snorts bubbles into the clear eddy that stings with cold, then sucks his fill.

It is not his country, not the country he knows or likes. He moves back, away from the stream, and regards with tilted ears and bold, clear eyes what he hears and sees. He scuffs the ground and lowers his head to nudge my shoulder, coaxing me gently, suggesting, I suspect, that we go back the way we came.

But, for a little while, this is the place for us — a good place too — a place of good omen, a place of beginning things — and of ending things I never thought would end.

XII

Hodi!

T<small>HE</small> trees that guard the thatched hut where I live stand in disorganized ranks, a regiment at ease, and lay their shadows on the ground like lances carried too long.

They are tall trees shouldering the late sun on its way before its light is done, urging the evening into their circle. Sun shafts pry through the close guard and touch the door of the hut, or the window, or the chimney, but they are as weak as the glow of my hurricane lamp, smug and dowdy in the centre of my cedar table. Night comes early at Molo. In my house it comes earlier still, but the stables are unshaded and I can see them from where I sit. I can see the safely closed doors, a stretch of the paddock fence, a tired syce trudging to his dinner. The workday is finished, dead as the calendar page that bore its number. But the year is thick with other pages, full with other work.

There are orders for tomorrow. The girth gall on Collarcelle requires a different saddle — item for her syce. Wrack, the chestnut colt, is coming along — I'll send him a mile and a quarter, three-quarter speed; carries head too low for running martingale — rings only — chain snaffle.

There's Welsh Guard. He'll do — he is the son of Camciscan. Tendon boots? His legs are as sound as steel hinges. Gallop day tomorrow, but not for him; there's weight in his

143

neck — slow work with sweating hood. He'll pull — the good ones always pull. I'll ride Welsh Guard, and that's three.

There are two others. I train them in exchange for my hut and stable space. Dull horses, too old and 'handicapped out,' but a job's a job. Let me see ...

I think. I scribble notes. I wonder about the high price of feed, and chew my pencil. I am a trainer of race-horses, I have already got my licence. Six weeks to the Race Meeting at Nairobi — the little hotels filled, the streets humming, each day the grandstands mottled with the costumes and the colour of a dozen tribes and peoples. Winners. Losers. Money changing hands. Trainers big-chested, trainers flat-chested, explaining how it might have happened, 'except just for this.' All of them men. All of them older than my eighteen years, full of being men, confident, cocksure, perhaps offhand. They have a right to be. They know what they know — some of which I have still to learn, but not much, I think. Not much, I hope. We shall see, we shall see.

Pencil-chewing leads to nothing. My scribbles are complete, the price of feed is adamant; it is hard, it can't be changed by thinking.

I rise from my chair, stretch, and look once more toward the stables, once more toward the humourless regiment of trees that surround me. But it is not so bad. Next week I am promised two more horses to train, so my stable is growing. Only the work grows too.

I am as fond of my syces as it is possible to be. Each has followed me from Njoro, knowing that salaries might be slow in coming, food and other things not so plentiful as they had been. But still they followed, barefoot up the long trail, ragged, shyly presenting themselves for work and, of course, finding it.

Yet syces can do only certain things. They are stable boys;

they can ride, they can groom, they can clean what has to be cleaned. They cannot apply a pressure bandage, or treat lameness, or judge fitness, or handle an overwilling horse, not even a sulky one. These things belong to me, but five o'clock in the morning until sundown, long as it seems, is not long enough. If only there were someone to trust — someone I know. But, of course, there isn't. Not now. This is not Njoro in past days when I was a child and had a friend or two. This is Molo in the new days with new friends still in the making. Where are the old? Where are they ever?

I take the alarm clock off the shelf near my iron bed and begin to wind it. The hurricane lamp on the table no longer has competition from the sun. It squats in the amber corona of its nearly futile light, twisting decent shadows into tortured shapes, shedding yellow on the walls of the thatched hut, the chair, the earthen floor.

It is an ancient lamp, not of my own things. Its base is cheap metal, nicked in places, its chimney is smudged with soot. How has it lighted the hours of how many men? How many men have scribbled under it, eaten under it, got drunk under it? Has it ever seen success?

I think not. It is crumpled and slatternly, enured to failure, as if no man with hope in his fingers had ever trimmed its wick. It gives a joyless light; it is a dissolute eye. Watching it burn I am at last depressed. I make it a symbol of despair, only because it is not brighter, perhaps because it cannot talk.

But at least I can talk, if only on paper. I rummage in a saddlebag swung from a nail on the wall, find my father's last letter from Peru, spread it open to read again and answer.

Silence is never so impenetrable as when the whisper of steel on paper strives to pierce it. I sit in a labyrinth of solitude jabbing at its bulwarks with the point of a pen — jabbing, jabbing.

As always, my door is open. It may as well be closed —
there is nothing to see but night. There is nothing to hear
for a long time, and then I hear what I know to be naked
feet walking toward me. But there is no stealth in the
sound, neither is there any noise. It is the honest sound of
one used to darkness, moving through my palace guard of
trees.

I do not lift the pen from the paper nor raise my head. I
wait for a word, and it comes.

'Hodi.'

The voice is soft. It is deep with a timbre I almost remember, but do not know. It is respectful and warm and there is
shyness in it. Through the single Swahili word it says, 'I am
here,' and the echo of it adds, 'Am I welcome?'

I do not have to think. Now I leave the pen and raise my
head from the half-covered sheet of paper. Somehow that
word is always to be trusted. 'Hodi' — we who have used it
know it would scorch the lips of a liar and make a cinder of a
thief's tongue. It is a gentle word, a word of honour, asking
an answer gently. And there is an answer.

I rise from the chair and look out through the door, seeing
no one, and give the answer.

'Kaaribu!'

I have said, 'Come — you are welcome.'

I do not know the man who appears — the young man who
halts at my threshold draped in a warrior's shuka. He is tall,
and he wears a belt of beads hung with a club, and a sword in
a bright red scabbard. The tails of Colobus monkeys circle his
ankles; a strand of chain supporting a hollowed lion's claw
swings from his throat. He is tall and as silent as the night at
his back. He does not move forward; he stands at the threshold.

There is nothing for me to say. I stand and wait, letting the

146

deceitful light make a fool of my memory. I advance around
the cedar table. I look at the dark hair, plaited to a heavy
pigtail, the forward-tilted chin — the eyes — the cheekbones
— the hands . . .

My own hand goes forward as if it were no part of me. The
young man says, 'I have come to help — to work for you, if
you can use me. I am Arab Ruta.'

But now I see; now I know.

It is little Kibii of the Egret's secret, Kibii of the vanished
days, born once again.

I wonder now how long we talked, how long we sat at the
cedar table with the lamp at our elbows — the good lamp, the
gay lamp transformed in character, no longer bent, but only
leaning toward us to lend its light to an old companionship?
Perhaps an hour — perhaps three. Each of us had a diary to
read, unwritten but remembered well, and each had an audience.

I told of Njoro, of the farm's end, of things that had been
and of things I hoped would be. We laughed at some things
because we had grown so much older; we were serious about
others because we were still so young.

He spoke of his life since they had given him that spear he
had always wanted and had made a Murani of him — and had
renamed him Arab Ruta. Kibii was someone he barely knew.
Kibii was gone, Kibii was literature. This was a warrior and a
man of solemn thoughts.

'The world is a big place,' he said. 'I have been north as
far as the Uasin Gishu, farther south than Kericho, and I
have walked on the slopes of Ol Donia Kenya. But everywhere a man goes there is still more of the world at his shoulder, or behind his back, or in front of his eyes, so that it is useless to go on. I have hunted buffalo and lion, and traded sheep
near the place called Soyamu, and I have talked with other

men in all these places. After such things a man comes back
to his home, and he is not much wiser.'

'Then you are disappointed — Arab Ruta? When you were
a boy — when you were Kibii — you did not speak like this.'

'A boy does not speak like a man. The world has taught
me not more than my father taught me — and not more than
I learned from Arab Togom.'

'I do not know Arab Togom.'

'It was he my father chose to prepare me for my circumcision, and I think he prepared me well. He is a Murani of
my father's age-grade and a very wise man. He told me the
history of my people and of how a man should live his life,
keeping his voice soft and his anger sheathed until there is
just need for it — like this sword that hangs from my belt.
He told me how God delivered the first seed of all the cattle
that live into the keeping of my people and of how my tribe
cannot die if they husband this gift. He told me of war and of
how the soul of a man withers like the face of an aged woman
if the will to fight is lost. Arab Togom told me these things.
What shall a man eat and how shall a man love so that he re-
mains a man and is yet not like a bull in the herd or like a
hyena clawing at a feast?

'I am married now, at last — but first I learned these ways
of life. Obedience to law is among them; obedience to my own
heart is a part of them. I have met men that have seen more
of the world than I. One I know has even stood up to his
knees in the water that never ends and tastes like salt on the
tongue; another has lived in a village so big that only one man
out of a hundred men knows the name of his neighbour. These
men have wisdom too. It is another wisdom, and I do not say
it is bad wisdom, but that which I have learned from my
father, Arab Maina, whom you remember well, and from Arab
Togom, seems enough to live by.

'Have you in these years, Memsahib, learned more than this?'

Kibii into Arab Ruta — Beru into Memsahib! — this stilted word that ends my youth and reminds me always of its ending ——

What a child does not know and does not want to know of race and colour and class, he learns soon enough as he grows to see each man flipped inexorably into some predestined groove like a penny or a sovereign in a banker's rack. Kibii, the Nandi boy, was my good friend. Arab Ruta, who sits before me, is my good friend, but the handclasp will be shorter, the smile will not be so eager on his lips, and though the path is for a while the same, he will walk behind me now, when once, in the simplicity of our nonage, we walked together.

No, my friend, I have not learned more than this. Nor in all these years have I met many who have learned as much.

So the days that followed at Molo became easier days. Arab Ruta had not forgotten what he knew about horses. Part of my work became his work, in time he brought his wife to live there. In time my responsibility grew from five to eight horses, then to ten, until my thatched hut, the modest stables, even the quarters of Ruta and the syces, seemed no longer the place for us and I thought of other places. I thought of Nakuru, deep in the Rift Valley — a place where there were bigger stables, a race-course of sorts, and warmer weather. And in this I conceded to Pegasus the argument he never left, but still pressed home, day after day, by stubbornly striving, whenever I mounted him, toward the trail that had brought us to Molo. This, he continued to say, this of all places is no place for us!

149

But still it was — because of a thing that happened.

I am incapable of a profound remark on the workings of Destiny. It seems to get up early and go to bed very late, and it acts most generously toward the people who nudge it off the road whenever they meet it. That is an easy conclusion and it will not put to rest all further speculation on the subject, but whenever I wonder nowadays about Molo, I am forced to wonder a little about Destiny — and I achieve no progress whatever toward explaining anything. It seems remarkable to me at least that if I had not gone to Molo, I might never have seen New York, nor learned to fly a plane, nor learned to hunt elephant, nor, in fact, done anything except wait for one year to follow another.

I had always believed that the important, the exciting changes in one's life took place at some crossroad of the world where people met and built high buildings and traded the things they made and laughed and laboured and clung to their whirling civilization like beads on the skirts of a dervish. Everybody was breathless in the world I imagined; everybody moved to hurried music that I never expected to hear. I never yearned for it much. It had a literary and unattainable quality like my childhood remembrance of Scheherazade's Baghdad.

But Molo was the other end of the dream — the waking end. It was attainable, it was placid, it was dull.

What but commonplace things could follow the meeting of two people on that elevated scrap of earth? How can the course of a life be changed by a word spoken on a dusty road — a pin-scratch of a road, itself short-lived and feeble against the mountain-calloused crust of Africa? Where would a word fall except on the wind?

Pegasus and I went along the road one day and met a stranger. He rode no horse. He stood in the dirt track beside an automobile bogged and powerless, trying with grimy hands to coax the roar of life back to its dead engine. He worked in a welter of sun and grease and sweat, the only moving figure in an uninspired scene of small frustration, but his hands were patient. The man was young and unperturbed, but he was not otherwise unlike any man bent over the same task.

In Africa people learn to serve each other. They live on credit balances of little favours that they give and may, one day, ask to have returned. In any country almost empty of men, 'love thy neighbour' is less a pious injunction than a rule for survival. If you meet one in trouble, you stop — another time he may stop for you.

'Can I help?'

I had dismounted from Pegasus; the pony stood stiff-legged, straining against the reins, eyeing the angular apparition of steel and rubber with fear and distrust. For myself, I had seen engines before — the big mill engines at Njoro, and, as for automobiles, my father owned one of the first, and I had seen others on occasional visits to Nairobi. They were rolling in, but few had rolled as high as Molo. I knew what happened; I knew they ran out of petrol, or got flat tires, or just broke down.

The stranger turned from his tinkering and smiled and shook his head. No, I couldn't help. Engines were moody things. They had to be nursed. He had nursed this one for weeks and was getting used to it.

'Not bored with it?'

He wiped grease from a pair of pliers and shrugged, squinting upward at the sun. No. Well, yes — at times, of course. At times he got damned bored with it. But you had to have something to worry about, didn't you? You couldn't just sit on this window ledge of Africa and watch the clouds go by?

'I suppose you couldn't.'

I sat down on a hummock of grass, holding my reins, leaning almost against the forelegs of Pegasus. There was no place to tether a horse; there was nothing but rolling downs that went on and on in easy waves until they broke against the wall of the sky. There were no clouds to watch. The automobile so sharply sketched against this simple canvas was an intrusion; it was as if a child had pasted the picture of a foolish toy over a painting you had known for years.

The young man dropped his pliers and sat on his heels. He had intelligent eyes lit gently with humour. He was older than I by six or seven years, but he had the kindness not to show tolerance.

'I know what you're thinking. The motorcar looks silly here — your horse looks natural. But you can't stop things, you know. One day, when roads are built, this whole country will be rumbling with trains and cars — and we'll all get used to it.'

'I don't think I will. The trains I've seen are filthy — and even you can't think much of the motorcar ——'

He smiled in agreement. 'Not much really. I've got a little farm near Eldama Ravine. If it ever pays off, I'll get an aeroplane — I flew one in the war and got to like it; in the meantime the car is something to keep me busy . . .'

I had heard of aeroplanes — they too belonged to Baghdad. People talked about them, my father had talked about them — most times with a shake of his head. They were interesting inventions, it seemed, and there were men who got into them and went from place to place — why, I never knew. It seemed such a far step away from the warmth and the flow of life and the rhythm of flowing with it. It was too much outside of the things one knew — to like, or even to believe. A man was not a bird — how Arab Maina would have laughed at that — men wishing themselves into wings! It would have reminded him of a legend.

'When you fly,' the young man said, 'you get a feeling of

possession that you couldn't have if you owned all of Africa. You feel that everything you see belongs to you — all the pieces are put together, and the whole is yours; not that you want it, but because, when you're alone in a plane, there's no one to share it. It's there and it's yours. It makes you feel bigger than you are — closer to being something you've sensed you might be capable of, but never had the courage to seriously imagine.'

What would Arab Maina have said to that? — Arab Maina, with his wish to walk an even path on naked feet, keeping his eyes on the earth, his great spear in his hand and his vanity buried in his heart? He would have found a legend for that. He would have said, 'Lakwani — listen! Once there was the child of a leopard who found the ways of his kind too small to live by . . . and one day this child of a leopard . . .'

That is what Arab Maina would have said — that and more. But I said almost nothing. I saw that this man, tinkering with his battered engine on that pin-scratch of a road under a sun that burned the metal in his hands, was no fool — at most, a dreamer. He meant these things — not for me, of course (I was just an audience for his dreaming), but for himself. And his were solemn dreams. They were solemn dreams and in time he made them live.

Tom Black is not a name that ever groped for glory in a headline or shouldered other names aside for space to strut in. It can be found in the drier lists of men who figured flights in terms of hours or days, instead of column inches. There was fanfare when he and Charles Scott hurled the sleek red 'Comet' across eleven thousand miles of the world in 1934. There were other flights that found the public fancy. All these were diversions. If a man has any greatness in him, it comes to light, not in one flamboyant hour, but in the ledger of his daily work.

I saw the ledger written. But so many days followed that one on the road at Molo — so many intervened before we met again.

I mounted Pegasus and waved good-bye and, behind me, heard the tired engine stir to life and sing with a broken voice that had no music in it. And the happy tinker who had revived it again jostled on his dreamy way wrapped in a nebula of dust.

He had been lavish with a stranger. He had left me a word, tossed me a key to a door I never knew was there, and had still to find.

'All the pieces are put together, and the whole is yours . . .' A word grows to a thought — a thought to an idea — an idea to an act. The change is slow, and the Present is a sluggish traveller loafing in the path Tomorrow wants to take.

Jumbled thoughts — restless thoughts — absurd thoughts! Pull yourself together. Whoever heard of Destiny with pliers in his hand?

'Come, Pegasus — stretch those handsome legs — it's almost feeding time!'

XIII

Na Kupa Hati M'zuri

THE red-jawed Russian squints over his glass of vodka, swallows, and snorts from the bottom of his belly.

'Leopard?' he says. 'Pah! I have fought Siberian wolves with a clasp-knife. Listen, my friend — once at Tobolsk...'

'Oxford myself,' the man at his elbow says, 'shall we sing?'

'Wait until the orchestra stops.'

'White hunter? You'll want the best, old man. Get Blixen if you can, or Finch-Hatton. The Rift Valley isn't Hyde Park, you know...'

'In America we make the biggest there are. Take Chicago now...'

'Champagne, Memsahib?'

'Only a little... thanks. Now what were you saying, dear? Is that Lord Delamere with the glasses on?'

'No. The one with the long hair. He never misses a Race Meeting. He never misses anything.'

'Good old Muthaiga Club!'

'Good old Haig and Haig!'

'Good old Harrow — a toast to Harrow!'

'Eton, you mean — swing, swing together — steady from stroke to bow...'

'Forty years on...'

'Gentlemen! Gentlemen!' A tipsy fellow, swaying like a wind-rocked palm, frowns over the sea of fun and commands it to subside, but he has no magic. The sea rises, engulfs him in a single swell of laughter, and rolls on and on.

Let there be music. And there is music.

'Beryl! — I've been looking for you . . .'

The lean, easy figure of Eric Gooch looms at my shoulder. There is economy in the straight lines of his face, his eyes are blue and candid, and lacking worry. He is a farmer who has farmed for years without crying about it. He likes it. He likes all animals and especially horses. His filly, Wise Child, is in my stable. Now that I have moved to Nakuru, leaving Molo with its smells of Scotland, its cold nights and its contours so unorthodox — except to a Calvinistic eye — I am in closer touch with the owners of the horses I train. This is the big race, the important race — the Saint Leger, and most of my hopes (and Eric's) hang on the satin-sleek shoulders of Wise Child.

Eric finds a chair and somehow crowds it up to my table. We put our heads together and talk of what to us are serious things; we mumble under the raucous chorus of voices that blend somehow and rise to the rafters of Muthaiga Club in a crescendo that lacks only a conductor to time its swell.

We can talk elsewhere. Nairobi has outgrown its swamp and tin-roof days. There are other places for discussing a horse-race, but none more appropriate, none more congenial. Poet or ploughman, statesman or derelict — every man has his Mermaid's Tavern, every hamlet its shrine to conviviality, and in the image of the common spirit of those who haunt it, the character of the shrine is fashioned.

A Claridge's in London or a pub, a Cirro's in Paris or a bistro — alehouse, coffee-house, bodega, caravansary — by any name each is a sanctuary, a temple for talk, and for the observance of the warming rites of comradeship. Around this samovar, over those crystal goblets or beside that skin of wine, not much is said that, morning after, will stir a sleepy world to thoughtfulness. What music there was is vanished with the vanished hours, what words were uttered are dead with the fallen dust and are as prudently whisked away.

The Old Days, the Lost Days — in the half-closed eyes of memory (and in fact) they never marched across a calendar; they huddled round a burning log, leaned on a certain table, or listened to those certain songs.

Muthaiga Club may nowadays be changed. 'Na Kupa Hati M'zuri' (I Bring You Good Fortune) was, in my time, engraved in the stone of its great fireplace. Its broad lounge, its bar, its dining-room — none so elaborately furnished as to make a rough-handed hunter pause at its door, nor yet so dowdy as to make a diamond pendant swing ill at ease — were rooms in which the people who made the Africa I knew danced and talked and laughed, hour after hour.

But there were occasions for this. Not every night was a gay night at Muthaiga; not many of its members or habitués were idle people. Farms need farmers, safaris need hunters, horses need horsemen. There, as everywhere, work was work, but there were intervals — and a tavern in the town.

'Days of toil and nights of gladness!' I do not know the author of that simplest of all designs for living, but I know the man who made it half a creed and half a toast. Glad nights were few on which Sandy Wright — son of Scotland, husband of the soil, and pioneer of my own Njoro — did not lift his glass and exact the pledge, once more, from his often pledged disciples.

Naval officers from battleships anchored at Mombasa could steer an unerring course, on land, to the threshold of Muthaiga. Politicians escaping their fresh-built corridors of small connivance and enormous words lounged in the alcoves of Muthaiga. District Commissioners — leather-brown, the drone of some frontier wind still singing in their ears, their minds free for a while from deserts and decisions, black men's ways and white men's edicts — found solace at Muthaiga. Lion, elephant, buffalo, kudu — some dead a day, some dead for years — were revived again and shot again in copses of Wedgwood saucers, behind hillocks of table linen, or in jungles of swizzle sticks.

'I stood here ... my gun-bearer there ... Tusks? — just under two hundred ...'

'Black-maned devil — big as they come — my heavy rifle in camp ...'

'Ah!' says the red-jawed Russian, 'lion? Listen, my friend, I have fought Siberian wolves ...'

Let there be music.

At Race Meetings there is more than music. At Race Meetings there is even more than racing, though the trumpeter who heralds each start seems no mere member of the K.A.R., but a pied piper toward whose high, repeated notes hurry all the keepers of the land, for if they are not children, they must nonetheless respond to an irresistible ditty.

Just as Arab Ruta was once Kibii, British East Africa is now Kenya. Nairobi has a frontier cut to its clothes and wears a broad-brimmed hat, but it tends an English garden; it nurtures the shoots of custom grafted from the old tree. It dresses for dinner, passes its port-wine clockwise, and loves a horse-race.

'And so,' says Eric Gooch, 'what are our chances?'

I frown and shake my head. 'Without Wrack to run against us, they would be perfect.'

What a thing to have to say! My own skill and labour have moulded every muscle on the hard, dynamic body of the chestnut colt. Wrack's prowess is the product of my own hands; he is far and away the favourite for the Leger — but he will run against me. Part of that conversation buzzing around these wide, white walls is gossip about Wrack — little words of speculation droning like bees in a bottle.

Eric and I think back.

Just twelve weeks ago Wrack had been taken from my stable at Nakuru by his owner and put into the care of another trainer — a man who knew a good thing when he saw it. In the year Wrack had been with me, he had developed from a leggy, headstrong colt into a full-formed race-horse, swift, haughty, and contemptuous of competition. Wrack could run and knew it. Nervously, his owner had listened to the argument that a girl of eighteen could not be entrusted with those precise finishing touches, that careful shading of muscle against bone, that almost sophistical task of persuading a horse that nothing in his own world of probabilities was so improbable as another horse's ability to beat him past the post. Wrack had been taken from me on the strength of the doubt, and my reputation as a trainer, which had only begun to take firm root, was hardly encouraged by the act.

But gossip has its better points. Whispers are not restricted to the bearing of bad news and there are men who smell injustice however softly it walks.

Eric Gooch had known that I would bring about fifteen horses to Nairobi for the big Race Meeting, and that some of these would win the lesser races. He had also known that, without Wrack, I had nothing to enter as a serious contender for the classic — the single race that really mattered. Eric had thought hard, and then he had come to my stable from his farm at Nyeri.

'I've worried about this thing,' he had said, 'but I don't know any way out. Wrack is already being backed to win, and, so far as I can see, there is nothing to stop him. Of course, there's Wise Child — but, hell, you know about Wise Child.'

Know about her? Like Pegasus, she had been born into my hands. Her Thoroughbred blood had filtered through twenty generations of winners. Hers was the metal to match the metal of Wrack. Only there was the question of legs.

Wise Child, as a two-year-old, had been mishandled by her first trainer. Her tendons had been concussed — jarred too early against too hard a track. With all that fire in her heart, all that energy in her tidy bay body, she could barely carry a man on her back. Would it be possible in twelve weeks' time to strengthen those willing but ailing legs — to build them up so that she could drive them a mile and three-quarters — and win?

Eric had thought not — but she was mine if I would have her.

Well, I would have her. It cost only work to try, but to watch Wrack, my own Wrack, sweep the field, bearing alien colours, would cost much more.

And so it had been settled. Wise Child of the gentle manner, the soft, kind eyes and the will to win (if only those legs could be strengthened again), had come into my care at Nakuru. Together we had worked and worried — Arab Ruta, myself, and the little bay filly; but at least we had been blessed with a world of our own to work in.

It was a world of absolutes. It held no intermediate shades, neither of sound nor of colour. There were no subtle strokes in the creation of Nakuru.

The shores of its lake are rich in silence, lonely with it, but the monotonous flats of sand and mud that circle the shallow water are relieved of dullness, not by only an occasional bird or a flock of birds or by a hundred birds; as long as the day lasts Nakuru is no lake at all, but a crucible of pink and crimson fire — each of its flames, its million flames, struck from the wings of a flamingo. Ten thousand birds of such exorbitant hue, caught in the scope of an eye, is a sight that loses credence in one's own mind years afterward. But ten thousand flamingos on Lake Nakuru would be a number startling in its insignificance, and a hundred thousand would barely begin the count.

Menegai Crater overlooks the township and the lake. In the time of man it has breathed no brimstone, and barely a wisp of smoke. But in the annals of the Rift Valley which contains all this as a sea contains a coral atoll or a desert a dune, the time of man is too brief a period to deserve more than incidental recording. Tomorrow, next day, or next year, Menegai may become again the brazier over which some passing Deity will, for a casual aeon or so, warm his omnipotent hands. But until then, one can stand safely on its edge, watching the lake of pink and scarlet wings, so far below — the lake that seems to have stolen for the moment, at least, all the mountain's fire.

This was the lavish background against which I worked my horses at Nakuru. My entrance with Arab Ruta and Wise Child on the flat shore each morning just after daylight must have been as anticlimactic as the spectacle of three mice crossing a stage gigantically set for the performance of a major Wagnerian opera. I used the shore because it was the only place soft and yielding enough for Wise Child's sensitive legs.

My quarters were hardly so elaborate as the hut at Molo had been. By day I lived in a stable I had renovated for my own use, and by night I slept at the very top of the modest little grandstand, built, as was the race-course, by stolidly British members of the district, who, like all the others of our immutable clan, were allergic to the absence of horses.

And each time I had watched Wise Child test her tendons on the moist ground while flamingos rose and settled on the surface of the lake or sluggard hippopotami waddled into it, I had thought of Wrack — disdainful Wrack. How well I knew him!

But the twelve weeks had hurried on, the work had been done as skilfully as I could do it.

And now, at last, we are here. Now Eric fingers his glass and questions me hopefully, while the music of Muthaiga marches through our talk, and festive people clasp hands, revive old toasts — and make bets on tomorrow's Leger.

One hundred pounds — two hundred pounds...

'Has the filly a chance?'

'Against Wrack? Of course not.'

'Don't be too sure... don't be too sure. Why, I remember...'

Well, that's what makes a horse-race.

Jockey: Sonny Bumpus.

What's in a name? At least there's no weight in this one. There's an airy insolence in it. Who would be so heedless as to run a horse against such a happily cocksure combination as — Sonny Bumpus on Wise Child?

And if this were not enough to ponder, what about Arab Ruta? Arab Ruta, the mystic, the conjurer, the wizard of Njoro?

'Ah-yey!' he says, as he grooms the filly with inspired hands, 'I will make these muscles like the muscles of a Murani ready for battle. I will make them tough as the bow of a Wandorobo. I will put my own strength into them!' He spits contempt. 'Wrack — I warn you! You are a colt, but God has given our filly the blade of a Nandi spear for a heart, and put the will of the wind in her lungs. You cannot win, Wrack. I, Arab Ruta, say so!'

He turns to me. He is solemn. 'It is settled, Memsahib. Wrack will lose.'

I look up from the plaiting of Wise Child's mane, and smile.

'There are times, Ruta, when you sound like Kibii.'

With hesitance my smile is returned. Ruta is thoughtful, but unchastened. 'No, Memsahib — it is only that I have the power to make truths of my beliefs. It is a thing only a Murani can do.'

We are in our stable at the race-track. Within two hours the Leger will be run. While Ruta grooms, I plait the silky mane and the blacksmith spreads out his tools to put on Wise Child's aluminum racing plates. The filly stands quiet as a nodding kitten, but she is not asleep. She knows. She is thinking. Perhaps she is wondering, as I am, about those weakened tendons. She cannot feel them; it is not a matter of pain. It is only a question of how long they will take the strain of speed, the piston-pounding of hooves against the hard track, the long way from that excited start to that distant finish.

She straightens at the touch of the blacksmith's hand, then yields a foot with graceful resignation. She will do whatever is asked of her, as she always has done. She turns her head, nudging me, speaking to me — do not worry; I will run. As long as these legs will bear me up, I will run. But have we long to wait?

Not long, Wise Child, not very long.

When the blacksmith is finished, I leave the stable, and, for a few minutes, inspect the course again — as if I had not already done it a dozen times. Other trainers, and owners, stand alone or in pairs about the paddock gates or lean on the white rails that enclose the oval track. Syces are busy, a jockey wearing the colours of Lady MacMillan's stable scurries through the bustle — an important, a resplendent midget. Bookmakers tread on each other's toes, on mine, on anybody's, or stand flat-footed scowling at scraps of paper clutched like passports to El Dorado.

A cloud of people, growing darker, creeps over the course, across the grandstands, muffling in its billows the martial thunder of the K.A.R. Band.

To the north looms Mount Kenya, throne of the Kikuyu God, jewelled in sunlight, cushioned in the ermine of lasting snow. And, to the northeast, lying lower, like a couch of royal purple awaiting the leisure of this same prodigious God, spread the Aberdares. Under the shadow of such sovereign furnishings sprawl the ignoble stamping grounds of little people — the Indian Bazaar, the Somali Village, Nairobi itself in its microcosmic majesty. And the inhabitants of these, coloured as variously as unsorted beads, stream through the open gates of the race-course, paying for passage, eager for pleasure.

I have wondered sometimes if it is the beauty of a running-horse that brings so many people of so many kinds to such a makeshift amphitheatre as this is, or if it is the magnetism of a crowd, or if it is only the banal hope of making an easy shilling? Perhaps it is none of these. Perhaps it is the unrecognized expectation of holding for an instant what primordial sensations can be born again in the free strength of flashing flanks and driving hooves beating a challenge against the ground.

A keeper of an Indian duka — a Government clerk — a Lord Delamere — an Eric Gooch, all cogs of a kind, in a life of a kind, have made for themselves here, and everywhere, places where they can sit with folded arms and pay regular tribute to an animal so humble that he can be bought for a banknote.

Yet I wonder if he is ever bought? I wonder if the spirit of Camciscan, the sturdy integrity of Pegasus, the wise and courageous heart of Wise Child can ever be bought?

Is this too much to say of horses?

I remember the things they did; I remember this Saint Leger.

In the large talk of Continental sweepstakes, it is a trivial thing. It is not trivial to Wrack, to Wise Child, to the eight other horses who will leave the starting post; it is not trivial to me as I make the final preparations.

I feel the filly's legs, a little puffy, but not feverish. I kneel down and strap the tendon boots on them, firmly, carefully. I slip on the light racing bridle with my blue-and-gold colours striping the forehead band; I put the martingale over her head, onto her neck.

Arab Ruta fixes the protective pad on her withers, the number cloth over that, and then the saddle. At last I tighten the girths. We do not talk very much. It is only a matter of minutes before the bell will ring calling the horses to the paddock.

Sonny Bumpus has had his instructions. The lean, dark haired boy has listened earnestly to every word. He is a grand horseman, honest as daylight.

I have explained the strategy over and over: 'Lie two or three lengths behind Wrack for the first couple of furlongs — until the filly gets warmed up. Steady her round the first bend; if her legs are still standing after that, let her go on the far stretch. Get the lead — keep it. She's willing and fast. She'll stay forever. If Wrack challenges, don't worry — so long as her legs can take the drive she'll never quit. If they fail — well — it won't be your fault, but whatever happens don't use your whip. If you do, she'll stop in her tracks.'

That's all. That's all there can be. A bell rings and I nod to Ruta. He takes Wise Child's reins in his hands and leads her slowly toward the paddock. The small fleck of sweat on her flanks is the only indication that she shares with us our anxiety, our unmentioned fears, and our quiet hopes.

It is only coincidence that in the paddock she falls in line behind Wrack, giving me a chance to compare them closely. I do not even bother about the others — Lady MacMillan's entries, one of Delamere's, a couple entered by Spencer Tryon, one of the best of trainers. They are all good horses, but I admit none as a threat. Wise Child has but two threats — Wrack, and her own weak tendons.

Wrack is triumphant in advance of victory. He is a beautiful colt, sleek as speed itself, dancing like a boxer on quick, eager feet, flaunting his bright body in front of the steady and demure Wise Child. I look at him and take credit for that impressive form, but allow myself the comfort of small malice at the sight of too much sweat streaming from his chestnut coat — a coat that looks as if it might be otherwise a bit too dry under the touch of experienced fingers. Has Wrack been overtrained since he left me? Has someone been too anxious? Or am I smothering reason with a wish . . .

I recognize Wrack's owner a few yards down the rail — at the elbow of the colt's new trainer. We nod to each other all around, with about the same warmth one might expect of so many robots. I can't help it. I'll be doubly damned if I will try to help it.

Eric Gooch touches my shoulder. 'I couldn't resist,' he says; 'the filly looks so good I've placed a bet on her for myself — and another for you. I won't have to mortgage the old homestead if she loses, but we'll both be a little richer if she wins. Will she?'

'Her legs are weak as oat straws, but she'll try.'

'Wrack's the horse!' A dogmatic gentleman next to me hurries off to place his bet on Wrack. I wince a little, but the man's no fool.

Comments are being made on the splendid condition of Wise Child, but the filly is as deaf to flattery as a hitching post. She's deaf to everything. She circles round the paddock before the critical gaze of five hundred pairs of eyes. She moves modestly, even shyly, as if her being there at all is a matter she can only hope will be regarded as an excusable error.

Suddenly the crowd mumbles and shifts, the paddock opening is cleared, and the lead horse — a black stallion — prances in pompous style toward the track. In a few minutes it will all be over.

Eric and I hurry through the grandstand into Delamere's box. We wait; we watch; we brace ourselves against the wooden ledge.

The horses canter briskly past the stands. Wise Child, with Sonny riding feather light, trips like a shy schoolgirl behind the others. She is without ego, but she can afford vanity. There's not a prettier one in the field — nor one more thoughtful. I strain forward, trying foolishly to make her aware of me, to make her feel somehow that the burden of her secret is a little shared — the secret of those smartly bound legs that may have to yield so soon.

'She's in wonderful shape!'

Eric is radiant, but there's no answer from me. I unbuckle my binocular case and find that my hands are shaking. She won't win; she can't win. I know Wrack's form. I try to be casual, nodding to my friends, fumbling my program as if I could really read it. But the pages are blank. I read nothing. I stand staring down at the little group of horses with humourless anxiety, not as if this were just a race held under the African sun in a noisy settlement between Lake Victoria and the Indian Ocean, but as if this were the greatest race of all time, held on the greatest course, with the world looking over my shoulder.

Incongruously the band blares out the nerve-tightening

notes of 'Mandalay' and some of the crowd beat the floor boards in heavy time. I wish the band would stop — and I love bands. I wish people would stop humming that dreary tune — and I love the tune. I can see perfectly well without glasses, but I lift the binoculars to my eyes and watch.

They're at the post — some of them eager, some of them stubborn, some of them not quite sure. Atop their gleaming backs the jockeys look like gaudy baubles, secured with strings. They bob up and down, they rise, lean forward, then settle again. A horse rears, or whirls, striking plumes of dust from the track until the bright marionette he carries is swallowed in it, but appears again, transformed now — stubbornly human now, controlling, guiding, watching.

I find Wrack. Look at Wrack! He's fighting to run, dying to run. As always, he's impatient with delay. Arrogant devil — he wants it over with; it's his race and he wants to hammer it into our heads once and for all. Why the ceremony? Why the suspense? Let's run! He's doing a pirouette; he'll plunge if his boy can't hold him. Easy Wrack — quiet, you elegant fool!

The starter is ready, the crowd is ready, Eric and I are ready. The band has stopped and the grandstand is a tabernacle of silence. This is the moment — this should be the moment. Steady, Sonny — the end may hang on the beginning, you know. Steady, Wise Child. All right. Everybody on their feet; everybody crane their necks.

Beautiful line-up; their noses are even as buttons on a tape. Watch the flag. Watch...

No! False start. Wrack, you idiot; I'd hammer that out of you. I had it out of you once. You can't start that way; you've got to be calm. Don't you remember? You've got to...

'Be calm,' says Eric, 'you're trembling.'

So I am. Not quite like a leaf, but anyway like a branch.
I don't see how I can help it much, but I turn to Eric and
smile vacuously as if somebody just past eighty had asked me
to dance.

When I turn again, they're off with Wrack in the lead.
That's fine. That's what I expected. It's what the crowd expected too. Five thousand voices, each like a pipe in an immense, discordant organ, swell and roll over the single, val-
iant note of the trumpeter. They roll over me, but they sound
like a whisper — a bit hoarse, but still like a whisper. I have
stopped trembling, almost breathing, I think. I am calm now
— wholly composed. They're off, they're on their way, swinging down the long course, leaving behind their heels a ripple
of thunder.

How can I compare a race like this to music? Or how can I
not? Will some perfectionist snug in the arms of his chair
under the marble eyes of Beethoven shudder at the thought?
I suppose so, but if there's a fledgling juggler of notes and
cadences, less loyal to the stolid past, who seeks a new theme
for at least a rhapsody, he may buy a ticket at any gate and
see how they run. He will do what I cannot. He will transpose
and change and re-create the sound of hooves that pelt like
rain, or come like a rolling storm, or taper like the rataplan of
fading tympani. He will find instruments to fit the bellow of
a crowd and notes to voice its silence; he will find rhythm in
disorder, and build a crescendo from a sigh. He will find a
place for heroic measures if he watches well, and build his
climax to a wild beat and weave the music of excitement in
his overtones.

A race is not a simple thing. This one is not. There are not
just ten horses down there, galloping as fast as they can.
Skill and reason and chance run with them. Courage runs with
them — and strategy.

You do not watch a race; you read it. There is cause in every flux and change — jockeys have ability or they haven't; they bungle or they don't. A horse has a heart or he lacks it.

Questions must be answered before the rap of one hoof follows another — when to hold back, when to coax, when to manoeuvre. More speed? All right, but will he last?

Who can tell? A good boy — a sound judge of speed can tell. Slow pace, medium pace, fast pace — which is it? Don't let a second-rater snatch the race! Sonny shouldn't; he's sensitive as a stop-watch. But he might.

What's that behind — trick or challenge? Don't be fooled, don't be rattled, don't be hurried. Mile and three-quarters, you know — with ten in the field, and every one a winner until you prove he's not. There's time, there's time! There's too much time — time for errors, time for a lead to be stolen, time for strength and breath to vanish, time to lose, with the staccato insistence of forty hooves telling you so. Eyes open — watch the score!

Wrack's first, then the black stallion pulling hard. A brown horse with more style than speed clings to a precarious third. It's Wise Child at his flank, on the rails. She's smooth. She's leopard smooth.

'God, she's going well!' Eric yells it, and I smile. 'Be calm — you're trembling.'

He isn't, perhaps, but he's hopping up and down as if he'd won the race, and he hasn't. He hasn't won anything yet. Tendons. Tendons — remember the tendons! Of course she's going well, but...

'Come on, Wrack!'

Support for the enemy, unidentified. I snort and mumble in my mind. Silly man, don't yell — watch. They're in the far stretch now. My jockey's no fool — Sonny's no fool. See that? See Wise Child easing up, gliding up? Where's your Wrack now? Don't yell — watch. She's catching him, isn't she? She's closing in, isn't she?

She is; she does. The crowd stirs, forgetting bets, and roars for blood. They get it too. Wrack is a picture of driving power — Wise Child a study in coordination of muscle and bone and nerve. She's fast, she's smooth. She's smooth as a blade. She cuts the daylight between Wrack and herself to a hand's breadth — to a hair's breadth — to nothing.

'Come on, Wrack!'

A diehard, eh? All right, roar again — howl again, but bet again if you can!

The filly streaks past the colt like a dust devil past a stone, like a cheetah past a hound. Poor Wrack. It will break his heart.

But it doesn't — not Wrack's heart! His head is up a little and I know he's giving all he has, but he gives more. He's a stallion, and the male ego kindles a courage that smothers the pain of his burning muscles. He forgets himself, his jockey, everything but his goal. He lowers his head and thunders after the filly.

Without seeing, I know that Eric gives me a quick glance, but I cannot return it. I can only watch the battle. I am not yet so callous that the gallantry of Wrack seems less than magnificent.

Gallop, Wrack! — faster than you can, harder than you can. My own Wrack — my stubborn Wrack — six lengths behind.

But for how long? Wise Child's still against the rails — a small shadow against the rails, moving like a shadow, swift as a shadow — determined, quiet, steady. My glasses are on her. Thousands of eyes are on her when she sways.

She sways, and the groan from the crowd absorbs my own.

171

The filly swings from the rails and falters. Her legs are going, her speed is going, her race is going!

Wrack's jockey sees it. Wrack sees it. The whip smarts against his quarters, but he needs no whip. He closes fast, narrowing the distance — length by length.

'Come on, Wrack!' The cry is almost barbaric now, and it comes from a hundred places.

Scream — yell! Cheer him on! Can't you see her legs are going? Can't you see she's running only on her heart? Let him have the race — let him win. Don't push her, Sonny. Don't touch her, Sonny ...

'Eric ...'

But he's gone. He's jumped over the box and run down to the rails. For myself, I can't move. I exist in a cauldron of screams and cheers and waving arms. Wrack and the filly are down the last stretch now, and he's on her flank, overtaking her, passing her, shaming her — while she breaks.

My glasses dangle on their strap. I bend over the edge of the box, clamping my fingers on the wooden ledge. I can't shout, or think. I know this is only a horse-race. I know that tomorrow will be the same as yesterday, whoever loses. I know the world won't turn a hair, whoever wins — but it seems so hard to believe.

I suppose for an instant I'm in a trance. My eyes see everything, but register nothing. Not a noise, but the sudden hush of the crowd jars me to consciousness again. How long is an instant? Could it be long enough for this?

I see it happen — clearly, sharply, as a camera must see things happen. I am as cold and as bloodless. As rigid too, I think.

I see Wise Child falter once more, and then straighten. I see her transformed from the shadow she was to a small, swift flame of valour that throws my doubt in my teeth. I see her

172

scorn the threat of Wrack and cram the cheers for his supporters back in their throats. I see her sweep the final furlong on swollen legs, forging ahead, feeding him the dust of her hooves.

And I hear the crowd find its voice again, hurling her past the winning post in a towering roar of tribute.

And then it's over. Then it's silent, as if somebody closed the door on Babel.

I feel my way down to the unsaddling enclosure. A grey mass of people clings to the rails — a foggy, but articulate jungle of arms, heads, and shoulders surrounding the winner — chanting, mumbling, shifting. They stare, but I think they see nothing. They see only a bay filly, standing quietly with quiet eyes — and that is nothing. That is ordinary; it can be seen anywhere — a bay filly that won a race.

The crowd dwindles as I talk to Eric, to Sonny, to Arab Ruta, and stroke the still sweating neck of Wise Child. The movement of my hand is mechanical, almost senseless.

'She didn't just win,' Eric says; 'she broke the Leger record.'

I nod without saying anything, and Eric looks at me with kindly impatience.

Weighing out of the jockeys is finished; everything is over and the last notes of the band have whimpered into silence. All the people press toward the gates, the emblems of their holiday litter the course, or scamper in a listless dance before the wind. Half the grandstand lies in a shadow, and the other half is lit with the sun. It is like a pod emptied of its seeds. Eric takes me by the arm and we jostle toward the exit with the rest.

'She broke the record — and with those legs!' says Eric.

'I know. You told me.'

'So I did.' He walks along, scuffing the ground, and scratches his chin in a masculine effort not to look sentimental — a futile effort, but at least he can inject a note of gruffness into his voice.

'Maybe it's silly,' he says, 'but I know you'll agree that no matter how much money we could make with Wise Child, she deserves never to race again.'

And she never does.

XIV

Errands of the Wind

THE dooryard of Nairobi falls into the Athi Plains. One night I stood there and watched an aeroplane invade the stronghold of the stars. It flew high; it blotted some of them out; it trembled their flames like a hand swept over a company of candles.

The drumming of the engines was as far away as the drumming of a tom-tom. Unlike a tom-tom, it changed its sound; it came closer until it filled the sky with a boastful song.

There were pig-holes and it was dark. There were a thousand animals strolling in the path of an aeroplane searching for a haven; they were like logs in a lightless harbour.

But the intruder circled and swung low with articulate urgency. Time after time it circled and swung low, and its voice said: I know where I am. Let me land.

This was a new thing. The rest of the world may have grown complacent by then about aeroplanes flying in the night, but our world had barren skies. Ours was a young world, eager for gifts — and this was one.

I think there were four of us standing there, staring upward, watching the rigid shadow wheel and return again. We lighted fires and made flares. The flames of these burned holes in the darkness, and when they were at their highest, the plane came down but could not land.

Wildebeest and zebra detached themselves from their res-

175

tive herds, like volunteers in a People's Army, and moved under the dipping wings.

The plane swung low again and climbed again, blaring its frustration. But it returned with vindictive fury and shattered the front of the animal legions and made first conquest of their ancient sanctuary.

More people had driven out from the town, compelled by the new romance of a roaring propeller — a sound that was, for me, like a white light prying through closed eyes, disturbing slumber I did not want disturbed. It was the slumber of contentment — contentment with a rudimentary, a worn scheme of life — slumber long nurtured by a broad and silent country, effortless and fruitful in the sun, and whose own dreams were the fabric of its history. I had curiosity, but there was resentment with it. And neither of these could be translated into reason.

A dozen hands went out to help the pilot from his monoplane — a mechanical hybrid with high wings and a body the commonest jay would have jeered at. Two motorcars, manoeuvred into position, provided a somewhat less than celestial aura as an accessory to the visitation, and the pilot descended into this — unshaven, unsmiling, and apparently long unwashed.

With one hand he waved away the questions that greeted him; with the other he clutched an ordinary biscuit tin — a bedraggled, a spurious Galahad nursing a fraudulent grail.

I moved closer and stared into his face. One side was lit by an oil flare and the other by the beam of a car. Even so, the stubbornly confident features were recognizable. When I had seen him last, the hand that held the biscuit tin had brandished a pair of pliers, and his chariot, a more earthy thing than this one, had no more exalted aspiration than to travel a dirt-track road at Molo with respectable speed.

The happy tinker had got his aeroplane. But either the thrill of having it had already dulled or he had accepted what seemed to me a major triumph as anyone else might accept the tedious dependability of daybreak.

He nodded to the half-dozen of us grouped around him, yawned as if he had never yawned before, and asked for two things — a cigarette and an ambulance.

'There's a wounded man in the cabin ... could somebody drive to the hospital?'

A car left at once, the whine of its gears rising to the pitch of heroic hysteria, and people stepped back from the plane as if Death had crooked a finger from its cockpit.

Still holding his biscuit tin, Tom Black, late of Molo, of Eldama Ravine, and of other places whose names I had not the temerity to ask, ministered to the needs of his machine, puffed at his cigarette and maintained a thoughtful silence. It was a preoccupied silence that no one attempted to disturb.

When the ambulance came, the injured passenger, sheathed in a cocoon of blankets, was handed out of the cabin. Still more onlookers arrived, the animals, conceding armistice, but not peace, had returned in cautious groups, their eyes burning like lanterns in a poorly lighted dream.

Even the flares persisted — hopeful yet of staring down the night. But the night had begun to grumble. There was thunder, and the stars took cover.

The wounded man was borne in silence, while wildebeest, ostrich, and zebra circled the ceremony, unholy hyenas whimpered their frustration, and the visionary whose visions came true directed the disposition of the semi-rigid bundle, like a priest of Baal offering a sacrifice.

An hour later, in commemoration, I suppose, of our first meeting, Tom Black and I sat at the only all-night coffee stand in Nairobi, and I yielded to curiosity; I asked questions.

177

Something about that irreverent contrivance of fabric and wires and noise, blustering through the chaste arena of the night, had stirred the course of my thoughts to restless eddies.

Where had he been? Why had he come?

He shrugged, looking at me out of eyes that, for the first time, I saw were disturbing in their clarity. They were blue and they seemed to dissolve all questions and all answers within themselves. And they laughed when they should have been solemn. They were eyes that might have followed the trajectory of a dead cat through a chapel window with more amusement than horror, but might at the same time have expressed sympathy for the fate of the cat.

'I flew the plane down from London,' he explained, 'and landed at Kisumu. That was yesterday. Before I could take off again for Nairobi, a runner came with a message from a safari near Musoma. Same old thing — somebody proving how fatal it is to be a fool. Lion, rifles — and stupidity. You can imagine the rest.'

I could, almost, but I preferred to listen. I looked around the little coffee stand where we sat. A corporal of the K.A.R. and an Indian clerk stood at the counter, yards apart, eating solemnly as if each were to be hanged at dawn. But there was no one else. We four were the only acolytes at the shabby midnight altar — we four and its silent mullah who moved among the pots and dishes, clothed in a vestment of tarnished white.

Through my own insistence, fortified by coffee transparent as tea, I got the details of what I suppose was hardly more than an incident, but which somehow proved that Africa is capable of a sardonic smile, that it accepts new things, but allows no thing to escape its baptism.

Tom Black had flown six thousand miles with a new aeroplane and a new idea. His dream had sprouted wings and wheels. It had an authentic voice that he hoped would wake other dreamers, and silence the sleepy sounds, of a roused but still too lazy land.

If the towns and villages of Kenya lacked roads to unite them, like threads in a net, then at least there was land enough for the wheels of planes and sky enough for their wings and time enough for their propellers to beat back the barriers of doubt they flew against. Everywhere in the world, highways had come first — and then the landing fields. Only not here, for much of Kenya's future was already the past of other places. New things that shone with the ingenuity of modern times were superimposed upon an old order, contrasting against it like a chromium clock against a rawhide shield. The mechanistic age impended over an horizon not hostile, but silently indifferent.

Into this horizon Tom Black had flown his aeroplane. One day it would carry mail, as he intended it to do. It would soar above old paths tamped by the feet of Native runners; it would cleave wakes in the wind.

But first, in homage to its ancient host, it had already performed an errand; it had carried a message of enterprise, a cargo of pain, and a vessel of death through an African night.

'Lion, rifles — and stupidity' — a simple story as he told it, and as it was.

None of the characters in it were distinguished ones — not even the lion.

He was an old lion, prepared from birth to lose his life rather than to leave it. But he had the dignity of all free creatures, and so he was allowed his moment. It was hardly a glorious moment.

The two men who shot him were indifferent as men go, or perhaps they were less than that. At least they shot him without killing him, and then turned the unconscionable eye of a camera upon his agony. It was a small, a stupid, but a callous crime.

When Tom Black, sacrificing a triumphant arrival at Nairobi, landed instead at the camp site near Musoma, one man lay dead and a second, mangled and helpless, was alive only by the caprice of chance. A third white man and a couple of Native boys stood about the burdened canvas cot performing feeble incantations and attempting sorcery against gangrene with bandage, iodine, and water. The camera was a ruined mass of glass and metal, the lion was dead, though some kind of elemental retribution had armed him with strength for the last blow. There was a human corpse to be disposed of and a life to be saved — if that were possible.

Messages were sent by runner and by telegraph from Kisumu. And messages were received. The dead man, it was requested, was to be cremated and his ashes brought to Nairobi.

Cremation is a smooth word that seeks to conceal the indelicate reality of a human body being baked in fire. In print and in the advertisements of mortuaries equipped with silver-handled kilns, it is a successful word. In mid-afternoon on the African veldt under a harsh and revealing sun, it is at best a euphemism. Still, since men cherish the paradox requiring that to insure immortality they must preserve what is most mortal about them, wood was gathered and a fire was built.

The wounded man, wrapped in his bandages and his pain, could smell at intervals the heavily significant smudge of the embers. The Natives vanished.

Tom Black, who liked Life too much to be patient with Death, squatted on his heels through the long afternoon, solaced by an occasional jigger of tepid whisky, while a pencil of smoke rising from the pyre wrote endlessly its dismal little tale in disturbing and legible script.

If there were vultures — those false but democratic mourners at every casual bier — they were not mentioned in his recounting. There were no tears, no fumbling over a prayer book. The third white man who had accompanied the abortive safari had nothing to say; there couldn't have been much.

It was a tragedy with too petty a plot to encourage talk, too little irony to invite reflection. It was a scene whose grand climax consisted of the scooping of a few miserable ashes into a bent and unsanctified biscuit tin, and whose final curtain, wove from ribbons of dusk and a few thin threads of smoke, rolled down upon a shiny aeroplane straining toward the sky.

The injured man lived to tell (but I think not to boast) about his encounter with the lion, and the ashes of his companion repose now, I suspect, in an urn of Grecian elegance far from any path a creature more ominous than a mouse might choose to wander. Perhaps above that urn there hangs a picture salvaged from the broken camera — a picture of a great beast frozen forever in an attitude of bewildered agony by the magic of a lens. And, if this is so, then those who pause before these otherwise unmeaning trifles may consider that they speak a moral — not profound, but worthy of a thought; Death will have his moment of respect, however he comes along, and no matter upon what living thing he lays his hand.

African tragedy — melancholy trivia. What's in a point of view?

Tom Black sipped his coffee, stared into the cup as if it were a crystal ball, and grinned at his own story.

'There's a technique about distinguishing one kind of ash from another,' he said, 'known only to myself and the early Egyptians. So don't ask questions. Just remember never to fly without a match or a biscuit tin. And of course you're going to fly. I've always known it. I could see it in the stars.'

'Ruta,' I said, 'I think I am going to leave all this and learn to fly.'

He stood in a loose-box beside a freshly groomed colt — a young colt gleaming like light on water. There was a body-brush in Ruta's hand, its bristles intertwined with hairs from the colt. Ruta removed the hairs with slow fingers and hung the brush on a peg. He looked out the stable door into the near distance where Menegai shouldered a weightless cloud. He shrugged and dusted dustless hands, one against the other.

He said, 'If it is to be that we must fly, Memsahib, then we will fly. At what hour of the morning do we begin?'

BOOK FOUR

XV

Birth of a Life

WE BEGAN at the first hour of the morning. We began when the sky was clean and ready for the sun and you could see your breath and smell traces of the night. We began every morning at that same hour, using what we were pleased to call the Nairobi Aerodrome, climbing away from it with derisive clamour, while the burghers of the town twitched in their beds and dreamed perhaps of all unpleasant things that drone — of wings and stings, and corridors in Bedlam.

Tom taught me in a D. H. Gipsy Moth, at first, and her propeller beat the sunrise silence of the Athi Plains to shreds and scraps. We swung over the hills and over the town and back again, and I saw how a man can be master of a craft, and how a craft can be master of an element. I saw the alchemy of perspective reduce my world, and all my other life, to grains in a cup. I learned to watch, to put my trust in other hands than mine. And I learned to wander. I learned what every dreaming child needs to know — that no horizon is so far that you cannot get above it or beyond it. These I learned at once. But most things came harder.

Tom Black had never taught another soul to fly, and the things he had to teach beyond the simple mechanics that go with flying are those things that have not lent themselves to words. Intuition and instinct are mysteries still, though pre-

185

cisely spelled or rolled precisely off the tongue. Tom had these — or whatever qualities they signify.

After this era of great pilots is gone, as the era of great sea captains has gone — each nudged aside by the march of inventive genius, by steel cogs and copper discs and hair-thin wires on white faces that are dumb, but speak — it will be found, I think, that all the science of flying has been captured in the breadth of an instrument board, but not the religion of it.

One day the stars will be as familiar to each man as the landmarks, the curves, and the hills on the road that leads to his door, and one day this will be an airborne life. But by then men will have forgotten how to fly; they will be passengers on machines whose conductors are carefully promoted to a familiarity with labelled buttons, and in whose minds knowledge of the sky and the wind and the way of weather will be extraneous as passing fiction. And the days of the clipper ships will be recalled again — and people will wonder if clipper means ancients of the sea or ancients of the air.

'Trust this,' said Tom, 'but nothing else.' He meant the compass.

'Instruments can go wrong,' he said. 'If you can't fly without looking at your airspeed and your altimeter and your bank-and-turn indicator — well, then you can't fly. You're like somebody who only knows what he thinks after reading his newspaper. But don't mistrust the compass — your judgement will never be more accurate than that needle. It will tell you where you ought to be going and the rest is up to you.'

There were ear-phones in the Gipsy Moth, but Tom never used them. While I sat in the rear cockpit, a fumbling beginner, apprehensive and wondering how my hands, so used to strips of leather and my feet so used to stirrups, would ever get used to this, Tom might have eased the task a little by talking into those ear-phones — but he never would. He rolled them up and put them in a corner out of reach. He said: 'It's no good my telling you where you go wrong each time you do. Your own intelligence will tell you that. Speed sense, sense of height, and sense of error will come later. If they don't, well ... but they will.'

That they did was due to him. There was never a more careful pilot nor yet a more casual one. His confidence never shrank beside the bullying roar of a plane. He wasn't a tall man, but he had a quiet, convincing manner that made him look bigger than any job he ever held and more capable than any craft he ever flew.

Wilson Airways — the first commercial enterprise of its kind in East Africa — had been the child of Tom's imagination and foresight. When he undertook to teach me to fly, he was managing director, chief pilot, and guiding spirit of the hopeful little company, but the somewhat pompous executive title had nothing to do with polished desks and swivel chairs.

Tom's job was to pioneer new routes, to probe inland Africa, seeking footholds for the future. More often than not, he took off from Nairobi, flying over country as unused to wheels as it was to wings, with no more than a modest expectation that there might be some place to land at the end of his flight.

And not all of this was done by daylight; he flew without beams, without beacons or radio, through whatever darkness the night could offer — and through whatever weather. There was rarely a light of a village for guidance, nor any highways, nor rails, nor wires, nor farms. He did not call it blind flying; he called it night flying, though when fog or storm required it of him, he flew blind for hours without special instruments, yet not failing on his course. He had what those thick books with dull gray covers call 'sensory reaction.'

We flew down into Tanganyika once just after I had got my 'A' licence, and it may have been that I was a bit full with the sense of achievement. Or, if I wasn't, Tom suspected that I might be.

Near the end of the return trip, flying north toward the Ngong Hills over the Rift Valley, the Gipsy Moth was afflicted with a strange lethargy. I was at the controls and, as the hills (which rise about eight thousand feet above sea level) came closer so that their ravines and green slopes emerged from the lazy haze they live in, I opened the throttle and drew back the stick for altitude. But, it seemed, there wasn't any more.

The little plane was doing a respectable eighty miles an hour — hardly record speed even then, but still fast enough to make me appreciate the sad and final consequences of not getting over that close horizon. As I blundered on, the trees of the Ngong Hills began to separate one from another, to stand out individually — even magnificently; the ravines got deeper.

More stick, more throttle.

I was calm. Most beginners, I thought, might have got a bit rattled — but not I. Certainly not Tom. He sat in front of me motionless as a drowsing man.

You can open a throttle just so far and increase the angle of a joy-stick to just such a degree — and if your plane does not respond to this, you had better think of something else. The Moth was not gaining altitude; she was losing that, and her speed. She was heading straight for the implacable hills like a moth hypnotized by light. There was a weight on her wings that I could feel, bearing her down. She could not lift the weight. Tom must have felt it, but he never moved.

When you can see the branches of trees from a cockpit, and the shape of rocks no bigger than your own hands, and places where grass thins against sand and becomes yellow, and watch the blow of wind on leaves, you are too close. You are so close that thought is a slow process, useless to you now — even if you can think.

The sound of our propeller got trapped between a wall of rock and the plane before Tom straightened in his seat and took the controls.

He banked sharply, dusting the trees and rock with blue exhaust. He put the nose of the Gipsy down and swung her deep into the valley while her shadow rode close on the hill. He lost altitude until the valley was flat. He climbed in spirals until we were high above the Ngong Hills, and then he went over them and home.

It was all so simple.

'Now you know what down-draft is,' said Tom. 'You get it near mountains, and in Africa it's common as rain. I could have warned you — but you shouldn't be robbed of your right to make mistakes.'

It was a right he protected as long as we flew together, so that in the end I never did anything in a plane without knowing what might have happened if I had done some other thing.

A 'B' licence is a flyer's Magna Carta — it delivers him from the bondage of apprenticeship; it frees him to make a living. It says, in effect: 'We, the undersigned, believe that you are now competent to carry passengers, mail, etc., and we approve of your accepting pay for doing so. Please report to the examiners within three months and, if you have not contracted strabismus, or a melancholy point of view in regard to this Board, we will be happy to renew your permit.'

About eighteen months after I began to fly, I was granted my 'B' licence. Under British regulations, this is the ultimate diploma. I had nearly a thousand flying hours to my credit at

the time and, if my eyesight had failed me during my preparations for the examinations, it would have been due to the ad-
ditional hundred or two hours I spent studying navigation out
of books whose authors must have been struck dumb in the
presence of a one-syllable word. Everything those authors
said was sound and sane and reasonable, but they went on the
theory that truth is rarer than radium and that if it became
easily available, the market for it would be glutted, holders of
stock in it would become destitute, and gems of eternal verity
would be given away as premiums.

My life had been, and was, a physically active life, spent
in a country many of whose first settlers still tilled their own
fields, and whose aboriginals were imaginative enough and
legion enough to necessitate the keeping of a King's regiment
in permanent residence at Nairobi, in the outposts, and along
the frontiers. Childhood environment had not inclined me toward a bookish existence, nor did flying seem to me, at first,
anything but adventure on wings. That textbooks had to
arch their ugly backs in the midst of this pretty dream was a
mild blow.

I had abandoned race-horse training altogether, keeping for
myself only Pegasus. Arab Ruta had come with me to Nairobi.
He lived in a small house in the native quarter, not far from
my own cottage at Muthaiga, and he flew with me often. I do
not think that, emotionally at least, the transition from horses
to planes was ever complete in Arab Ruta; a thing that moved
was a thing alive. He never wiped a plane — he groomed it;
and what he couldn't accomplish easily with his hands, he attempted with soft words. Whenever my Avian came home
from a long flight and was dull with dust, Ruta was saddened,
not by thoughts of the work at hand, but by the aspect of so
vital a creature being used so hard. He would shake his head
and touch the fuselage the way he used to touch the loins of a

horse — not impulsively, but with animal respect for animal dignity.

When he had undertaken the care of the plane for only a month, Ruta had already acquired a small entourage of Somalis, Nandi friends, and Kikuyu urchins who hung more or less on his heels, and I suspect on his words. He was not above condescension, but he never stooped to swagger. In any case the pride he took in his new work was wholly genuine. And yet, even in the face of the materialistic and brightly cynical environment of Nairobi, his spiritual integrity held strong. He never deserted his childhood beliefs, and I think they never deserted him.

Before Tom left Wilson Airways to fly for Lord Furness in England (and later for the Prince of Wales), we used to meet in the evenings over a drink or dinner and talk of our flying or of a thousand other things. I was free-lancing then, carrying mail, passengers, supplies to safaris, or whatever had to be carried, and Tom still worked and sweated away as Ambassador of Progress to the hinterland. Often we left the Nairobi Airfield just after dawn — Tom perhaps bound for Abyssinia and I for the Anglo-Egyptian Sudan, Tanganyika, Northern Rhodesia, or wherever somebody would pay me to go. Sometimes it would be two or three days before we saw each other again, and then there was a lot to talk about. I remember Arab Ruta on these occasions — serving the drinks, or the dinner, understanding very little English, but hovering still about the table, not like a servant, or even like a friend, but like an animate household god, quite as bronze, quite as omniscient, and quite as profound.

Oddly enough, Ruta the Nandi Murani and Tom Black the English flyer had in common a peculiar quality. Loosely, it might be called a premonitory sense. Tom was not given to psychic revelation, and Ruta — child of Africa or not — was no apostle of black magic, but each was nevertheless sensitive and had an awareness of things to come whenever those things were to affect them closely. One instance of this comes to my mind still, with disturbing frequency.

Many people who lived in Kenya at that time, or who live there now, remember Denys Finch-Hatton. As a matter of fact there are people all over the world who remember him, because he was of the world and his culture was of it — though I suppose Eton and Oxford might argue a more specific source.

Denys has been written about before and he will be written about again. If someone has not already said it, someone will say that he was a great man who never achieved greatness, and this will not only be trite, but wrong; he was a great man who never achieved arrogance.

I met him first when I was about eighteen, though he had been in Africa for several years — intermittently, at least — and had already got himself a reputation as one of the ablest of White Hunters. He had a physique still remembered in British athletic circles; he was a foremost cricketer. He was a scholar of almost classic profundity, but was less pedantic than an untutored boy. There were occasions when Denys, like all men whose minds have encompassed among other things the foibles of their species, experienced misanthropic moments; he could despair of men, but find poetry in a field of rock.

As for charm, I suspect Denys invented it, but the meaning of it was a bit different — even in his recent day. It was a charm of intellect and strength, of quick intuition and Voltarian humour. He would have greeted doomsday with a wink — and I think he did.

My story about his death is simple enough, but it proves for my own satisfaction the truth of a line contained in a remembrance of him which appeared in the London *Times*:

'Something more must come from one so strong and gifted; and, in a way, it did. . . .'

What came from him, if emanate is not the better word, was a force that bore inspiration, spread confidence in the dignity of life, and even gave sometimes a presence to silence.

I had flown with him often in the plane he had brought by boat from England and which he had added to the little nucleus of wings and fins and fragile wheels on the Nairobi Airfield.

Denys' plane was a Gipsy Moth. He had taken up flying too recently to be expert, but the competence which he applied so casually to everything was as evident in the air as it was on one of his safaris or in the recitations of Walt Whitman he performed during his more sombre or perhaps his lighter moments.

He asked me to fly with him to Voi, one day, and of course I said I would. Voi presumed to be a town then, but was hardly more than a word under a tin roof. It lies south by southeast of Nairobi in the depth of the elephant country — a dry spot in a pocket of dryer hills.

Denys said he wanted to try something that had never been done before. He said he wanted to see if elephant could be scouted by plane; if they could, he thought, hunters would be willing to pay very well for the service.

It seemed a good idea to me, even a thrilling idea, and I brought it to Tom in some excitement.

'I'm going down to Voi with Denys. He wants to see how efficiently elephant can be spotted from the air, and if it would be possible to keep a hunting party more or less in touch with a moving herd.'

Tom leaned against a workbench in the newly built Wilson Airways hangar, jotting figures on a scrap of paper. Archie Watkins, high priest of engine magicians, a big, blond man with a stutter and an almost holy reverence for the hymn of purring pistons, grinned good morning through a thicket of wires and bolts. It was a flyer's day. The open hangar looked out on the airfield, on the plains, and on a square of sky lonely for clouds.

Tom stuffed the bit of paper in the leather jacket he always wore, and nodded. 'Sounds practical enough — up to a point. You'd find a lot more elephant than places to land after you'd found them.'

'I suppose so. But it seems worth trying — Denys' idea always are. Anyway, we're just going to fly out from Voi and back again. No rough landings. If it works out, there should be a good living in it. When you think of all the people who come out here for elephant, and all the time that's spent, and . . .'

'I know,' said Tom, 'it's an excellent idea.' He moved away from the bench and went out of the hangar door and looked at the field. He stood there a minute or so without moving, and then came back.

'Make it tomorrow, Beryl.'

'Weather?'

'No. The weather's all right. Just make it tomorrow — will you?'

'I suppose I will, if you ask me to, but I don't see why.'

'Neither do I,' said Tom, 'but there it is.'

There it was. I went back to my cottage at Muthaiga and worked at bringing my logbook up to date. Denys took off for Voi without me. He took his Kikuyu boy along and flew first to Mombasa, where he had a place on the coast. Landing there, his propeller was chipped by a coral fragment and he wired Tom for a spare.

Tom sent it down with a Native mechanic, though Denys had been adamant about needing no help. In any case the

194

new propeller was fitted and, a day later, Denys and the Kikuyu boy took off again, back-tracking inland to Voi.

On the evening of the day they arrived there, Tom and I had dinner at Muthaiga. He was neither silent nor morose, but not much was said about Denys. I had the feeling that Tom felt a bit foolish about preventing me from making the trip. Anyway, we talked about other things. Tom was thinking of returning to England, so we thought about that and talked about it together.

I had lunch the next day in my cottage. Arab Ruta cooked it as usual, served it as usual, and acted as usual. But about an hour later, while I was working out some unworkable nuggets of navigation, Ruta knocked at my door. It was a very shy knock and he looked shy when he came in. He looked like someone with a lot to think about, but nothing to say, though he got it out at last.

'Memsahib, have you heard from Makanyaga?'

Makanyaga was Denys. To Arab Ruta, and to most of the Natives who knew Denys, he was Makanyaga. It seemed an opprobrious epithet, but it wasn't. It means, 'To Tread Upon.' Bwana Finch-Hatton, the argument ran, can tread upon inferior men with his tongue. He can punish with a word — and that is a wonderful skill.

It was indeed, since Denys rarely used it on any but those whose pretensions, at least, marked them as his equals. And then he used it with profligate generosity.

I closed my books. 'No, Ruta. Why should I hear from Makanyaga?'

'I do not know, Memsahib. I wondered.'

'Is there something to hear?'

Ruta shrugged. 'I have heard nothing, Memsahib. It may be that there is nothing. It occurred to me to ask you — but, of course, Bwana Black would know.'

Bwana Black knew soon enough, and so did I. We sat in the Wilson Airways office later that same afternoon when the Voi District Commissioner telephoned to say that Denys and his Kikuyu boy were dead. Their plane had taken off from the runway, circled twice, and then dived to the earth, where it burned. No one ever learned why.

Tom had kept me from a trip and Arab Ruta had asked a question. They had known, and I have wondered how they knew, and I have found an answer for myself.

Denys was a keystone in an arch whose other stones were other lives. If a keystone trembles, the arch will carry the warning along its entire curve, then, if the keystone is crushed, the arch will fall, leaving its lesser stones heaped close together, though for a while without design.

Denys' death left some lives without design, but they were rebuilt again, as lives and stones are, into other patterns.

XVI

Ivory and Sansevieria

O<small>NE</small> day, when the world was many months older, which is to say ages older, the mail brought a letter from Tom. He had long since flown to a new job in England and had not come back.

Three times I had flown the same six-thousand-mile route, but each time I had returned like the needle on my own compass returning to its magnetic meridian. There was no opiate for nostalgia, or at least no lasting cure, and my Avian — my little VP–KAN — shared with me the homing sense.

Things had changed too in Kenya. My father was there again, back from Peru, and I had a farm at Elburgon, where he lived. The farm was not like the farm at Njoro, but it made the memory of that more real, and the Rongai Valley and the Mau Forest were close on its edges.

Life had a different shape; it had new branches and some of the old branches were dead. It had followed the constant pattern of discard and growth that all lives follow. Things had passed, new things had come. The wonder of my first fledgling hours of flight was lost in the many hundreds of hours I had sat making my living at the controls of my plane. Month after month I had piloted the mail for East African Airways — until that optimistic commercial effort had itself died and been buried under the growing success of Wilson Airways. I had carried passengers in all directions, and because there were more than could be carried, I had leased a bigger plane — a Leopard Moth — and added that to my fleet of one.

I flew the Leopard when I had two passengers. Each paid me a shilling a mile — and there are miles and miles of Africa. I got the same rate, of course, when I used the Avian for one passenger, and between the two planes I managed a monthly income of about sixty pounds sterling.

For a while I had thought that this was good enough — but five times that was better. Seventy-five pounds a month and three pounds for each flying hour was better. It didn't matter much that no one else wanted the job. Life itself could be better, and I had made it so.

Elephant! Safari! Hunting! Denys Finch-Hatton had left me a legacy of excitement — a release from routine, a passport to adventure. Elephant *could* be scouted by air. Denys had thought it, I had proved it — and Tom warned against it. This is his letter:

> The Royal Aero Club
> 119 Piccadilly
> London, W.1.

My dear Beryl:

I have just come up from the Newmarket races and found your last letter waiting at the Club. I am awfully upset to hear that you have been so ill, but trust that by now you have completely recovered. It seems to me that you are rather overdoing it — living on your nerves too much ... you have got to be capable of accepting non-hazardous, ordinary, sane, dull, everyday work that requires a balanced brain and steady reasoning.

All this is really to tell you that if you had one grain of sense, you wouldn't make a regular habit of flying for elephant in elephant country. Financial worry may be eased by one or two safaris, but as a steady business it's sheer madness and damnably, bloodily dangerous.

You won't listen, but anyway I'm glad the Avian seems a faithful servant. I only hope it keeps ticking over and serving you loyally for just as long as you need it. ....

I badly want to get into harness again. Duke is in the South
of France and I haven't heard from him for a long time. I want
the opportunity of busting the Cape record, but it's hard to
make money with such a flight unless you sell your shirt and
your soul to advertising agents — which I have no intention of
doing. . . .

Did you get your spares in time? I telephoned your cable-
gram to Avros and they told me they would get on with the
order immediately. . . .

Give up the elephant flying — it's not worth the chances you
have to take. Good luck, and my very best,

TOM

By wire (same day)

MAKINDU
KENYA COLONY

BERYL

BE AT MAKINDU TOMORROW SEVEN A.M. STOP
BRING WINSTON'S MAIL STOP CALL AT MANLEY'S AND
COLLECT FIFTY ROUNDS AMMUNITION SIX BOTTLES
GIN SIX BOTTLES WHISKY TWO BOTTLES ATEBRIN TWO
BOTTLES PLASMA QUININE STOP MAKULA REPORTS
HERD ELEPHANT WITH BIG BULL STOP BABU AT MA-
KINDU WILL SUPPLY WRITTEN DIRECTIONS FROM ME
ON ARRIVAL STOP IF FISH DAY BRING FISH

BLIX

Stop. Everything is available, including the fish, shipped
up from Mombasa. I'm available too. Tom Black's letter
glares at me from my desk at Muthaiga Club — and he's right
as rain. He's always right. What I have learned about flying
I have learned from him and he knows the Ukamba elephant
country better than I do. He knows about the quick storms
sweeping inland from the coast; he knows about dysentery,
tsetse fly, and malaria; he knows about the sansevieria — that

199

placid, but murderous weed, jutting up like an endless crop of sabres from the wide waste that sinks to the Indian Ocean.

Land on sansevieria and your plane is skewered like a duck pinned for taxidermy — land in it and walk away. Only not fast, nor far. Rest for a moment; take your time. There are no lion to speak of, and few, if any leopard. There is only the Siafu ant.

What eulogies have been written about the ant! 'Sturdy fellow, honest fellow, thrifty fellow!' I would not wish, even upon a misguided entomologist, no matter what his extra-academic sins might be, a single night in company with Siafu ants.

The Siafu is sturdy enough, God knows, but he is neither honest nor thrifty — he is a thief, a wastrel, and a man-eater. The biggest of his species is half the length of a matchstick, and, given time, he can (and would) gnaw through all the matchsticks in Christendom if there were a bit of meat, live or otherwise, at the end of his labours.

Siafu don't just sting — they bite chunks out of you. Within a few hours a normal, healthy horse, if he is unable to escape his stable, can be killed and half-eaten by even a reserve division of Siafu.

I have dreamed about a lot of unpleasant things — as I suppose we all have — snakes, drowning, leopard, falling off high places; but the dreams I have had about Siafu, in my bed, under the floor, in my hair, relegate all other bad dreams to the category of unlikely but tranquil hallucinations. Give me beetles and bugs, spiders, puff-adders, and tarantulas like buttons of cosy wool — but not Siafu. They are minions of the Devil — red, minute, numberless, and inexorable.

I think about them, and about all the disadvantages attendant upon the business of scouting elephant by plane. Tom's letter is not detailed — but then it needn't be. Neither he nor

I have any illusions about the availability of clear places to land anywhere south, or east of Makindu. Most people in East Africa have heard about that country.

The Ukamba is flat enough on a map — even on my flying map. It spreads east from Nairobi, north to the frontier, southeast to the Indian Ocean. It is circled by the Tana River and by the Athi — both sucking their lazy lives from the Kenya Highlands. They enclose the Ukamba like a frayed noose dropped to earth by an intrigued Satan, to mark a theatre for later labours. The country is bush, sansevieria, fever, and drought. The sansevieria is everywhere; the bush is fathoms deep, impenetrable as submarine growth in the buried fields of the sea. It is no country for men, but it is country for elephants. And so men go there.

Blix went there often, but Blix was Blix. Tom, on the other hand was Tom, level-headed for all his dreaming, only perhaps he hadn't realized how committed I had already become to the business of scouting for game. The cheques, at the end of each safari, were pleasant narcotics against what disturbing memories I may have brought back, the work was exciting — and life was not dull.

BABU AT MAKINDU WILL SUPPLY WRITTEN DIRECTIONS

BLIX

Blix — Blickie — Baron von Blixen. He is, and was, known variously by any of these names, and by several others — none of them harsh. He is six feet of amiable Swede and, to my knowledge, the toughest, most durable White Hunter ever to snicker at the fanfare of safari or to shoot a charging buffalo between the eyes while debating whether his sundown drink will be gin or whisky. If Blix has ever yielded to embarrassment before any situation, it must have been when he confronted himself with the task of writing his admirable, but all too shy, record of his work in Africa. The book, to those who know him, is a monument of understatement. In it he has made molehills out of all the mountains he has climbed, and passed off as incidents true stories that a less modest man might enlarge to blood-curdling sagas.

Blix's appreciation of the melodramatic is non-existent. So far as I know, he has never stood off an attack by two or three hundred naked savages (single-handed with only one bullet in his rifle) while bleeding profusely from the left thigh, and such imperfections in his hunting career may mark him as pretty poor cinema material. When, as often happened, he met certain Natives more or less committed to nudism, not to say mayhem, he invariably ended up by swapping yarns with the chief, while the young warriors tiptoed past the conversation, and gourds full of tembo were served in the shade of whatever hut or tree did service as the Throne Room.

To say that Baron von Blixen, as a White Hunter, was cool in the face of danger is both hackneyed and slightly inaccurate. In the first place, he never threw himself into the face of danger if that could be avoided; secondly, if by chance he found himself (or anyone else) in a dangerous situation, he was inclined to grow hot rather than cold, blasphemous rather than silent.

But these outward manifestations were so much less important than the fact that he never did the wrong thing — and never missed what he shot at.

'Bwana Blixen' is still a name that, in many places, from Rhodesia to the Belgian Congo, to the Sahara Desert, would fall upon more than a few ears with the quick familiarity of an echo.

To find it appended to a telegram from Makindu, even after a long friendship, was still too compelling a thrill to be disregarded.

Ivory and Sansevieria

Muthaiga Club
Nairobi
Kenya Colony

Dear Tom:

The parts for the Avian arrived here in time — due entirely
to your quick action. One day I'l' have a tail wheel instead of a
skid and won't tear it off on rough landings.

Don't worry about the elephant scouting. I know you're
absolutely right, and I intend to quit it as soon as I can — but
Blix wired today from Makindu and I'm going down in the
morning. It's Winston Guest's safari.

Tail winds and happy landings.

As always

BERYL

By the aid of a blue string of smoke, indicating, though half-
heartedly, the list of the wind, I land the Avian on the muram
clearing at Makindu, clamber out, and walk over to the
station.

Makindu doesn't look like anything; it isn't anything. Its
five tin-roofed huts cling to the skinny tracks of the Uganda
Railway like parasites on a vine. The biggest of them — the
station — contains a table and Blix's Babu, wearing his forefinger out on a telegraph key.

One day there will be a small but select company of Hindus
wandering about Africa — each possessing the distinctive at-
tribute of a thwarted forefinger. They will be the descendants
of the original station masters on the original Uganda Railway.
I have arrived by plane, foot, or horse during all hours of the
day or night at one or another of the thirty-odd stations in
Kenya and have never yet found the telegraph key without
its Babu leaning over it, pounding like mad, as if the whole of
East Africa were rapidly sliding into the Indian Ocean and he
alone had observed the phenomenon.

I have no idea of what they really talked about. Possibly I
do the Babus an injustice, but I think at best they used to

203

read the novels of Anthony Trollope to each other over the wire.

The Babu at Makindu reeled off an impressive lot of dots and dashes before he looked up from his table. He had kind, brown eyes, a little weary from squinting, and a small head wrinkled like a well-cured nut. He wore cheap twill trousers that were dirty and a cotton shirt that was clean. He stood up, finally, and bowed: 'I have message for you from Baron.'

There was a spindle on his table containing three pieces of paper of different colour, size, and shape. I could recognize Blix's handwriting on the top one, but the Babu shuffled importantly through the three scraps as if they were a hundred. At last he handed me my directions with the exultant smile of a bank manager handing you the notation of an overdraft.

'My wife — she have tea for you.'

Tea, as brewed by the wives of station Babus, is mostly sugar and raw ginger, but it is always hot. I had tea and read Blix's directions.

'Get to Kilamakoy. Look for smoke.' Underneath was a quickly scribbled drawing, complete with arrows and a circle labelled 'Camp.'

I thanked my hosts for their tea, went out to my plane, swung the propeller, flew straight to Kilamakoy (which is not a settlement, but a Wakamba word for a stretch of country without residential possibilities), and looked for smoke.

After a while I saw a miserly runway, walled in bush, with a white man at either end — each beckoning with such enthusiasm that I concluded the gin, rather than the quinine, was the nostrum immediately required.

XVII

I May Have to Shoot Him

I SUPPOSE, if there were a part of the world in which mastodon still lived, somebody would design a new gun, and men, in their eternal impudence, would hunt mastodon as they now hunt elephant. Impudence seems to be the word. At least David and Goliath were of the same species, but, to an elephant, a man can only be a midge with a deathly sting.

It is absurd for a man to kill an elephant. It is not brutal, it is not heroic, and certainly it is not easy; it is just one of those preposterous things that men do like putting a dam across a great river, one tenth of whose volume could engulf the whole of mankind without disturbing the domestic life of a single catfish.

Elephant, beyond the fact that their size and conformation are aesthetically more suited to the treading of this earth than our angular informity, have an average intelligence comparable to our own. Of course they are less agile and physically less adaptable than ourselves — Nature having developed their bodies in one direction and their brains in another, while human beings, on the other hand, drew from Mr. Darwin's lottery of evolution both the winning ticket and the stub to match it. This, I suppose, is why we are so wonderful and can make movies and electric razors and wireless sets — and guns with which to shoot the elephant, the hare, clay pigeons, and each other.

The elephant is a rational animal. He thinks. Blix and I (also rational animals in our own right) have never quite agreed on the mental attributes of the elephant. I know Blix is not to be doubted because he has learned more about elephant than any other man I ever met, or even heard about, but he looks upon legend with a suspicious eye, and I do not.

There is a legend that elephant dispose of their dead in secret burial grounds and that none of these has ever been discovered. In support of this, there is only the fact that the body of an elephant, unless he had been trapped or shot in his tracks, has rarely been found. What happens to the old and diseased?

Not only natives, but many white settlers, have supported for years the legend (if it is legend) that elephant will carry their wounded and their sick hundreds of miles, if necessary, to keep them out of the hands of their enemies. And it is said that elephant never forget.

These are perhaps just stories born of imagination. Ivory was once almost as precious as gold, and wherever there is treasure, men mix it with mystery. But still, there is no mystery about the things you see yourself.

I think I am the first person ever to scout elephant by plane, and so it follows that the thousands of elephant I saw time and again from the air had never before been plagued by anything above their heads more ominous than tick-birds.

The reaction of a herd of elephant to my Avian was, in the initial instance, always the same — they left their feeding ground and tried to find cover, though often, before yielding, one or two of the bulls would prepare for battle and charge in the direction of the plane if it were low enough to be within their scope of vision. Once the futility of this was realized, the entire herd would be off into the deepest bush.

Checking again on the whereabouts of the same herd next

day, I always found that a good deal of thinking had been going on amongst them during the night. On the basis of their reaction to my second intrusion, I judged that their thoughts had run somewhat like this: A: The thing that flew over us was no bird, since no bird would have to work so hard to stay in the air — and, anyway, we know all the birds. B: If it was no bird, it was very likely just another trick of those two-legged dwarfs against whom there ought to be a law. C: The two-legged dwarfs (both black and white) have, as long as our long memories go back, killed our bulls for their tusks. We know this because, in the case of the white dwarfs, at least, the tusks are the only part taken away.

The actions of the elephant, based upon this reasoning, were always sensible and practical. The second time they saw the Avian, they refused to hide; instead, the females, who bear only small, valueless tusks, simply grouped themselves around their treasure-burdened bulls in such a way that no ivory could be seen from the air or from any other approach.

This can be maddening strategy to an elephant scout. I have spent the better part of an hour circling, criss-crossing, and diving low over some of the most inhospitable country in Africa in an effort to break such a stubborn huddle, sometimes successfully, sometimes not.

But the tactics vary. More than once I have come upon a large and solitary elephant standing with enticing disregard for safety, its massive bulk in clear view, but its head buried in thicket. This was, on the part of the elephant, no effort to simulate the nonsensical habit attributed to the ostrich. It was, on the contrary, a cleverly devised trap into which I fell, every way except physically, at least a dozen times. The beast always proved to be a large cow rather than a bull, and I always found that by the time I had arrived at this brilliant if tardy deduction, the rest of the herd had got another ten miles away, and the decoy, leering up at me out of a small, triumphant eye, would amble into the open, wave her trunk with devastating nonchalance, and disappear.

This order of intelligence in a lesser animal can obviously give rise to exaggeration — some of it persistent enough to be crystallized into legend. But you cannot discredit truth merely because legend has grown out of it. The sometimes almost godlike achievements of our own species in ages past toddle through history supported more often than not on the twin crutches of fable and human credulity.

As to the brutality of elephant-hunting, I cannot see that it is any more brutal than ninety per cent of all other human activities. I suppose there is nothing more tragic about the death of an elephant than there is about the death of a Hereford steer — certainly not in the eyes of the steer. The only difference is that the steer has neither the ability nor the chance to outwit the gentleman who wields the slaughter-house snickersnee, while the elephant has both of these to pit against the hunter.

Elephant hunters may be unconscionable brutes, but it would be an error to regard the elephant as an altogether pacific animal. The popular belief that only the so-called 'rogue' elephant is dangerous to men is quite wrong — so wrong that a considerable number of men who believed it have become one with the dust without even their just due of gradual disintegration. A normal bull elephant, aroused by the scent of man, will often attack at once — and his speed is as unbelievable as his mobility. His trunk and his feet are his weapons — at least in the distasteful business of exterminating a mere human; those resplendent sabres of ivory await resplendent foes.

Blix and I hardly came into this category at Kilamakoy — certainly not after we had run down the big bull, or, as it hap-

pened, the big bull had run down us. I can say, at once with
gratification still genuine, that we were not trampled within
that most durable of all inches — the last inch of our lives.
We got out all right, but there are times when I still dream.

On arriving from Makindu, I landed my plane in the shallow box of a runway scooped out of the bush, unplugged wads
of cotton wool from my ears, and climbed from the cockpit.

The aristocratically descended visage of the Baron von
Blixen Finecke greeted me (as it always did) with the most
delightful of smiles caught, like a strip of sunlight, on a familiar patch of leather — well-kept leather, free of wrinkles, but
brown and saddle-tough.

Beyond this concession to the fictional idea of what a White
Hunter ought to look like, Blix's face yields not a whit. He has
gay, light blue eyes rather than sombre, steel-grey ones; his
cheeks are well rounded rather than flat as an axe; his lips are
full and generous and not pinched tight in grim realization of
what the Wilderness Can Do. He talks. He is never signifi-
cantly silent.

He wore then what I always remember him as wearing, a
khaki bush shirt of 'solario' material, slacks of the same stuff,
and a pair of low-cut moccasins with soles — or at least ves-
tiges of soles. There were four pockets in his bush shirt, but I
don't think he knew it; he never carried anything unless he
was actually hunting — and then it was just a rifle and ammunition. He never went around hung with knives, revolvers,
binoculars, or even a watch. He could tell time by the sun,
and if there were no sun, he could tell it, anyway. He wore
over his closely cropped greying hair a terai hat, colourless and
limp as a wilted frond.

He said, 'Hullo, Beryl,' and pointed to a man at his side —-
so angular as to give the impression of being constructed entirely of barrel staves.

'This,' said Blix, with what could hardly be called Old-World courtesy, 'is Old Man Wicks.'

'At last,' said Old Man Wicks, 'I have seen the Lady from the Skies.'

Writing it now, that remark seems a little like a line from the best play chosen from those offered by the graduating class of Eton, possibly in the late twenties, or like the remark of a man up to his ears in his favourite anodyne. But, as a matter of fact, Old Man Wicks, who managed a piece of no-man's-land belonging to the Manoni Sugar Company, near Masongaleni, had seen only one white man in sixteen months and, I gathered, hadn't seen a white woman in as many years. At least he had never seen an aeroplane and a white woman at the same time, nor can I be sure that he regarded the spectacle as much of a Godsend. Old Man Wicks, oddly enough, wasn't very old — he was barely forty — and it may have been that his monkish life was the first choice of whatever other lives he could have led. He looked old, but that might have been protective colouration. He was a gentle, kindly man helping Blix with the safari until Winston Guest arrived.

It was a modest enough safari. There were three large tents — Winston's, Blix's, and my own — and then there were several pup tents for the Native boys, gun-bearers, and trackers. Blix's boy Farah, Winston's boy, and of course my Arab Ruta (who was due via lorry from Nairobi) had pup tents to themselves. The others, as much out of choice as necessity, slept several in a tent. There was a hangar for the Avian, made out of a square of tarpaulin, and there was a baobab tree whose shade served as a veranda to everybody. The immediate country was endless and barren of hills.

Half an hour after I landed, Blix and I were up in the Avian, hoping, if possible, to spot a herd of elephant before Winston's arrival that night. If we could find a herd within two or three days' walking distance from the camp, it would be extraordinary luck — always provided that the herd contained a bull with respectable tusks.

It is not unusual for an elephant hunter to spend six months, or even a year, on the spoor of a single bull. Elephant go where men can't — or at least shouldn't.

Scouting by plane eliminates a good deal of the preliminary work, but when as upon occasion I did spot a herd not more than thirty or forty miles from camp, it still meant that those forty miles had to be walked, crawled, or wriggled by the hunters — and that by the time this body and nerve-racking manoeuvre had been achieved, the elephant had pushed on another twenty miles or so into the bush. A man, it ought to be remembered, has to take several steps to each stride of an elephant, and, moreover, the man is somewhat less than resistant to thicket, thorn trees, and heat. Also (particularly if he is white) he is vulnerable as a peeled egg to all things that sting — anopheles mosquitoes, scorpions, snakes, and tsetse flies. The essence of elephant-hunting is discomfort in such lavish proportions that only the wealthy can afford it.

Blix and I were fortunate on our very first expedition out of Kilamakoy. The Wakamba scouts on our safari had reported a large herd of elephant containing several worth-while bulls, not more than twenty air miles from camp. We circled the district indicated, passed over the herd perhaps a dozen times, but finally spotted it.

A herd of elephant, as seen from a plane, has a quality of an hallucination. The proportions are wrong — they are like those of a child's drawing of a field mouse in which the whole landscape, complete with barns and windmills, is dwarfed beneath the whiskers of the mighty rodent who looks both able and willing to devour everything, including the thumb-tack that holds the work against the schoolroom wall.

Peering down from the cockpit at grazing elephant, you have the feeling that what you are beholding is wonderful, but not authentic. It is not only incongruous in the sense that animals simply are not as big as trees, but also in the sense that the twentieth century, tidy and svelte with stainless steel as it is, would not possibly permit such prehistoric monsters to wander in its garden. Even in Africa, the elephant is as anomalous as the Cro-Magnon Man might be shooting a round of golf at Saint Andrews in Scotland.

But, with all this, elephant are seldom conspicuous from the air. If they were smaller, they might be. Big as they are, and coloured as they are, they blend with everything until the moment they catch your eye.

They caught Blix's eye and he scribbled me a frantic note; 'Look! The big bull is enormous. Turn back. Doctor Turvy radios I should have some gin.'

Well, we had no radio — and certainly no gin in my plane. But just as certainly, we had Doctor Turvy.

Doctor Turvy was an ethereal citizen of an ethereal world. In the beginning, he existed only for Blix, but long before the end, he existed for everybody who worked with Blix or knew him well.

Although Doctor Turvy's prescriptions indicated that he put his trust in a wine list rather than a pharmacopoeia, he had two qualities of special excellence in a physician; his diagnosis was always arrived at in a split second — and he held the complete confidence of his patient. Beyond that, his adeptness at mental telepathy (in which Blix himself was pretty well grounded) eliminated the expensive practice of calling round to feel the pulse or take a temperature. Nobody ever saw Doctor Turvy — and that fact, Blix insisted, was bedside manner carried to its final degree of perfection.

I banked the Avian and turned toward camp.

Within three miles of our communal baobab tree, we saw four more elephant — three of them beautiful bulls. The thought passed through my head that the way to find a needle in a haystack is to sit down. Elephant are never within three miles of camp. It's hardly cricket that they should be. It doesn't make a hunter out of you to turn over on your canvas cot and realize that the thing you are hunting at such expense and physical tribulation is so contemptuous of your prowess as to be eating leaves right in front of your eyes.

But Blix is a practical man. As a White Hunter, his job was to produce the game desired and to point it out to his employer of the moment. Blix's work, and mine, was made much easier by finding the elephant so close. We could even land at the camp and then approach them on foot to judge more accurately their size, immediate intentions, and strategic disposition.

Doctor Turvy's prescription had to be filled, and taken, of course, but even so, we would have time to reconnoitre.

We landed on the miserly runway, which had a lot in common with an extemporaneous badminton court, and, within twenty minutes, proceeded on foot toward those magnificent bulls.

Makula was with us. Neither the safari nor this book, for that matter, could be complete without Makula. Though there are a good many Wakamba trackers available in East Africa, it has become almost traditional in late years to mention Makula in every book that touches upon elephant-hunting, and I would not break with tradition.

Makula is a man in the peculiar position of having gained fame without being aware of it. He can neither read nor write; his first language is Wakamba, his second a halting Swahili. He is a smallish ebon-tinted Native with an inordinately wise eye, a penchant for black magic, and the instincts of a beagle hound. I think he could track a honeybee through a bamboo forest.

No matter how elaborate the safari on which Makula is engaged as tracker, he goes about naked from the waist up, carrying a long bow and a quiver full of poisoned arrows. He has seen the work of the best rifles white men have yet produced, but when Makula's nostrils distend after either a good or a bad shot, it is not the smell of gunpowder that distends them; it is a kind of restrained contempt for that noisy and unwieldy piece of machinery with its devilish tendency to knock the untutored huntsman flat on his buttocks every time he pulls the trigger.

Safaris come and safaris go, but Makula goes on forever. I suspect at times that he is one of the wisest men I have ever known — so wise that, realizing the scarcity of wisdom, he has never cast a scrap of it away, though I still remember a remark he made to an overzealous newcomer to his profession: 'White men pay for danger — we poor ones cannot afford it. Find your elephant, then vanish, so that you may live to find another.'

Makula always vanished. He went ahead in the bush with the silence of a shade, missing nothing, and the moment he had brought his hunters within sight of the elephant, he disappeared with the silence of a shade, missing everything.

Stalking just ahead of Blix through the tight bush, Makula signalled for a pause, shinned up a convenient tree without noise, and then came down again. He pointed to a chink in the thicket, took Blix firmly by the arm, and pushed him ahead. Then Makula disappeared. Blix led, and I followed.

The ability to move soundlessly through a wall of bush as tightly woven as Nature can weave it is not an art that can be acquired much after childhood. I cannot explain it, nor could Arab Maina who taught me ever explain it. It is not a matter of watching where you step; it is rather a matter of keeping your eyes on the place where you want to be, while every nerve becomes another eye, every muscle develops reflex action. You do not guide your body, you trust it to be silent.

We were silent. The elephant we advanced upon heard nothing — even when the enormous hindquarters of two bulls loomed before us like grey rocks wedded to the earth.

Blix stopped. He whispered with his fingers and I read the whisper. 'Watch the wind. Swing round them. I want to see their tusks.'

Swing, indeed! It took us slightly over an hour to negotiate a semicircle of fifty yards. The bulls were big — with ivory enough — hundred-pounders at least, or better.

Nimrod was satisfied, wet with sweat, and on the verge, I sensed, of receiving a psychic message from Doctor Turvy. But this message was delayed in transit.

One bull raised his head, elevated his trunk, and moved to face us. His gargantuan ears began to spread as if to capture even the sound of our heartbeats. By chance, he had grazed over a spot we had lately left, and he had got our scent. It was all he needed.

I have rarely seen anything so calm as that bull elephant — or so casually determined upon destruction. It might be said that he shuffled to the kill. Being, like all elephant, almost blind, this one could not see us, but he was used to that. He would follow scent and sound until he *could* see us, which, I computed would take about thirty seconds.

Blix wiggled his fingers earthward, and that meant, 'Drop and crawl.'

It is amazing what a lot of insect life goes on under your nose when you have got it an inch from the earth. I suppose it goes on in any case, but if you are proceeding on your stomach, dragging your body along by your fingernails, entomology presents itself very forcibly as a thoroughly justified science. The problem of classification alone must continue to be very discouraging.

By the time I had crawled three feet, I am sure that somewhere over fifty distinct species of insect life were individually and severally represented in my clothes, with Siafu ants conducting the congress.

Blix's feet were just ahead of my eyes — close enough so that I could contemplate the holes in his shoes, and wonder why he ever wore any at all, since he went through them almost in a matter of hours. I had ample time also to observe that he wore no socks. Practical, but not comme il faut. His legs moved through the underbrush like dead legs dragged by strings. There was no sound from the elephant.

I don't know how long we crawled like that, but the little shadows in the thicket were leaning toward the east when we stopped. Possibly we had gone a hundred yards. The insect bites had become just broad, burning patches.

We were breathing easier — or at least I was — when Blix's feet and legs went motionless. I could just see his head close against his shoulder, and watch him turn to peek upward into the bush. He gave no signal to continue. He only looked horribly embarrassed like a child caught stealing eggs.

But my own expression must have been a little more intense. The big bull was about ten feet away — and at that distance elephant are not blind.

Blix stood up and raised his rifle slowly, with an expression of ineffable sadness.

'That's for me,' I thought. 'He knows that even a shot in the brain won't stop that bull before we're both crushed like mangos.'

In an open place, it might have been possible to dodge to one side, but not here. I stood behind Blix with my hands on his waist according to his instructions. But I knew it wasn't any good. The body of the elephant was swaying. It was like watching a boulder, in whose path you were trapped, teeter on the edge of a cliff before plunging. The bull's ears were spread wide now, his trunk was up and extended toward us, and he began the elephant scream of anger which is so terrifying as to hold you silent where you stand, like fingers clamped upon your throat. It is a shrill scream, cold as winter wind.

It occurred to me that this was the instant to shoot.

Blix never moved. He held his rifle very steady and began to chant some of the most striking blasphemy I have ever heard. It was colourful, original, and delivered with finesse, but I felt that this was a badly chosen moment to test it on an elephant — and ungallant beyond belief if it was meant for me.

The elephant advanced, Blix unleashed more oaths (this time in Swedish), and I trembled. There was no rifle shot. A single biscuit tin, I judged, would do for both of us — cremation would be superfluous.

'I may have to shoot him,' Blix announced, and the remark struck me as an understatement of classic magnificence. Bullets would sink into that monstrous hide like pebbles into a pond.

Somehow you never think of an elephant as having a mouth, because you never see it when his trunk is down, so that when the elephant is quite close and his trunk is up, the dark red-and-black slit is by way of being an almost shocking revelation. I was looking into our elephant's mouth with a kind of idiotic curiosity when he screamed again —and thereby, I am convinced, saved both Blix and me from a fate no more tragic than simple death, but infinitely less tidy.

The scream of that elephant was a strategic blunder, and it did him out of a wonderful bit of fun. It was such an authentic scream, of such splendid resonance, that his cronies, still grazing in the bush, accepted it as legitimate warning, and left. We had known they were still there because the bowels of peacefully occupied elephant rumble continually like oncoming thunder — and we had heard thunder.

They left, and it seemed they tore the country from its roots in leaving. Everything went, bush, trees, sansivera, clods of dirt — and the monster who confronted us. He paused, listened, and swung round with the slow irresistibility of a bank-vault door. And then he was off in a typhoon of crumbled vegetation and crashing trees.

For a long time there wasn't any silence, but when there was, Blix lowered his rifle — which had acquired, for me, all the death-dealing qualities of a feather duster.

I was limp, irritable, and full of maledictions for the insect kind. Blix and I hacked our way back to camp without the exchange of a word, but when I fell into a canvas chair in front of the tents, I forswore the historic propriety of my sex to ask a rude question.

'I think you're the best hunter in Africa, Blickie, but there are times when your humour is gruesome. Why in hell didn't you shoot?'

Blix extracted a bug from Doctor Turvy's elixir of life and shrugged.

'Don't be silly. You know as well as I do why I didn't shoot. Those elephant are for Winston.'

'Of course I know — but what if that bull had charged?'

Farah the faithful produced another drink, and Blix produced a non sequitur. He stared upward into the leaves of the baobab tree and sighed like a poet in love.

'There's an old adage,' he said, 'translated from the ancient Coptic, that contains all the wisdom of the ages — "Life is life and fun is fun, but it's all so quiet when the goldfish die."'

XVIII

Captives of the Rivers

THE only disadvantage in surviving a dangerous experience lies in the fact that your story of it tends to be anticlimactic. You can never carry on right through the point where whatever it is that threatens your life actually takes it — and get anybody to believe you. The world is full of sceptics.

Blix is the only man I know who could write posthumously about a fatal happening without arousing doubtful comment. He went about for years in Africa with enough malaria in his system to cause the undoing of ten ordinary men. Every now and then, when the moment seemed propitious, the malaria demon would go through all the formalities of a coup de grâce and then walk away, leaving Blix, more often than not, huddled motionless on a forest path without even Doctor Turvy for comfort. A day later, Blix would be on his way again, resembling a half-brother to Death, but shooting just as straight as he always had and performing his job with his usual competence.

Like the Irish, of whom it is said that they never know when they are beaten, Blix never knew when he was dead. He was charged by a bull elephant once and fell against a tree in attempting a sidestep. Blix lay flat on his back while the bull tore the tree from its roots, ground most of it into the earth within inches of Blix's body, and then stormed away in the blind conviction that his puny enemy was dead. To

219

this day, Blix argues that the bull was wrong, but everybody is aware that Nordic blood sometimes bestows a stubbornness, impervious to conviction, upon its bearers.

But there were occasions when Blix was the victim of more commonplace, even tedious, hardships.

Winston had got the elephant that had almost got Blix and me. That elephant was big, but not big enough for the dynamic Mr. Guest, who seems to wring from each moment of his life its ultimate squeal of excitement, so Blix and I took off together again and went scouting toward a place called Ithumba.

For a long time we saw nothing, but on the way back, flying over the Yatta Plateau, we found a colossal bull grazing in majestic loneliness amongst the thorn trees and the thicket.

A bull like that is a challenge to a hunter. It is one thing to track down a herd with its cows and calves and its republican method of formulating communal policy, but it is another thing to tackle a seasoned individualist unfettered by responsibility — selfish, worldly-wise, and quick to act.

We returned to camp about mid-afternoon and Winston decided to go straight after the bull. Big as Winston is and physically powerful as he is, he could hardly have hesitated, with honour, in ordering the advance. There was the elephant and there was Winston — with a possible fifteen miles between them. Man and beast, notwithstanding, it brought to mind those two mutually respectful sons of Greece who meet so often in print without anybody's ever knowing the outcome. Winston heard, in our description of the lone colossus, the call of Destiny. Late as it was, he commanded action.

Blix fixed up a light safari, using about fifteen porters. This contingent, organized for mobility, carried mostly non-edible supplies, and would strike out across country, while, with Farah and Arab Ruta in joint command, a couple of lorries

were sent around, over what roads there were, to establish new
headquarters at Ithumba. The plan had an almost military
flavour.

Some idea of the kind of terrain and difficulty of organization may be got from the fact that, while the foot party might
expect to force its way a distance of only thirty miles in order
to reach Ithumba, the lorries would have to travel more than
two hundred miles in a great circle to reach the same point.

The Yatta Plateau, rising about five hundred feet from the
plain, is caught between the Athi River on the west and the
Tiva on the east. The plateau itself is a man-trap of bush,
thicket, and thorn trees fifteen to twenty feet high, inter-
locked like steel mesh, dark enough and deep enough to swal-
low an army.

Blix's strategy had to be simple, and was. The party would
camp on the banks of the Athi for the first night, climb the
plateau at dawn, hunt down the spoor and, with luck, bring
Winston's bull to bay before dark in a kind of lightning
manoeuvre. Having been successful (any other expectation
was of course fantastic), the party would descend the eastern
slope of the plateau, wade the narrow Tiva, and arrive at
Ithumba joyously bearing its treasure of ivory.

For my part, needing some servicing on the Avian, I prepared to fly back to Nyeri (about sixty miles north of Nairobi)
and then return to Ithumba within three days.

'When the plane is ready,' Blix said, 'fly straight to
Ithumba. We'll be waiting there.'

I took off from our camp near Kilamakoy just as Winston
and Blix, like the twin heads of a determined dragon, made off
through the bush with a long tail of burdened porters dragging closely behind.

I flew the hundred and eighty-odd miles up to Nyeri and
landed at John Carberry's coffee farm, Seramai.

Lord Carberry, an Irish peer with an African anchorage and an American accent, was a brilliant flyer in the days when it was still considered a noteworthy feat to drive an automobile a hundred miles and then be able to walk away from it reasonably erect. Carberry was a pilot in the First World War — and before it. After the war, he came out to British East Africa and bought and developed Seramai.

The place borders the Kikuyu Reserve near the southern hem of Mount Kenya's foothills and lies at an altitude of nearly eight thousand feet. The country is cool, misty, and lush with rich soil and a wealth of rain. Blue-green coffee trees cover it like a geometrically tufted counterpane.

I am not sure whether the name Seramai is an ancient one bestowed by the Kikuyu or whether John Carberry thought of it himself; it means 'Place of Death.' If the name did have a Kikuyu origin, though, it is not likely that Carberry would have been intimidated by its hardly subtle significance. He would, I believe (if the price were reasonable and the opportunity existed), be happy to purchase, and live in, Mr. Poe's House of Usher — granted permission to build a landing field beyond the tarn. John Carberry is an extremely intelligent and practical man, but his unorthodox sense of humour makes him, at times, almost literally a bedfellow of the dead French author who liked to use a human skull for an inkpot. 'J. C.' is a man who snickers when circumstances pointedly indicate the propriety of a shudder.

'J. C.' is what he likes to be called. Lord of the realm or not, he is fired throughout his lanky frame with a holy passion for democratic ways and manners. He has lived in the United States and loves it. He will never write one of those books comparing England and America, only to conclude that the culture of the latter offers the same clinical interest as a child prodigy born of congenitally daft backwoods parents. When

John Carberry says that something has gone 'haywire,' he says it with full appreciation of the succinct quality of American expression — with such enthusiasm, in fact, that a New York taxi-driver might count him as no more alien than a visitor from Tennessee after a month's exposure to Times Square.

J. C. had a wonderful airplane mechanic in a Frenchman by the name of Baudet, and beyond that he had an adequate runway, a good hangar, and facilities for making minor repairs on planes. Since Tom had gone to England, it was, regardless of the distance, easier for me and more pleasant to fly to Seramai for servicing on the Avian than to use Wilson Airways. The Carberry house was always open to friends and its landing field to pilots.

June Carberry, small, nimble-minded, and attractive, presided over evenings at Seramai like a gracious pixy over a company of characters snatched from an unfinished novel originally drafted by H. Rider Haggard and written by Scott Fitzgerald, with James M. Cain looking over his shoulder. Conversation drifted from phantom elephants to the relative potency of various cocktails, to Chicago gangsters — but usually ended on aeroplanes.

John Carberry, in spite of his wife's lack of enthusiasm for flying, could (and would) talk straight through three highballs on an aeronautic subject so relatively simple as wingflaps.

'Watch the Amurricans,' said J. C., 'their commercial planes have got it over ours like a tent. Say! Listen! when I was in California...'

And we listened.

On the morning I was to return to Ithumba, I listened to J. C.'s almost gleeful chortle as we regarded the weather out of the sitting-room windows of Seramai. Normally, you could see Mount Kenya and the Aberdares; abnormally, you could at least see the Gurra Hill, not ten miles from the runway.

But on that morning you could see nothing; mountain mist had stolen down from Kenya during the night and captured the country.

J. C. shook his head and affected a deep sigh. 'I don't know,' he said. 'I've always maintained that nobody could get out of here unless he could see the Gurra. Of course I'm not sure about it, because nobody has ever been jackass enough to try. I wouldn't do it for a million dollars.'

'That's encouraging. What do you suggest?'

J. C. shrugged. 'Well, there always has to be a first time, you know. I think if you bear a bit to the west and then a bit to the east, you might just get through all right. That's only a guess, you know, but hell, Burl, you're a good blind flyer and with a little luck — who can tell? Anyway, if you get through, just give this bottle of gin to Old Man Wicks, will you?'

It has always been a question in my mind as to whether J. C.'s nature is sadistic, or if only he prefers to paint a gloomy picture in the hope that the subsequent actuality will seem brighter by contrast. Many German flyers, having a superstition that to wish good luck brings bad luck, will see a fellow pilot off with the cheering remark, 'Farewell — but I hope you break your arms and legs!' Perhaps J. C. has that superstition. At least, when I did take off, his longish face — more aristocratic, I suspect, than suits his humble taste — had a grin. But his grey eyes, in spite of it, had a flyer's concern for a flyer's worries.

They needn't have had. I was pretty good at hedge-hopping. It's only natural to be pretty good when you're flying two feet above the treetops beneath sixty miles of fog. Your sense of self-preservation becomes extremely acute if you know that your margin of safety is barely wider than your own shoulders. You feel trapped. You can't allow yourself any altitude or you'll be absorbed in the fog, just as the mountains somewhere ahead of you are absorbed in it. So you manage to hang just under the roof of the narrow corridor of visibility and above the tops of the trees that look like inverted clouds, black and ready to rain. I coasted down the slopes that run from Seramai to the plains, swinging east or west to round the swell of a hill or to cling on the misty curves of a valley. And in a little while I found a blue hole and went up and through it and consulted my compass — and got to Ithumba.

The runway there was better than most and the landing was easy. Our camp was set up in the lee of a hill of rock and the tents were open and waiting. The canvas chairs were out, the lorries were side by side and empty. Everything was ready — and had been for two days. Neither Bwana Blixen, reported Arab Ruta, nor Bwana Guest had been seen or heard from since the moment they had so bravely set forth to storm the Yatta.

The trouble is that God forgot to erect any landmarks. From the air every foot of the Yatta Plateau looks like every other foot of it, every mile is like the next mile, and the one after that, and the one after that.

Years of free-lancing, scouting for elephant and flying the mail in Africa, have made me so used to looking for a smudge of smoke that even now I have a particular affinity for chimneys, campfires, and stoves that puff.

But nothing puffed on the morning I looked for Winston and Blix; nothing stirred. It seemed to me that two intelligent white men with fifteen black porters could have managed a small corkscrew of smoke at least, unless the whole lot of them had been struck dead like the crew of the *Flying Dutchman*.

I knew that the hunting party had taken only enough food

for a couple of meals, which, according to my calculations, left
them about seven meals short. That might, unless something
were done about it, lead to sad, not to say morbid, consequences. What I could not understand was why they had insisted on remaining on top of the plateau when the camp at
Ithumba lay just across the Tiva River. I banked and lost
altitude and flew low over the Tiva to see if I could find them,
perhaps in the act of fording it.

But the river had swallowed itself. It wasn't a river any
more; it was a proud and majestic flood, a mile-wide flood, a
barrier of swift water defying all things that move on legs
to cross it. And yet, beside the Athi, it was a lazy trickle.

The Athi, on the other side of the plateau, had got illusions of grandeur. It was sweeping over the parched country
above its banks in what looked like an all-out effort to surpass
the Nile. Far up in the Highlands a storm had burst, and
while the sky I flew in was clean and blue as a Dutch roof-
top, the Yatta was a jungle island in a rain-born sea. The
gutters of Mount Kenya and the Aberdares were running
deep. Winston and Blix and all their men were caught like
kittens on a flooded stump; they were marooned in driest Africa.

In all likelihood the elephant they hunted was marooned
as well if he had not already been shot. But in either case,
dead or alive, he would have afforded small comfort.

Edible game is scarce on the Yatta, and the swollen rivers
would hardly subside within a week. Given time, I knew Blix
would be resourceful enough to figure a way out — possibly
on rafts built of thorn trees. But, in order to work, men must
eat. I nosed the Avian down toward the endless canopy of
bush and zigzagged like a homeless bee.

In twenty minutes I saw their smoke. It was a wizened
little string of smoke, sad and grey, and looking like the after-
glow of a witch's exit.

Blix and Winston stood by a fire, frantically heaping it with weeds and branches. They waved and swung their arms, and signalled me to come down. They were alone, and I saw no porters.

I swung lower and realized that a narrow clearing had been sculptured out of the jungle growth, but a landing seemed impossible. The runway was short and walled with thicket and rough enough to smash the Avian's undercarriage.

If that happened, contact with the camp at Ithumba — and everything beyond Ithumba — would be cleanly broken. And if it didn't happen, how could I take off again? Getting down is one thing, but getting up again is another.

I scribbled a note on the pad strapped to my right thigh, popped the note into a message bag, and aimed the bag at Blix.

'Might get down,' I said, 'but runway looks too short for take-off. Will return later if you can make it longer.'

It seemed a simple message — clear and practical; but, judging from its reception, it must have read like an invitation to arson or like an appeal to warn the countryside by beacon that the fort had been stormed and massacre was imminent.

XIX

What of the Hunting, Hunter Bold?

Blix heaped foliage and wood on his fire until the smoke from it could be smelled in the cockpit as I flew over the clearing, and I think that in the end he cast his terai hat into the blaze, or perhaps it was Winston's. The smoke rose in enormous grey mushrooms, and I could see pink whips of flame snap in the sunlight. Both men leapt up and down and gesticulated with their arms as if, for months past, they had fed altogether upon flowers that conferred a kind of inspired lunacy.

Quite plainly I was to have no larger runway, and just as plainly, there was a reason for it. Blix would not ask me to chance a landing in a spot like that unless other possibilities had first been explored.

By now I was pretty sure I could land if I had to, but not at all sure I could get off again in the same space. There was no wind to check a landing nor to aid a take-off. I had to think.

I banked the plane and circled several times, and each time I did it the dark balloons of smoke grew fatter and soared higher and the dance below achieved the tempo of ecstasy. I still could see no porters.

It breaks my heart to land a plane on rough ground; it is like galloping a horse on concrete. I considered side-slipping in, but remembered Tom's admonition that to do it expertly (to straighten up from the slip and flatten out a few inches from the earth) is impracticable when you have to land on a broken surface. More often than not this is courting a damaged undercarriage or a cracked longeron. 'Save your sideslips for a time when the approaches are such that you can't possibly get in any other way,' Tom used to say, 'or for a day when your motor has quit. But so long as your motor can help you — fly in.' So I flew in.

I flew in and the Avian hit the roots and clods and buried stumps with gentle groans and creaks of protest. She churned the loose dust to billows that matched the billows of the fire. She roared to the edge of the thicket as if she meant to leap it, but decided not. Eventually the drag of the tail-skid and manipulation of the rudder pulled her up, and she stopped with a kind of apprehensive shudder.

Blix and Winston stormed her sides like pirates storming a sloop. They were unshaved and dirty. I had never realized before how quickly men deteriorate without razors and clean shirts. They are like potted plants that go to weed unless they are pruned and tended daily. A single day's growth of beard makes a man look careless; two days', derelict; and four days', polluted. Blix and Winston hadn't shaved for three.

'Thank God, you got here!' Winston was smiling, but his normally handsome face was half-mooned in whiskers and his eyes were definitely not gay. Blix, looking like an unkempt bear disturbed in hibernation, gave me his hand and helped me out of the cockpit.

'I hated to ask you to land, but I had to.'

'I guessed that. I saw you couldn't get off the plateau. But what I don't understand . . .'

'Wait,' said Blix, 'everything will be explained — but first, have you brought anything?'

'I'm afraid not — nothing to eat, anyway. Haven't you shot *anything?*'

'No. Not even a hare. The place is empty and we haven't

eaten for three days. That wouldn't matter so much, but...'

'But no word from Doctor Turvy? Well, I'm betraying a trust, but J. C. did send a bottle of gin for Old Man Wicks. I suppose you need it more than he does. What happened to your porters?'

It was the wrong question. Blix and Winston exchanged glances and Blix began to swear rhythmically under his breath. He reached into the locker and got Old Man Wicks's bottle of gin and pulled the cork out. He handed the bottle to Winston and waited. In a minute Winston handed it back and I waited, watching the largesse from Seramai go the way of all good things.

'The porters are on strike,' Winston said.

Blix wiped his mouth and returned the bottle to his companion in exile.

'Mutiny. They haven't lifted a hand since they missed their first meal! They've quit.'

'That's silly. Porters don't go on strike in Africa. They haven't got a union.'

Blix turned away from the plane and looked back across the runway. 'They didn't need one. Empty bellies constitute a common cause. Winston and I cleared that runway ourselves. I don't think we could have made it any longer even if you had insisted on it.'

I was impressed. Limited as it was, the runway was nevertheless a good hundred yards long and ten yards wide, and the clearing of such a space with nothing but Native pangas to use was a herculean job of work. Some of the growth must have been fifteen feet high, and all of it so dense that a man could barely force his body through it. I suppose that more than a thousand small trees, with trunks three to five inches in diameter, had been felled with those ordinary bush knives. Once the trees had fallen, their stumps had to be dug out of the earth and thrown to the side and an effort made to level the cleared ground.

I learned later from Makula — who had diplomatically remained aloof from the labour controversy (as well as from the labour itself) — that for two nights running Blix had slipped out of his blankets when everyone else was presumably asleep and had worked straight into the morning on the clearing. Certainly he deserved his nip of gin.

Every one of Blix's porters, in what still is, to my knowledge, the most wonderful example of nose-slicing to spite the face, had insisted that since they had no food they could do no work. They had lounged around the makeshift camp day after day while Blix and Winston had slaved at the clearing, though it had been explained to the porters very carefully (and no doubt with some heat) that if there were no clearing, they might not see a bowl of posho for weeks to come.

Nevertheless, Blix was worried about his porters. I think that a less just man might have been tempted to say, 'Starve, damn you!' But not Blix. His reputation as a White Hunter wasn't entirely built in the cocktail bar at Muthaiga. He said, 'Beryl, I know it's asking a lot, but you've got to get Winston out of here first, then come back for me — and then for Makula. Get Farah to give you all the beans and dry food you can carry for the porters, and bring it here after you've dropped Winston. It means two more landings in this hole and three take-offs. But if I didn't think you could manage, I wouldn't ask you to do it.'

'I suppose if I ask what happens if I don't manage, you'll tell me how quiet it gets when the goldfish die?'

Blix grinned. 'Terribly quiet,' he said, 'but *so* peaceful.'

It was small comfort to know that Winston took the same chance that I did when we attempted the take-off from the runway. I shouldn't think that Winston weighs much less than a hundred and eighty pounds (dismounted and lightly clad), and that much weight made a lot of difference to the Avian under conditions prevailing that day on the Yatta. I insisted on waiting for a breeze, and finally got one strong enough to just bend the column of smoke that still rose from Blix's fire.

Winston got into the front seat, Blix swung the prop, and the Avian moved down the runway — slow, fast, faster. The wall of thicket came nearer and began to look more solid than a wall of thicket ought to look. I saw Winston shake his head and then lower it slightly. He was staring straight before him — a little like a prizefighter in a crouch.

I held the stick forward trying to gather what speed I could before the take-off. I'm afraid I thought of Tom's letter, but a second later I was thinking of Tom's brilliant judgement in suggesting the Avian for African work. No other plane that I knew could have been pulled off the ground, almost literally, the way I pulled her off, without stalling. She responded like a Thoroughbred steeplechaser, missing the thicket with inches to spare. Winston abruptly came out of his crouch, swung around in the seat and winked at me — a little like the same prizefighter having won a decision in the fifteenth round. I gained altitude, throttled down, and swung toward the Tiva. It had no recognizable banks. It looked like a lake wandered from home.

It would not be quite true to say that Arab Ruta and Farah were nervous wrecks when we arrived at Ithumba, but they were pretty obviously relieved. Farah, who is a lean, energetic Somali, inclined to talk so fast that you are still coping with his first sentence while he is waiting for an answer to the last, was of the opinion that his Bwana Blixen was touched with immortality. He did not think that anything serious could have happened to Blix, but he was aware that anyone else's misfortune would be, in a way, also Blix's. Farah greeted us with inquiring rather than worried eyes, while Arab Ruta rushed up to the plane and immediately inspected the landing gear, the wings, and the tail-skid. Then, a little tardily, he smiled at me.

'Our plane is unhurt, Memsahib! — and you also?'

I admitted that I was intact, at least, and prepared to take on the food needed for Blix's rebellious porters.

It takes a lot of practice to make perfect, but a little helps. I had no difficulty in picking up Blix or in putting him down again in the camp at Ithumba. And on the third trip, to get Makula, everything went smoothly too, except for Makula himself, who hesitated to go at all.

'Ai-Ai!' he complained in garbled Swahili, 'how strange that hunger makes a man shake like a stick in the wind. Hunger does bad things to a man!' He regarded the plane with a disquiet eye. 'When one is hungry, it is better, I think, not to move.'

'You won't have to move, Makula. You can just sit in front of me until we get to camp.'

Makula tugged at his shuka and ran his fingers up and down the sleek surface of his golden bow. He thumbed his rawhide string and made it sing a cautious song. 'Each man is a brother to the next, M'sabu, and brothers must lean upon each other. All the porters are alone. Can I leave them?'

The day was shorter than it had been, Blix's fire was dead, and 'all the porters' were feeding in happy silence. They had won their strike and they had food enough and time enough, with no cares. What I had brought would last until the floods were down — and there was no work.

But we needed Makula. I remembered an old Swahili phrase, and I said it: 'A wise man is not more than a woman — unless he is also brave.'

233

The old tracker regarded me carefully for a long moment — as if I had uttered a truth from a cabala previously known only to himself and the lost ages. Then he nodded solemnly and spat on the ground. He stared at the spittle and then at the failing sun. At last he rubbed his hands on his shuka and climbed into the Avian. I swung the propeller, ran around to the rear cockpit, and got in behind him. His naked neck was rigid and ringed with glinting metal bands. White beads dangled from the bands and glinted too against his black skin. He held his bow in firm fingers and it tapered gracefully up from the cockpit like the magic wand he hoped it was. He waited until the plane moved and then he snatched from somewhere about his waist a thin blanket and bound his head with it, around and around, until he was blind as night and shapeless as fear. And then I took off.

All the way to Ithumba my bundle never moved. Makula had always cultivated the suspicion that he was as deft at witchcraft as at tracking. He carried a little bag of wooden amulets and feathers and odd bones which, because they were rarely seen and never explained, had taken on for his confrères the quality of talismans contrived in hell. I could almost believe that Makula was using them now, calling on their darkly potent powers to suspend sense and consciousness just this once — oh, God or Devil! — for just this little time.

I landed gently and taxied smoothly and stopped, and my bundle stirred. Blix and Winston were on hand, both relieved to see us — and both shaved. At the sound of their voices above the sound of the propeller that still ticked over with lazy ease, Makula began to unwind the blanket that his witchcraft had saved from a shroud's duty. When his head appeared, he did not sigh nor blink his eyes; he stared at the palms of his hands and then at the sky, and nodded at nothing in a gesture of restrained approval. Things had worked out about as he had planned them; he would forgo, for the time, any minor complaints. He climbed out of the plane with a certain grace and arranged his shuka and smiled at everybody.

'Well, Makula,' said Blix, 'how did you like your first trip through the air?'

I think it was less a question than a pleasant gibe — and there was an audience to hear the answer. Not only Farah and Ruta, but those porters who had stayed with the camp, had joined the circle that honoured old Makula. We thought the glibness of his tongue was being put to test, but he thought it was his dignity. He made himself a little taller and skewered Blix with a glance.

'Baba Yangu (Father of Mine), I have done many things — and so this was no great thing to me. To a Kikuyu, or a Wandorobo, or a Kavirondo, it might be a great thing to fly through the air. But I have seen much of the world.'

'As much as you saw today, Makula?'

'Not so much at one time, Baba Yangu. Today, it is true, I saw the great sea down there by Mombasa, and the top of Kilamanjaro, and the place where the Mau Forest ends — but those things I had seen before, by myself.'

'You saw all those things today?' Farah's scepticism went undisguised. 'You could not have seen those things, Makula. You did not fly so far, and we all know that your head was wrapped in your own blanket! Can men see, then, through darkness?'

Makula let his long fingers caress the little bag of witchery that hung from his waist. He turned to his accuser and smiled with magnificent forgiveness.

'Not *all* men, Farah. Who could expect so much of God?'

You could expect many things of God at night when the campfire burned before the tents. You could look through and beyond the veils of scarlet and see shadows of the world as God first made it and hear the voices of the beasts He put there. It was a world as old as Time, but as new as Creation's hour had left it.

In a sense it was formless. When the low stars shone over it and the moon clothed it in silver fog, it was the way the firmament must have been when the waters had gone and the night of the Fifth Day had fallen on creatures still bewildered by the wonder of their being. It was an empty world because no man had yet joined sticks to make a house or scratched the earth to make a road or embedded the transient symbols of his artifice in the clean horizon. But it was not a sterile world. It held the genesis of life and lay deep and anticipant under the sky.

You were alone when you sat and talked with the others — and they were alone. This is so wherever you are if it is night and a fire burns in free flames rising to a free wind. What you say has no ready ear but your own, and what you think is nothing except to yourself. The world is there, and you are here — and these are the only poles, the only realities.

You talk, but who listens? You listen, but who talks? Is it someone you know? And do the things he says explain the stars or give an answer to the quiet questions of a single sleepless bird? Think of these questions; fold your arms across your knees and stare at the firelight and at the embers waning on its margin. The questions are your questions too.

'Sigilisa!' (Listen!) 'Simba is hungry tonight.'

So a Native boy interprets the first warning of a distant lion stalking in a distant silence. A jackal skirts the red pool of comfort that warms you, a tent flap chatters in the wind.

But Simba is not hungry. He is alone, too, companionless in his courage, friendless in his magnificence — uneasy in the night. He roars, and so he joins our company, and hyenas join it, laughing in the hills. And a leopard joins it, letting us feel his presence, but hear nothing. Rhino — buffalo — where are they? Well, they are here too — somewhere here — just there, perhaps, where that bush thickens or that copse of thorn trees hides the sky. They are here, all are here, unseen and scattered, but sharing with us a single loneliness.

Someone stands up and stirs the fire which needs no stirring, and Arab Ruta brings more logs, though there are logs enough. Another fire burns a little distance from our own where the black porters squat as if they are fitted into niches of the night.

Somebody attempts to break the loneliness. It is Blix, asking a simple question that everybody answers, but nobody has listened to. Winston stares at the tips of his boots like a child who has never before had boots and never wants to lose them. I sit with a notebook on my knee and a pencil in my hand, trying to write a list of what I need, and writing nothing. I must answer Tom, too. He has written to say that he has entered for the International Air Race from Mildenhall to Melbourne. Eleven thousand and three hundred miles — half around the world almost. England to Australia. I should be in England. I ought to fly to England again. I know the route: Khartoum — Wadi Halfa, Luxor, Cairo, Benghazi, Tobruk... Tripoli and the Mediterranean... France and England. Six thousand miles — only a quarter around the world, and take your time. Well... I wonder.

'Want to fly to London, Blix?'

He says yes without even looking up from the rifle he's fiddling with.

'It's funny about that elephant,' says Winston.

Winston is still up there on the Yatta. 'Not even a spoor!' He shakes his head. 'Not a single sign,' he says.

Arab Ruta stands just behind me and Farah is next to him. They are there on the pretext of serving, but actually they are there just as we are there — thinking, talking, dreaming.

'In Aden,' says Farah to Ruta, 'where I was born, there by the Red Sea in Arabia, we used to go out on the water in boats that had each one wing, brown and very high, and the wind pushed this wing and carried us along. Sometimes at night the wind would stop — and then it was like this.'

'I have seen the sea at Mombasa,' says Arab Ruta, 'and at night too. I do not think the sea is like this. It moves. Here, nothing moves.'

Farah thinks, Blix whistles a few low notes from a knock-about tune, Winston ponders his phantom elephant, and I scribble by the light of the fire.

'The sea at Mombasa,' Farah says, 'is not the same sea.'

Momentarily the categorical pronouncement confounds Ruta. He bends to pick a log from the ground and toss it into the fire, but he is thoughtful.

'How big would you say that bull was?' Winston looks at Blix and then at me.

Blix shrugs. 'The one on the Yatta? Very big.'

'Tusks over a hundred?'

'Nearer two,' says Blix. 'He was very big.'

'Well, it's damned funny we never even saw his spoor.'

Winston relapses into silence and stares at the night as if his elephant might be there, swinging his huge trunk from side to side in soundless derision. Up on the plateau, the meeting place of Greek and Greek waits with no Greeks at hand.

I return to my list of things needed, but not for long. I wonder if I should have a change — a year in Europe this time — something new, something better, perhaps. A life has to move or it stagnates. Even this life, I think.

It is no good telling yourself that one day you will wish you had never made that change; it is no good anticipating regrets. Every tomorrow ought not to resemble every yesterday.

Still, I look at my yesterdays for months past, and find them as good a lot of yesterdays as anybody might want. I sit there in the firelight and see them all.

The hours that made them were good, and so were the moments that made the hours. I have had responsibilities and work, dangers and pleasure, good friends, and a world without walls to live in. These things I still have, I remind myself — and shall have until I leave them.

I nod stupidly at something Blix says and idly contribute a twig to our fire.

'Are you falling asleep?'

'Asleep? No. No, I am just thinking.' And so I am. I spend so much time alone that silence has become a habit.

Often, except for Ruta and Farah, I am alone at safari headquarters day after day, night after night, while the hunters, following a herd that I have found or waiting for me to find one, are camped miles away. At dawn they expect the sound of my Avian, and it always comes.

I awaken long before dawn at such times and always find Ruta ready with my cup of steaming tea, and I drink it, looking at the fading stars that are caught in the triangle of my open tent.

It is always misty when Ruta and I remove the canvas covers from the engine, the propeller, and the cockpit. Each humid, tropic day is stillborn, and does not breathe, however lustily pregnant the night that gave it birth. I take off in dead air with the accessories of my singular occupation arranged in their proper places.

There are the message bags stacked in two specially made boxes of teak that stand on either side of me on the floor of the cockpit. The bags are handsome things, in their way. I carry over a dozen of them — tough little brown pouches, leaded, and fitted with long streamers of blue-and-gold silk, for visibility. Blue-and-gold had been my racing colours; they are flying colours now.

There is my note pad fixed on a board and hung with straps to fasten on my thigh, and the quiver of pencils I carry with it. What frantic scribbling that pad and those pencils are a party to!

And there is my vial of morphine. I keep it, like a fetish, in the pocket of my flying jacket because the senior medical officer at Nairobi has told me to keep it, and has mumbled of forced landings in inaccessible wastelands and crackups in the depths of forests that men could hardly reach — in time. He has been insistent about this precaution, making me return the unopened vial at intervals, exchanging it for a fresher one. 'You never can tell,' he invariably says, 'you never can tell!'

And so equipped, I wave kwaheri to Ruta each day in the rheumy morning light, fly until I sight the smoke of the hunters' camp, and dip my wings to greet them. Then I am off over the rolling ocean of bush to find their quarry — and, when I find it, what a thrill it is, what a satisfying moment!

Sometimes I circle a herd for nearly an hour, trying to determine the size of its largest bull. If at last I decide that he carries enough ivory, my work begins. I must figure the course from the herd to the hunters' camp, reverse the course, jot it down on my pad, judge the distance, give details of terrain, warn of other animals in the vicinity, note water holes, and indicate safest approach.

I must find my smoke signal again, keeping an eye on the compass, a hand free for scribbling, and my course and distance calculator ready, should I need it. I feel triumphant when I can drop a note like this which Blix has returned to me and is still folded in my logbook:

> *Very* big bull — tusks quite even — my guess over 180-pounder. In herd of about 500. Two other bulls and many

babies in herd — grazing peacefully. Dense growth — high trees — two water holes — one about half-mile from herd NNE. Other about two miles WNW. Fairly open ground between you and herd, with open glade halfway. Many tracks. Large herd buffalo S.W. of elephant. No rhino sighted. Your course 220 degrees. Distance about ten miles. Will be back in one hour. Work hard, trust in God, and keep your bowels open — Oliver Cromwell

Well, Cromwell *did* say it, and it still makes sense.

All of it makes sense — the smoke, the hunt, the fun, the danger. What if I should fly away one morning and not come back? What if the Avian fails me? I fly much too low, of necessity, to pick a landing spot (assuming that there might be a landing spot) in such a case. No, if the engine fails me, if a quick storm drives me into the bush and sansivera — well, that is the chance and that is the job. Anyway, Blix has told Farah and Ruta what to do if I am ever gone for a longer time than my supply of petrol might be expected to last — get to a telegraph by foot or lorry, and wire Nairobi. Maybe somebody like Woody would begin the search.

Meanwhile, haven't I got two quarts of water, a pound of biltong — and the doctor's bottled sleep (should I be hors de combat and the Siafu hungry that night)? I certainly have, and, moreover, I am not defenceless. I have a Lüger in my locker — a gun that Tom has insisted on my carrying, and which can be used as a short rifle simply by adjusting its emergency stock. What could be better? I am an expedition by myself, complete with rations, a weapon, and a book to read — *Air Navigation*, by Weems.

All this, and discontent too! Otherwise, why am I sitting here dreaming of England? Why am I gazing at this campfire like a lost soul seeking a hope when all that I love is at my wingtips? Because I am curious. Because I am incorrigibly, now, a wanderer.

'Beryl — wake up!' Blix roars. Winston stirs and something scuttles through the bush in fright.

'I'm not asleep, I tell you. I'm thinking.'

'About England?'

'Yes — about England.'

'All right.' Blix stands up and yawns and stretches so that the shadows of his arms before the firelight embrace all of the Africa our eyes can see.

'All right,' he says again — 'when do we leave?'

'I'm going to Elburgon first,' I say, 'to see my father. After that, if you really want to come along, we're off.'

Elburgon is not a town; it is just a station on the Uganda Railway, one of many entrances to a broad, familiar country. There, as at Njoro, my house looks over the Rongai Valley and, as at Njoro, the Mau Forest broods in resigned silence, close on the edges of fields fresh robbed of their ancient trees. I have a gallop where my father still trains his horses and where I can land my plane. Everything has been done — every material thing — to give this place the aspect of benignity, of friendship, of tolerance and conviviality, but the character of a dwelling, like that of a man, grows slowly.

The walls of my house are without memories, or secrets, or laughter. Not enough of life has been breathed into them — their warmth is artificial; too few hands have turned the window latches, too few feet have trod the thresholds. The boards of the floor, self-conscious as youth or falsely proud as the newly rich, have not yet unlimbered enough to utter a single cordial creak. In time they will, but not for me.

My father takes me by the arm and we desert the veranda and the sundown shadows advancing on the valley and go inside to the big room whose hearth of native stone is neither

worn nor stained with ash. In these surroundings it will not
be so hard to say good-bye as it once was at Njoro.

My father leans against the mantelpiece and begins to load
his pipe with tobacco whose aroma bestows a presence on
thirty vanished years. That aroma and the smell of the smoke
that follows it are to me the quintessence of memory.

But memory is a drug. Memory can hold you against your
strength and against your will, and my father knows it. He
is sixty-four years old now, and well deserving of deep chairs
and care and dottle dreams and carping cronies — should he
desire these. He might say, with ample reason: 'I'm old now.
I've earned my rest.'

But he doesn't. He says: 'You know, I like South Africa.
I like Durban. I'm going down there to start training. The
racing's good and the stakes are high. I think it's a good
chance.' He announces his intention with the sanguine ex-
pectancy of a schoolboy.

'So, when you come back,' he says, 'I'll be there.'

He allows me no misgiving nor a moment's remorse — not
the luxury of feeling young nor himself the maudlin misery of
feeling old.

We sit together through the evening and discuss the things
that each has saved for the other to hear. We talk of Pegasus
— and of how he had died, quietly one night in his stall, for
no reason that anyone could ever find.

'Snake, perhaps,' says my father. 'Yellow mambas are
deadly.'

It may have been a mamba, or it may not have been.
However, or whatever it was, Pegasus — so expectantly
christened so long ago — is gone now, yielding his ethereal
wings to the realization of wood and steel ones that fly as high
and higher, but, for all that, are never so buoyant or capable of
bearing quite such cargoes of hope.

So we talked about that and about other things — about the forthcoming auction of my Avian, about Arab Ruta, and about Tom, who, with Charles Scott, had won the greatest air race ever staged — England to Australia — against the best pilots the world could muster.

'How strange it is,' says my father, 'that an old friend and neighbour of ours should have done such a wonderful thing! Eleven thousand miles and more — in seventy-one hours!'

It seems wonderful, but not strange to me. There are men whose failures surprise nobody, and others whose successes are as easily anticipated — Tom was of these.

I rise from my chair and my father glances at the clock. Time for bed. In the morning I will be off, but we have said nothing of good-bye. We have learned frugality — even in this.

In the morning I get into my plane, peer down the length of the gallop I use for a runway, and wave to my father. I am smiling and he is smiling, and he waves too. I have just one more stop at Nairobi (for Blix), and the next overnight stop after that will be Juba, in the Anglo-Egyptian Sudan.

The plane rolls forward and I salute once more and leave my father standing on the earth he has stood upon so long and so steadily. I circle and dip my wings, or rather I think the Avian voluntarily makes her last curtsey — her last, at least, to him.

He does not wave again. He stands, shading his eyes, looking upward, and I level off and take my course and follow it away.

XX

Kwaheri Means Farewell

A MAP in the hands of a pilot is a testimony of a man's faith in other men; it is a symbol of confidence and trust. It is not like a printed page that bears mere words, ambiguous and artful, and whose most believing reader — even whose author, perhaps — must allow in his mind a recess for doubt.

A map says to you, 'Read me carefully, follow me closely, doubt me not.' It says, 'I am the earth in the palm of your hand. Without me, you are alone and lost.'

And indeed you are. Were all the maps in this world destroyed and vanished under the direction of some malevolent hand, each man would be blind again, each city be made a stranger to the next, each landmark become a meaningless signpost pointing to nothing.

Yet, looking at it, feeling it, running a finger along its lines, it is a cold thing, a map, humourless and dull, born of calipers and a draughtsman's board. That coastline there, that ragged scrawl of scarlet ink, shows neither sand nor sea nor rock; it speaks of no mariner, blundering full sail in wakeless seas, to bequeath, on sheepskin or a slab of wood, a priceless scribble to posterity. This brown blot that marks a mountain has, for the casual eye, no other significance, though twenty men, or ten, or only one, may have squandered life to climb it. Here is a valley, there a swamp, and there a desert; and here is a river that some curious and courageous soul, like

245

a pencil in the hand of God, first traced with bleeding feet.

Here is your map. Unfold it, follow it, then throw it away, if you will. It is only paper. It is only paper and ink, but if you think a little, if you pause a moment, you will see that these two things have seldom joined to make a document so modest and yet so full with histories of hope or sagas of conquest.

No map I have flown by has ever been lost or thrown away; I have a trunk containing continents. I have the maps I always used en route to England and back. I have the log of my flight with Blix.

It was not a record flight either in speed or endurance; we took the time we needed and avoided no necessary stops; but it was not a dull flight. Even in March of nineteen-thirty-six, toward the close of that ignoble bit of brigandage which Italian euphemists of the moment were calling the Conquest of Ethiopia, it was still less than commonplace to fly from Nairobi to London. There were airfields along the way, but the terrain between them — or much of it, at least — had the same remote quality, the same barely plausible appearance as the surface of the moon through lenses. It differed from the moon in that it was so ominously accessible, and was similar in that its aspect was equally forbidding.

Flying due north, you had first to cross the entire Anglo-Egyptian Sudan, the whole of Egypt, and the desert of Cyrenaica in Libya. You were then at Benghazi, and happy to be there indeed, but before you still lay the Gulf of Sidra, Tripolitania, Tunisia, and the Mediterranean Sea — and beyond that, France. No matter how blithely you undertook to span that sixty-five hundred miles, or how casually you referred to it as a trip to England, you were aware that it was, in fact, no trip at all, but a major voyage; you had to navigate, you had to be weather-wise, you had to consider the handicaps.

Blix and I left at a pilot's hour, but on no pilot's day. Fog had spilled out of the sky by night and the morning found Nairobi and the Athi Plains bundled in mist. The town, the sunrise, and the ship were isolated each from the other by clouds that had no edges and refused to roll. They lay on the earth like sadness come to rest; they clung to people like burial clothes, white and premature. Blix found them gay.

He arrived at the airport carrying no more luggage than would see a schoolboy through a week-end trip. His face was cherubic in the company of faces grim and grey as those carved in a Gothic arch. When all was ready, he climbed into the rear seat of the Leopard Moth and sat there whistling and nursing in his lap a long, cylindrical object, wrapped in paper, and which gurgled when it was moved.

Arab Ruta went forward to swing the prop. I held my hand on the throttle and searched the fog with my eyes, but only from habit; I have never owned a carpet whose dimensions, imperfections, and limitations were more familiar to me than the surface of the Nairobi Airport. A lot of time had passed since the days of pig-holes, zebra herds, and oil flares. There were runways now, and hangars, and no audience to see the midnight landing of a plane or a dawn take-off; no Kikuyu youths to watch Ruta at his wonderful and mystic tasks. All was commonplace now. Adventure for Nairobi came in celluloid rolls straight from Hollywood, and adventure for other parts of the world went out from Nairobi in celluloid rolls straight from the cameras of professional jungle-trotters. It was a good time to leave.

I nodded, and the propeller whirred to life. Arab Ruta sidestepped with agility born of long practice. I could not hear him say kwaheri, but I saw his lips make the word. I said it too, and felt the small flat gift he had slipped into the cabin a moment before.

247

I have it still — a travelling clock bound in imitation leather, for which (I later learned) Ruta had hoarded five hundred of my cast-off cigarette coupons, collected quietly and patiently from wastebaskets, safari tents, and hangar sweepings.

The clock keeps time; it rings when you set it. But what a sad substitute, that hysterical jingle, for the soft and soothing voice that used to say, just after dawn, 'Your tea, Memsahib?' or long before, 'Lakwani, it is time to hunt!'

Harmony comes gradually to a pilot and his plane. The wing does not want so much to fly true as to tug at the hands that guide it; the ship would rather hunt the wind than lay her nose to the horizon far ahead. She has a derelict quality in her character; she toys with freedom and hints at liberation, but yields her own desires gently.

As we leave for London, swinging up to find the surface of the fog, and, finding it, the Leopard plays at her little game. The rudder bar resists the pressure of my feet, the stick inclines against my hand with almost truculent opposition. But this is momentary. A stern touch overcomes the urge to disobedience, and presently I settle back, flying with the craft and the craft with me.

Blix is already settled. He is comfortably drowsing in our closed cabin, with his feet on the unused seat beside him. It makes little difference to him whether this is the start or the end of a flight. Morpheus has never been his master; Blix is the master of Morpheus. He calls Sleep when he wants it, and it comes. When he does not want it, it stays away, no matter how late the hour or how tiring the day has been.

The first day is tiring enough, but only because the preparations for leaving have left me a bit weary. Night finds us at Juba, where my room in the Rest House, though it has the aspect of a prison cell, affords the fundamental comfort of a bed and protection from mosquitoes.

At dawn I tumble out and see that Blix has left his own room and is pacing back and forth in front of the plane where she is picketed with ropes and stakes. Her fuselage is yellow and her wings silver. Against the barely lighted sky she looks less like a bird than like a rare and brilliant insect, dead, and preserved on a cardboard mat.

We take off without breakfast because ahead of us lies country easier to face with ample time in reserve. Not that the crossing of it is a great aeronautical feat, but that to consider it indifferently might result in a sad aeronautical blunder.

I do not know what the regulations are now, but at that time no woman was allowed to fly solo between Juba and Wadi Halfa without express permission from the Royal Air Force Headquarters at Khartoum.

The reasons for this were plausible enough — a forced landing in the papyrus swamps of the Sudd was barely distinguishable from a forced landing on the banks of the Styx, and a forced landing beyond the Sudd, in the country of the Sudanese and Dinka tribes, might mean days or weeks of searching by the R.A.F., with the chances of recovering the cost of this being somewhat less hopeful than the chances of recovering the lost pilot.

I am a little vague as to why it was thought that women were less capable than men of avoiding these obvious dangers, though I suspect there was more of gallantry than reason in the ruling. In all, I flew the entire route between Nairobi and London six times — four of them solo (after convincing the R.A.F. of my ability to do it), and other women have flown it too. The outstanding error of judgement in flying over the Sudd, as a matter of fact, was made by a man — the late

Ernst Udet let himself run out of petrol while crossing it during the dry season and forced-landed on a ridge of hardened mud, where, after several anxious days, he was found by Tom Black, whose understanding of the Sudd was such that he was willing to spend days trying to get somebody out of it. Udet himself was hardly worse for the experience, but his mechanic was near death from mosquito bites.

If you can vizualize twelve thousand square miles of swamp that seethes and crawls like a prehistoric crucible of half-formed life, you have a conception of the Sudd. It is an example of the less attractive by-products of the Nile River, and one place in this world worthy of the word 'sinister.' Add to that, 'eerie' and 'treacherous,' and any other similar adjectives that occur, and the conception may become clearer. The surface of the Sudd, from the air, is flat and green — and inviting. If you should be either hypnotized or forced into landing upon it (and if, miraculously, and impossibly, you didn't turn over), the wheels of your plane would at once disappear into the muck, while your wings would, in all probability, rest upon the slowly heaving mat of decomposed — and living — growth that in many places is fifteen feet thick and under which flows a sluice of black water.

Assuming that you were thus nestled, unhurt, on the bosom of this interminable slough (whose stench came to your nostrils while you were still a thousand feet above it), and assuming that you had in your plane a radio transmitter through which you contacted Khartoum, giving your position and other details, you might, if you were naïve, expect something to happen. But nothing would, because nothing could.

Boats cannot move in the Sudd, planes cannot land in it, men cannot walk in it. In time a plane *would* arrive, circle a few times and drop provisions, but unless the aim of the pilot were such that he hit a part of your plane directly with his packet of manna, you would have gained nothing. If he did hit it, you would have gained little.

It is, of course, conceivable that, given enough food via bombardment, you might live to a ripe old age and achieve the ultimate in privacy while doing it, but it is more likely that those little minstrels of misery, the mosquitoes, not to say the Devil's own amphibian armada (crocodiles populate the Sudd), would discourage you long before your hair turned grey — a matter, I should think, of about two weeks.

In any case, the anticipation of such doleful prospects on the part of those civilian pilots permitted by the R.A.F. to chance the Sudd had led to extraordinary caution, and consequently there have been few, if any, lives lost in it.

Our flight contributed no new anecdote about the Sudd. During the four hours we flew over it, Blix and I spoke very little. The Leopard Moth had a closed cabin, and so conversation was possible, but we were in no mood for it.

Our silence was not an awed silence; I think we were simply depressed beyond words with the business of hanging for so long a time under such a flat blue sky and above such a flat virescent swamp. It was hardly like flying. It was like sitting in a plane which, by the aid of wires, dangled equidistant between the floor and the ceiling of a stage-set conceived without benefit of imagination.

Shortly after we left Juba, Blix, in the accepted dormouse style, roused himself long enough to mumble, 'I smell the Sudd!' — and then he was silent again until the Sudd was gone and both of us could smell the desert.

Beyond the Sudd there is the desert, and nothing but the desert for almost three thousand miles, nor are the towns and cities that live in it successful in gainsaying its emptiness. To me, desert has the quality of darkness; none of the shapes you see in it are real or permanent. Like night, the desert is boundless, comfortless, and infinite. Like night, it intrigues the mind and leads it to futility. When you have flown half-way across a desert, you experience the desperation of a sleep-less man waiting for dawn which only comes when the im-portance of its coming is lost. You fly forever, weary with an invariable scene, and when you are at last released from its monotony, you remember nothing of it because there was nothing there.

And after the desert, the sea. But long before we reached the sea, Blix and I had found that men alone can be more tire-some and give more hindrance than all the sand and all the water that may stretch over a quarter of the globe.

Malakal, Khartoum, Luxor — cities to their inhabitants, islands of regeneration to us. We stopped at each of them, and at each were blessed with that great triumvirate of blessings to the traveller — hot water, food, and sleep. But it was at Cairo that we were surfeited with these. After a flight of three thousand miles in three days, we were detained for an entire week by the majestic workings of the Italian Govern-ment. It was one of the incidents which Abdullah Ali had neg-lected to predict.

Abdullah Ali was in charge of the customs office at Alamza, the Cairo airport. He was also in charge of a small department in the Realm of Things to Come; he told fortunes, and told them well. He loved aviators with a paternal love and, in his way, he gave them guidance that put to shame even their compasses. He was a tall, spare column of a man, dark as a mummy and almost as inscrutable. He fumbled through our papers, glanced at our luggage, and affixed all the necessary stamps. Then he led us outside the customs shed, where the official glint faded from his eyes and in its place came the esoteric glow that illumines the eyes of all true seers. He kneeled in the yellow sand of the huge aerodrome and began to make marks upon it with a polished stick. 'Before she leaves,' he said, 'the lady must have her fortune.'

Blix sighed and looked wistfully toward the city. 'I'm dying of thirst — and he tells fortunes!'

'Shh! That's blasphemy.'

'I see a journey,' said Abdullah Ali.

'They always do,' said Blix.

'The lady will fly over a great water to a strange country.'

'That's an easy prediction,' mumbled Blix, 'with the Mediterranean just ahead.'

'And she will fly alone,' said Abdullah Ali.

Blix turned to me. 'If I am to be abandoned, Beryl, couldn't you make it a little closer to a bar?'

Abdullah Ali heard nothing of this irreverent comment. He went on making circles and triangles with his wizard's wand and unravelling my future as if it were already my past. His red fez bobbed up and down, his slender hands moved against the sand like foraging sparrows against snow. He was not really with us nor with the fortune either; he was back there under the shadow of the half-built Sphinx, making marks in the selfsame sand.

When we left him, the polished stick had disappeared and a pencil had taken its place. Abdullah Ali too had disappeared — or was at least transformed. That thin Egyptian with the grey suit and red fez, stooping as he walked through the door of the shed, was only a customs man.

'Do you believe him?' said Blix.

A taxicab had scurried across the airport to take us to Shepheard's Hotel. I got into the car and relaxed against the leather seat.

Who believes in fortune-tellers? Very young girls, I thought, and very old women. I was neither of these.

'I believe it all,' I said. 'Why not?'

XXI

Search for a Libyan Fort

Ｉｎ NINETEEN-THIRTY-SIX you could not fly over any Italian territory without permission from the Italian Government. It is true that you have to clear customs at each international border in any case, but the Italian idea was different.

The Italian idea was based upon the wistful suspicion that no foreigner (certainly no Englishman) could fly over Libya, for instance, and successfully resist the temptation to take candid camera shots of the newly contrived Fascist forts. The Italians, under Mussolini, would have been hurt indeed to know that a pilot existed (and many of them did) who had less curiosity about the Fascist forts than about the exact location of a bar of soap and a tub of hot water. The official reasoning seemed to run about like this: 'An aviator who shows an interest in our fortresses is guilty of espionage, and one who does not is guilty of disrespect.' I think the latter crime was, of the two, the more repugnant to the legionnaires of the flowing tunic and the gleaming button.

The symbols of war — impressive desert forts, shiny planes, beetle-browed warships — all inspire the sons of Rome, if not to gallantry, then at least to histrionics, which, in the Italian mind, are synonymous anyway. I sometimes think it must be extremely difficult for the Italian people to remain patient in the face of their armies' unwavering record of defeat (they looked so resplendent on parade). But there is little complaint.

The answer must be that the country of Caruso has lived a symbolic life for so long that the token has become indistinguishable from the fact or the deed. If an aria can suffice for a fighting heart, a riband draped on any chest can suffice for a general — and the theory of victory, for victory itself.

The one highly placed Italian I knew, and for whom I had respect — as did everybody else who knew him — was the late General Balbo. Balbo was a gentleman among Fascists, and, as such, his death was an act of Fate doubtless designed in the interests of congruity.

He was Governor of Tripolitania at the time Blix and I flew to England, but he had gone into the Southern Desert on routine inspection and so could not intercede, as he had twice done for me, in the matter of speeding our exit from Egypt into Libya.

However futile the Italian military, there is real striking power behind the rubber stamps of petty Italian officials — or there was. They kept Blix and me at Cairo, day after day, withholding our permits to cross the border into Libya. They had no reason, or gave none, and their maddening refusal to do anything whatever except to sit (I think literally) upon our passports, brought the profound observation from Blix that 'there is no hell like uncertainty, and no greater menace to society than an Italian with three liras worth of authority.'

It brought Blix to more than that. It exposed him to an incident that might have shattered the nerves of a less steady man.

Blix left Shepheard's Hotel each night well after dinner and disappeared into the honeycombs of Cairo. He is a gregarious individual who loves his fellows and hates to be alone. It is one of the minor tragedies of his life that, no matter in what gay companionship the night begins, not many hours pass before he is alone again — at least in spirit. His friends may still

be at his side around a table still graced by an open bottle —
but they are mute and recumbent; they no longer finger their
glasses, they no longer mutter about the vicissitudes of life,
nor sing the joys of living it. They are silent, limp, or
lachrymose, and in their midst sits Blix the Unsinkable — a
monument of miserable sobriety, bleak as a lonely rock jutting
from a lonely sea. Blix leaves them at last (after paying the
bill) and seeks comfort in the noises of the night.

One night in Cairo Blix came across an old friend and a
gentleman of doughty stock. He was the younger brother of
Captain John Alcock (who, with Lieutenant Arthur Brown,
made the first successful Atlantic flight), and moreover he was
a crack pilot for Imperial Airways. Alcock the younger, who
has rarely if ever been put hors de combat by anything that
can be poured from a decanter, was the realization of one of
Blix's most fervent hopes — a man to whom the undermost
side of a table was an unexplored region.

At some bar — I cannot remember which, any more than
Blix or Alcock could if they were asked — there began an historic session of comradely tippling and verbose good-fellow-
ship which dissolved Time and reduced Space to an ante-
room. On the table between those good companions the whole
of history was dissected and its mouldy carcass borne away
in an empty ice bucket. International problems were solved
in a word, and the direction of Fate foreseen through the
crystal windows of two upturned goblets. It was a glorious
adventure, but the only part I had in it came close on the
dawn.

I was asleep in my room at Shepheard's when a fist ham-
mered at my door. Ordinarily I should have climbed out of
bed and groped for my flying clothes. Ordinarily that knock
would have meant that somebody had forced-landed in a cotton field, probably in the middle of Uganda, and that they

had communicated with Nairobi asking for a spare part. But this was Cairo, and that insistent fist must be the fist of Blix.

I groped for lights, got into a dressing-gown, and let fly a few whispered maledictions aimed at the head of Bacchus But what I saw before me, when I opened the door, was no reeling Blix, nor even a swaying one. I have seldom seen a man so sober. He was grim, he was pale, he was Death warmed over. He shook like a harpstring.

He said: 'Beryl, I hated to do it, but I had to wake you. The head rolled eight feet from the body.'

There are various techniques for coping with people who say things like that. Possibly the most effective is to catch them just under the ear with a bronze book-end (preferably a cast of Rodin's 'Thinker') and then scream — remembering always that the scream is of secondary importance to the book-end.

Shepheard's in Cairo is one of the most civilized hotels in the world. It has everything — lifts, restaurants, an enormous foyer, cocktail rooms, a famous bar and ballroom. But it has no book-ends. At least my room had no book-end. It had a green vase with an Egyptian motif, but I couldn't reach it.

'The damned fools just stood there,' said Blix, 'and stared at the blood.'

I went back to my bed and sat on it. This was our sixth day in Cairo. Almost hourly either Blix or I had telephoned to see if our papers had been stamped for passage into Libya and each time we had got 'no' for an answer. It was wearing us down, both in cash and nerves, but I had thought that the most redoubtable White Hunter in Africa would have survived it a little longer. And yet, as I sat on the edge of the bed, there was Blix leaning against the wall of my room with all the vitality of a bundle of wrinkled clothes awaiting the pleasure of the hotel valet. I sighed with the sorrow of it all.

'Sit down, Blix. You're a sick man.'

He didn't sit. He ran a hand over his face and stared at the floor. 'So I took the head,' he muttered, in a low voice, 'and brought it back to the body.'

And so he had, poor man. He found a chair at last, and, as the daylight grew stronger, he grew stronger too, until finally I got the whole of what was in fact a tragic happening, but whose coincidence with Blix's homeward journey from his rendezvous with Alcock gave it, nonetheless, a comic touch.

Blix had not been left alone that night. Drink for drink and word for word, he had been met and matched according to the rules of his own making. At about four o'clock in the morning, hands were clasped and two suspiciously vertical gentlemen took leave of each other. I have Blix's word for it that he walked toward Shepheard's in a geometrically straight line — an undertaking that no completely sober man would even attempt. Blix said that his head was clear, but that his thoughts were complicated. He said that he was not given to visions, but that two or three times he had humanely stepped over small, nondescript animals in his path, only to realize, on looking back, how deceptive shadows can be in a dimly lighted city street.

It was not until he was within two blocks of Shepheard's, and doing nicely, that he saw at his feet a human head completely detached from its body.

Blix's presence of mind never left him on safari, nor did it here. He merely assumed that, being a little older than he had been, all-night revelry left him more shaky than it used to do. He squared his shoulders and was about to carry on when he saw that other people stood in a circle on the concrete walk — all of them staring at the severed head and babbling so idiotically that it came to Blix with violent suddenness that neither the people nor the head was an hallucination; a man had fallen across the tramlines in the path of an onrushing car and had been decapitated.

There were no police, there was no ambulance, there was no effort on anybody's part to do anything but gape. Blix, used to violence, was not used to indifference in the face of tragedy. He kneeled on the walk, took the head in his arms, and returned it to its body. It was the body of an Egyptian labourer, and Blix stood over it pouring Swedish imprecations on the gathered onlookers, like an outraged prophet reviling his flock. And when the authorities did arrive, he left his gruesome post, stole through the crowd, with his lips clamped tightly together, and came to Shepheard's.

All this he told me while he slumped in a chair and the morning traffic of Cairo began to hum beneath my windows.

After a while I ordered some coffee and, while we drank it, I thought that anyway there was hope for the world so long as the fundamental decency of a man was strong enough to triumph over all that the demon rum could do with six hours' start — and more cooperation than any demon has a right to expect.

'Are you giving up all-night parties, Blix?'

He shook his head. 'Oh, but I think that would be so very rash and so very unsociable. Walking home from them is the thing to avoid — I promise you!'

About noon on the sixth day of our stay in Cairo, the Italian authorities, having convinced themselves that our entrance into Libya would not result in a general uprising, returned our passports, and on the following morning we left, flying north to Alexandria, then west to Mersa Matruh, and on to Sollum.

From Sollum to Amseat is ten minutes by plane. Amseat is a post on the Italian Egyptian border; it consisted then of

wind, desert, and Italians, and I understand the wind and
desert still remain. You had to land there before proceeding
to the interior. The post is on a plateau and the landing field
is merely a piece of Libya bounded by imaginary lines.

We landed and were at once brought to bay by six armed
motorcyclists who plunged toward the plane as if they had
lain in wait behind the dunes for many anxious days before
springing their trap. This advance guard had barely dismounted before about thirty other cyclists roared smartly
across the sand, surrounded the Leopard, and thus completed
what, for them, was apparently a military manoeuvre of singular brilliance. Only one detail of organization seemed to
have been ignored: they lacked a leader. They all spoke,
argued, and waved their arms at once with great energy, dis-
playing a tendency toward republican methods that would
have been highly significant to a keen political observer. It
looked for a moment as if the first rift in Il Duce's tight-
seamed order was taking place right in front of our eyes. But
not at all. Eventually a swart soldier announced in a firm
tenor voice that he spoke English, which was an exaggeration,
but which served to quell the ripples of hysteria instantly.

'I will have this papers,' said the swart soldier. He extended his hand and collected our passports, special permits,
and medical certificates.

The sun was hot and, after Cairo, we were impatient, but
the inquisitor with the tenor voice was unhurried. With most
of the Amseat garrison peeking over his shoulder, he stared at
our papers while Blix swore first in Swedish, then in Swahili,
and finally in English. This is not an inconsiderable ability,
but it passed unnoticed. After half an hour or so, a man leapt
to the saddle of his motorcycle and spluttered away across the
desert. He was back in five minutes with a portable canvas
chair which was unfolded and set up in the sand. Everybody

waited in solemn silence. Blix and I had got out of the plane and we stood leaning against it, under the savage sun, thinking harsh thoughts. Minutes had begun to accumulate into an hour before still another machine arrived, complete with side-car, and out of which popped an officer draped in a long blue cloak that bore enough medals to afford about the same protection, during the heat of battle, as a bullet-proof vest. The man who supported all this glory also supported, we observed, the official posterior for which the canvas chair had been spread. He sat down and began to study our papers.

'I should have brought my rifle,' said Blix. 'I will bet you a gin and tonic I could hit the sixth medal on the left-hand side right there where the enamel is peeling.'

'You're casting ridicule on a Captain of Caesar's Legions. Do you know the penalty for that?'

'No. I think they condemn you to read a Gayda editorial daily, for life. But it would be almost worth it.'

'You don't know what you're saying.'

'Silence!' This was uttered in punctilious English by the Captain himself, who followed it with some crisp orders in Italian, and the effect was magical. Four soldiers dived into the Leopard, dragged out everything movable and spread it on the sand — and once more our papers vanished across the desert in the keeping of a dispatch rider who handled his machine with impressive skill.

Three and a half hours after our landing at Amseat, word came (I suspected directly from Rome) that we might proceed to Benghazi.

'*But,*' said the Captain, 'you do not follow the coast. It is required that you take the desert route and circle the forts — three times for each.'

'There is no desert route.'

'You will circle these forts,' said the Captain, 'or be arrested at Benghazi.' He clicked his heels, gave the Fascist salute, as did the entire garrison, and we took off.

Our map had been marked with three X's — each indicating a fort. The X's were at intervals across the Libyan Desert on a zigzag course. It was the first time I had been prevented from landing at Tobruk, and there could be no doubt that the Italians were making elaborate preparations, even then, for something more grandiose than just the defence of Libya. Their forts and their chests extended outward far beyond their usual confines.

From the air, the first fort looked like a child's conception of a fort, executed in sand with a toy shovel. But that was only because of the vast and empty stretches that surrounded it; any desert fort, regardless of the flag that flew over it, would look like that. But we had spent a lot of precious time searching for this one and done a lot of grumbling about it too. Having achieved the goal, we found it disappointing.

The barracks were set around a huge square which appeared to be quite empty, and there were turrets like those of a penitentiary. If there were guns, they were well hidden. Either by design or necessity, the material from which the fort was built was the exact colour of the desert itself. As we circled, men came out of the buildings, and some of them waved their arms. A few waved violently — half in anger, I thought, because of the tantalizing liberty of our plane as against their dry drudgery, and half in welcome of a sign that the world was still a reasonable world that left men free to fly — or some men, anyway.

No spirit of gallant adventure emanated from that dreary fort. It was peopled by men whose roots had been pulled up and planted again in the sand, and whose cheerless houses, too, rested precariously on the same uncertain stuff. The simulated belligerence of a passive people was symbolized there. Like the pompous medals on the Captain's chest, this fort was one of several medals pinned vaingloriously, if with doubtful permanence, on the great grey torso of the desert.

We circled again and levelled off and continued our search.

'One bomb,' said Blix, 'would wipe it out.'

We found the next fort, by the grace of God, but not the last. The word 'fort' presents a massive picture to the mind, but to the Libyan Desert a fort is hardly more than just another hump of sand. A fort is nothing. We had no course to follow — only a pencil mark to find; and the size of a thing is great or small in relation to its background. The sky has stars — the desert only distance. The sea has islands — the desert only more desert; build a fort or a house upon it and you have achieved nothing. You can't build anything big enough to make any difference.

Night falls like a dropped shutter in Libya in March. A plane without petrol falls too, or anyway spirals down into near oblivion.

'We won't bother about the last fort,' I said to Blix. 'I'd rather be jailed in Benghazi than stranded down there.'

'You're the pilot,' said Blix. 'Doctor Turvy and I are only passengers.'

XXII

Benghazi by Candlelight

The Greeks of Cyrenaica called it Hesperides. Ptolemy the Third was in love with his wife, so he called it Berenice. I don't know who changed it to Benghazi, but this is not the first act of vandalism the old city has suffered. The cornerstones of Benghazi are the tombs of its founders and their conquerors, and much of its history lies still buried in hand-hewn crypts of rock.

The city lives on an ancient spit of earth between the Gulf of Sidra and a marshy waste, and the shadow it casts has changed shape through the centuries. Once the shadow was slender and small; once it was broad and tipped with the arrogant spikes of a castle; once a monastery lent its quiet contours to the cool silhouette printed each day against the sand. But now, though this castle and this monastery still stand, their shadows are dissolved in the angular blur of modern buildings. The shape of the shadow has changed and will change again because Benghazi sprawls in the path of war. Mars kicks the little city to earth and it rises again, stubbornly, and is reduced again, but not for long. It is a small city with a soul — a grubby soul, perhaps, but cities with souls seldom die.

Like all seaports of the East, Benghazi is blatant and raw; it is weary and it is wise. Once it lived on ivory brought by caravan across the desert, trading this treasure and ostrich feathers and lesser things to an appreciative world, but now it deals in duller stuff — or deals in nothing, waiting for another war to pass, knowing that in reality it has no function except to provide hostelry for armies on the march.

Blix and I landed at Benghazi minutes before night. The Italian airport there is excellent, and so are the hangars. This latter convenience was especially satisfying to me, since I knew that our plane would be whisked away from us at once and put under lock and key (which it was). But there was no satisfaction in Blix's reminder that jail awaited us.

'If they are lenient,' he said, 'we oughtn't to get more than five years for ignoring that last fort. It was a serious breach of etiquette.'

But we got nothing. The frantic efficiency of the garrison at Amseat seemed to have burned itself out before anybody could telegraph the authorities at Benghazi that we were arriving and that our visit to each of the three forts ought to be verified. Nobody cared.

We were, of course, dragged through the usual tedious business of explaining to assorted officials just why we were there — not to say just why we were alive at all; but this had become routine for us as well as for them, and so they were stalemated.

When the order came allowing us to go to our hotel, we left the last of the Government buildings we had been filtered through, and hired a Fiat taxi whose Arab driver had lain in ambush before the official portals from the moment we had entered them. The driver knew most certainly that there was not a hotel room to be had in all of Benghazi, but he chose to break this disheartening intelligence to us gently; he drove from one hotel to another, sitting behind the wheel with a kind of anticipant leer on his face, mumbling in gulps and snatches of English that the next place would surely have rooms enough. But there were none. Mussolini's armies had outmanoœuvred us; Benghazi was occupied by fifty thousand polished boots.

In the end we gave up. We were hungry and thirsty and dead tired.

'Find *any place*,' said Blix, '*anywhere*, so long as it has a couple of rooms!'

'Anywhere' was the dirty fringe of Benghazi — the fringe that harbours the useless ones of twenty nations, the castoffs, the slag fallen to the side and forgotten until, out of necessity, it must sometimes be waded through or tread upon. 'Anywhere' was arrived at through a web-work of pinched and broken streets, dark, swept with the odours of poverty, the trapped and stagnant smells of stagnant life. 'Anywhere' was the anywhere of all cities — the refuse heap of human shards.

I sat with Blix in the back of the taxi and felt weariness turn to depression. The taxi slowed, wavered, and stopped.

We were in front of a square, mud building two stories high. A few of its windows had glass, some were spread over with rags. None was lighted. The structure had about it a mute quality; it stared at the street with the soulless expression of imbecility.

Our driver waved his arm toward the doorway which was open and had a yellow light burning somewhere behind it. 'Ah!' he said, 'I am lucky for you. No?'

Blix paid the fare without answering, and we went into a courtyard walled on all sides and festooned with tiers of tattered washing. The air was dead and smelled dead.

'Nice place,' said Blix.

I nodded, but we were not amused. We stood there stupidly, myself in white flying overalls no longer white, and Blix in wrinkled slacks and a shirt that had lost its shape. Everything about us was alien, and so we felt alien — almost apologetic, I think.

A door opened down the yard and a woman came toward us. She had a lighted candle and she lifted it close to our faces. Her own face held the lineage of several races, none of which had given it distinction. It was just a husk with eyes. She spoke, but we understood nothing. Hers was a language neither of us had ever heard.

Blix made gestures with his hands, asking for rooms, and the woman nodded quickly enough and led us into the house and up a flight of stairs. She showed us two rooms not even separated by a door. Each contained an iron bed that cowered under a sticky blanket and had an uncovered pillow at its head. One room had a white enamel basin on the floor, and the jug to match it was on the floor of the other. Everything lay under scales of filth.

'All the diseases of the world live here,' I said to Blix.

He was laconic. 'So do we, until tomorrow.'

He followed our hostess down the stairs in the hope of finding food and a drink while I cleaned my face with handkerchiefs until it was recognizable again. Later I followed too.

I found them both in a kind of musty cell at the rear of the house. The cell had a stove and two shelves and its walls were patrolled by cockroaches. Blix had got a tin of soup and a tin of salmon and he was prying one of these open while he talked to the tired woman and she to him. They had discovered a common language, not really familiar to either, but it served.

'We're talking Dutch,' Blix told me, 'and in case you haven't noticed it, this is a brothel. She runs it.'

'Oh.'

I looked at the woman, and then at the cockroaches on the wall, and then at Blix.

'I see,' I said.

It was somehow inevitable, in the scheme of things, that this place should be a brothel and this woman the keeper of it.

Inevitable, but hardly reassuring, I thought. The scheme of things was a shabby scheme.

Blix got the soup tin open and poured the contents into a pot. The brothel keeper pressed her fragile shoulders against the wall and stood there nodding her head like a pecking bird. She was dressed in purple rags and they hung upon her in the unmistakable manner of the livery of her trade. And yet, I thought that a transformation would have been easy. Put her in an apron and soak the mask of paint from her face and she could be used as a fit subject for any artist wanting to depict the misery and the despair and the loneliness of all women driven to drudgery. She might have been a seamstress, a farmhand's wife, a charwoman, a barmaid no longer maiden. She might have been anything — but of all things, why this?

Blix handed me a plate of soup and, as if it were a cue for her to retire, our hostess backed out of the room, grinning vapidly. She had long since forgotten the meaning of a smile, but the physical ability to make the gesture remained. Like the smile of a badly controlled puppet, hers was overdone, and after she had disappeared and the pad of her slippers was swallowed somewhere in the corridors of the dark house, the fixed, fragile grin still hung in front of my eyes — detached and almost tangible. It floated in the room; it had the same sad quality as the painted trinkets children win at circus booths and cherish until they are broken. I felt that the grin of the brothel keeper would shatter if it were touched and fall to the floor in pieces.

'You're thoughtful,' said Blix.

He ate some of his soup and looked thoughtful too. 'Centuries ago,' he said, 'Benghazi was called Hesperides — "The Garden of the Gods."'

'I know. The garden needs tending.'

Blix produced a bottle of white wine that some Italian

soldier had left and his successors had overlooked. We drank the wine out of enamel cups and ate the soup and the cold salmon, fighting a war of attrition against the cockroaches while the meal progressed.

The surface of our wooden table had the culinary history of the house inscribed upon it in grease. There was a candle stuck in a bottle, and a kerosene stove, and four walls, none with windows. The contrast to Shepheard's in Cairo was inescapable, but not mentioned.

Blix preferred to talk about the brothel keeper. With the patience of a hopeful novelist, he had coaxed out of her, through the exchange of tortured Dutch, a kind of synopsis of her life. It was a life better left in synopsis — too sordid and too miserable even to afford a framework for romance.

As a child of six or seven she had been stolen from her parents and had been brought to Africa on a boat. She remembered that the boat was white on the outside and that the journey had made her sick, but could recall nothing else. She had been beaten occasionally, but not often. There had not been any great, immemorable moments of terror or suffering, nor any particular interludes of happiness that stayed in her mind. None of it was very clear, she had told Blix. She felt no resentment about anything, but lately the thought of the early period, whose dates and places she couldn't remember, had begun to prey upon her mind.

'She was about sixteen,' Blix said, 'before she learned she had been sold into prostitution. I've read about white slavery, but I never expected to meet a victim of it. She didn't even know it was slavery until somebody told her; she just thought life was like that.'

'What does she think now?'

'She wants to get away from here, only she hasn't any money. She wants to get back to the country she was born in.

She thinks it might be Holland, but she doesn't know. She says it had trees with fruit on them, and that it got cold sometimes. It's about all she knows. I think she's gone half-witted trying to remember more. It's a hell of a thing to happen to anybody — like waking up and not knowing where you spent last night, only worse. Imagine not knowing where you came from!'

'What was her original language?'

'That's a mystery too,' Blix said; 'she learned Dutch from a Dutch sailor and picked up Arabic, Italian, and other smatterings in one brothel or another. She mixes them all.'

'Well, it's very sad, but you can't do anything about it.'

'I can do a little. I'm going to give her some money.'

While we were still back in Cairo, Blix had been robbed of two hundred pounds sterling in a barber shop. It was nearly all he had saved from his last safari. I judged that he had about fifty left, but I knew him to be incorrigibly philanthropic. I suppose that any man who attempted to cheat Blix out of a shilling would do it at the risk of life and limb, but if the same man asked for a shilling, he would doubtless get twenty.

'It's your money and your kind sentiment,' I said, 'but how do you know she's telling the truth?'

Blix stood up and shrugged. 'Anybody kicked as far down the ladder as she's been kicked isn't obliged to tell the truth, but I think she told some of it. Anyway, you can't expect gospel for a few pounds.'

We went upstairs and tried to get some sleep. I pulled the mattress off my bed and stretched out on the springs, fully dressed. In about ten minutes I could hear Blix snoring with magnificent resonance as he lay on the floor of his room, finding it quite as comfortable, I knew, as he had always found the forest earth that had made his bed for years.

I don't know when or how he gave the woman his contribution to the crusade against the downtrodden of this world; I think he had already done it when he announced his intention to me. At least, when we prepared to leave her sad and shabby house of infamy, at four-thirty in the morning, our hostess was awake and fumbling in the kitchen.

I can't say that her face was illumined by a new hope or that her eyes shone with any more inspiring light than they had held the night before. She was dull, slovenly, and as derelict as a woman could be. But she brewed a pot of tea and swept the ever-present cockroaches from the table with an indignant gesture. And after we had drunk the tea and had gone out of the courtyard and up the street, which was still almost completely dark, the brothel keeper stood in front of her brothel for a long time with the burning candle weeping tallow over her hands. It was the only light that we could see anywhere in the Garden of the Gods.

We crossed the Gulf of Sidra and landed first at Tripoli and then at Tunis, and then we saw green hills again and were finally at the end of the desert and at the end of Africa.

Perhaps, when we took off from the Tunis Airport, I should have circled once or twice and dipped my wings in salute, because I knew that, while Africa would be there forever, it would not ever be there quite as I remembered it nor as Blix remembered it.

Africa is never the same to anyone who leaves it and returns again. It is not a land of change, but it is a land of moods and its moods are numberless. It is not fickle, but because it has mothered not only men, but races, and cradled not only cities, but civilizations — and seen them die, and seen new ones born again — Africa can be dispassionate, indifferent, warm, or cynical, replete with the weariness of too much wisdom.

Today Africa may seem to be that ever-promised land, almost achieved; but tomorrow it may be a dark land again, drawn into itself, contemptuous, and impatient with the futility of eager men who have scrambled over it since the experiment of Eden. In the family of continents, Africa is the silent, the brooding sister, courted for centuries by knight-errant empires — rejecting them one by one and severally, because she is too sage and a little bored with the importunity of it all.

Imperious Carthage must once have looked upon Africa as its own province, its future empire; and the sons of the Romans who destroyed that hope, and are today no longer Romans, have retreated with a step rather less firm than Caesar's over routes that knew the rumble of cavalry long before Christ.

All nations lay claim to Africa, but none has wholly possessed her yet. In time she will be taken, yielding neither to Nazi nor to Fascist conquest, but to integrity equal to her own and to wisdom capable of understanding her wisdom and of discerning between wealth and fulfilment. Africa is less a wilderness than a repository of primary and fundamental values, and less a barbaric land than an unfamiliar voice. Barbarism, however bright its trappings, is still alien to her heart.

'We'll be back,' said Blix. And of course we would be, but, as we flew out over the Mediterranean toward the island of Sardinia with the coast of Tunisia still under our wings, there was no sign that Africa was aware that we were leaving, or cared. All things return to her — even such trivial things.

We found Sardinia — and Cagliari, its citadel that housed the last battalion of Fascist army officials we should have to face. But, after detaining us two more days, first, on the suspicion that I was not a woman, but a man in disguise, and secondly, on the inspired conjecture that, because our pass-

ports were stamped with old Ethiopian visas, we must both
be spies (hardly clever ones either), our inquisitors had finally
to set us free.

Their reluctance to do this was almost touching. Here
again were officers and men of 'the best-dressed army in the
world,' champing at the bit, fretting for weeks at a time before
the arrival of a foreign plane afforded them the opportunity of
surrounding its passengers and holding them captive beyond
the sights of a battery of snub-nosed rubber stamps. We left
Cagliari after computing that the Italian military had altogether detained us for ten extra days in the course of a six-
thousand-mile flight that should have taken us less than a
week.

Between Cagliari and Cannes, we flew into the first really
dangerous weather of the voyage. What had been a blue sky
became a ferment of clouds that clotted before a driving wind
and blacked out our vision with curtains of rain.

The Leopard Moth undertook the challenge with confident
gallantry, but when wind velocity reached sixty miles an hour
while we were still over Sardinia, and I was hedge-hopping
with the vague knowledge that the sea was somewhere ahead
and the specific knowledge that the island had only one airport
— the one behind us — it began to seem quite likely that the
French coast was more remote than it had been when we left
Nairobi.

I turned and smiled at Blix and he smiled back with equal
mirth — which is to say, none; and I realized how much more
difficult it is for a passenger than for a pilot to hang on to his
nerve in weather like that. Blix particularly was used to depending upon his own resources and his own two good hands
in any situation, but there he sat, useless as so much luggage
and quite as helpless, knowing at the same time that we had no
radio nor any special instruments to guide us to our goal.

A forced landing was impossible; the attempt would have resulted in what insurance companies so tenderly refer to as 'a complete write-off,' and at our backs the storm had already closed like a trap. We approached the sea with the plane flying crabwise. I held her nose on the course, judging her drift at twenty degrees. She was like a scrap of trash caught in a gale, and I experienced that sense of futility all pilots must sometimes feel when the natural forces that rule this planet reassert their sovereignty (and express their contempt) for Man the Pretender.

Flying at an altitude of a hundred feet, we saw the land break away to the sea, and saw the sea snatch at the wind with white, frustrated hands. The blue Mediterranean was not the Mediterranean of the travel books; it was the sea of Ulysses, with the escaped charges of Æolus running wild upon it. All the winds had burst their fetters.

'No chance to land now,' said Blix.

I shook my head. 'There hasn't been a chance since we hit the storm. We can't stay down, so we'll have to go up.'

I gauged my drift again as carefully as I could, reset my course for Cannes, and began to climb. We gained altitude, foot by foot, but it was not like flying — it was like running a gamut of unseen enemies, their blows falling, even in the dark, with unerring precision, and the plane groaned under each.

At five thousand feet it was still dark, and at seven and at eight. I began to think it would never be otherwise, but the Leopard was true to her name; she clawed her way up the steep bank of the storm until at ten thousand she found its crest. She found a sky so blue and so still that it seemed the impact of a wing might splinter it, and we slid across a surface of white clouds as if the plane were a sleigh running on fresh-fallen snow. The light was blinding — like light that in summer fills an Arctic scene and is in fact its major element.

I turned to Blix, but he had fallen asleep with the confidence of a child that in a world so bright there could lurk no evil.

For my part, I could not be sure that my drift calculations had been accurate. 'Ceiling zero' is a self-explanatory phrase that everybody understands, but the nomenclature of flying has always needed an equally terse description for complete lack of visibility below. 'Floor zero' seems hardly a happy solution, but I submit it for want of a better, and with equal generosity I suggest that 'cloud-hopping' may indicate the predicament of a pilot searching for a hole through which to descend and attain the earth again without blindly crashing into a part of it.

There were no holes in the white and endless prairie we sledded upon. It was an infinite prairie built of mist turned ice, and the shining light and the smoothness, and the stillness of the air made it appear neither probable nor desirable that down below, or anywhere, there should be another world. It was easy to believe and almost to wish that there wasn't, but indulgence in such feeble metaphysics was not wisdom; if we were off our course, even by a few degrees, we should land either on the coast of Spain or on the coast of Italy — and then there was always the sea.

I was about to check my instruments again — out of habit, because there was little they could tell me now without a fixed point against which to reset my compass — when the Leopard was so violently shaken that Blix was stirred out of his sleep. He shut his eyes to the white light and swore mildly.

'Where are we?'

A minute earlier I should not have been able to say, but bumps just then could only mean mountains and mountains meant Corsica to me. I had never before established my position in accordance with anything so intangible (not to say so invisible) as conflicting air currents, but this time I did.

I relaxed in my seat and announced that we were about an hour from the French coast and told Blix to keep his eyes open for the Maritime Alps. But we never saw them. In an hour we came down out of our ice-white world and at a thousand feet we could see Cannes, ten miles away. We spent that night in Paris, and on the afternoon of the next day, Tom Black, Blix, and I sat at the Mayfair in London surrounded by all the comforting accessories to civilization — and drank a toast to Africa because we knew that Africa was gone.

Blix would see it again and so should I one day. And still it was gone. Seeing it again could not be living it again. You can always rediscover an old path and wander over it, but the best you can do then is to say, 'Ah, yes, I know this turning!' — or remind yourself that, while you remember that unforgettable valley, the valley no longer remembers you.

XXIII

West With the Night

I HAVE seldom dreamed a dream worth dreaming again, or at least none worth recording. Mine are not enigmatic dreams; they are peopled with characters who are plausible and who do plausible things, and I am the most plausible amongst them. All the characters in my dreams have quiet voices like the voice of the man who telephoned me at Elstree one morning in September of nineteen-thirty-six and told me that there was rain and strong head winds over the west of England and over the Irish Sea, and that there were variable winds and clear skies in mid-Atlantic and fog off the coast of Newfoundland.

'If you are still determined to fly the Atlantic this late in the year,' the voice said, 'the Air Ministry suggests that the weather it is able to forecast for tonight, and for tomorrow morning, will be about the best you can expect.'

The voice had a few other things to say, but not many, and then it was gone, and I lay in bed half-suspecting that the telephone call and the man who made it were only parts of the mediocre dream I had been dreaming. I felt that if I closed my eyes the unreal quality of the message would be re-established, and that, when I opened them again, this would be another ordinary day with its usual beginning and its usual routine.

But of course I could not close my eyes, nor my mind, nor my memory. I could lie there for a few moments — remembering how it had begun, and telling myself, with senseless repetition, that by tomorrow morning I should either have flown the Atlantic to America — or I should not have flown it. In either case this was the day I would try.

I could stare up at the ceiling of my bedroom in Aldenham House, which was a ceiling undistinguished as ceilings go, and feel less resolute than anxious, much less brave than foolhardy. I could say to myself, 'You needn't do it, of course,' knowing at the same time that nothing is so inexorable as a promise to your pride.

I could ask, 'Why risk it?' as I have been asked since, and I could answer, 'Each to his element.' By his nature a sailor must sail, by his nature a flyer must fly. I could compute that I had flown a quarter of a million miles; and I could foresee that, so long as I had a plane and the sky was there, I should go on flying more miles.

There was nothing extraordinary in this. I had learned a craft and had worked hard learning it. My hands had been taught to seek the controls of a plane. Usage had taught them. They were at ease clinging to a stick, as a cobbler's fingers are in repose grasping an awl. No human pursuit achieves dignity until it can be called work, and when you can experience a physical loneliness for the tools of your trade, you see that the other things — the experiments, the irrelevant vocations, the vanities you used to hold — were false to you.

Record flights had actually never interested me very much for myself. There were people who thought that such flights were done for admiration and publicity, and worse. But of all the records — from Louis Blériot's first crossing of the English Channel in nineteen hundred and nine, through and beyond Kingsford Smith's flight from San Francisco to Sydney, Australia — none had been made by amateurs, nor by novices, nor by men or women less than hardened to failure, or less than masters of their trade. None of these was false. They were a company that simple respect and simple ambition made it worth more than an effort to follow.

The Carberrys (of Seramai) were in London and I could remember everything about their dinner party — even the menu. I could remember June Carberry and all her guests, and the man named McCarthy, who lived in Zanzibar, leaning across the table and saying, 'J. C., why don't you finance Beryl for a record flight?'

I could lie there staring lazily at the ceiling and recall J. C.'s dry answer: 'A number of pilots have flown the North Atlantic, west to east. Only Jim Mollison has done it alone the other way — from Ireland. Nobody has done it alone from England — man or woman. I'd be interested in that, but nothing else. If you want to try it, Burl, I'll back you. I think Edgar Percival could build a plane that would do it, provided you can fly it. Want to chance it?'

'Yes.'

I could remember saying that better than I could remember anything — except J. C.'s almost ghoulish grin, and his remark that sealed the agreement: 'It's a deal, Burl. I'll furnish the plane and you fly the Atlantic — but, gee, I wouldn't tackle it for a million. Think of all that black water! Think how cold it is!'

And I had thought of both.

I had thought of both for a while, and then there had been other things to think about. I had moved to Elstree, half-hour's flight from the Percival Aircraft Works at Gravesend, and almost daily for three months now I had flown down to the factory in a hired plane and watched the Vega Gull they were making for me. I had watched her birth and watched her growth. I had watched her wings take shape, and seen wood and fabric moulded to her ribs to form her long, sleek belly, and I had seen her engine cradled into her frame, and made fast.

The Gull had a turquoise-blue body and silver wings. Edgar Percival had made her with care, with skill, and with worry — the care of a veteran flyer, the skill of a master designer, and the worry of a friend. Actually the plane was a standard sport model with a range of only six hundred and sixty miles. But she had a special undercarriage built to carry the weight of her extra oil and petrol tanks. The tanks were fixed into the wings, into the centre section, and into the cabin itself. In the cabin they formed a wall around my seat, and each tank had a petcock of its own. The petcocks were important.

'If you open one,' said Percival, 'without shutting the other first, you may get an airlock. You know the tanks in the cabin have no gauges, so it may be best to let one run completely dry before opening the next. Your motor might go dead in the interval — but she'll start again. She's a De Havilland Gipsy — and Gipsys never stop.'

I had talked to Tom. We had spent hours going over the Atlantic chart, and I had realized that the tinker of Molo, now one of England's great pilots, had traded his dreams and had got in return a better thing. Tom had grown older too; he had jettisoned a deadweight of irrelevant hopes and wonders, and had left himself a realistic code that had no room for temporizing or easy sentiment.

'I'm glad you're going to do it, Beryl. It won't be simple. If you can get off the ground in the first place, with such an immense load of fuel, you'll be alone in that plane about a night and a day — mostly night. Doing it east to west, the wind's against you. In September, so is the weather. You won't have a radio. If you misjudge your course only a few

280

degrees, you'll end up in Labrador or in the sea — so don't misjudge anything.'

Tom could still grin. He had grinned; he had said: 'Anyway, it ought to amuse you to think that your financial backer lives on a farm called "Place of Death" and your plane is being built at "Gravesend." If you were consistent, you'd christen the Gull "The Flying Tombstone."'

I hadn't been that consistent. I had watched the building of the plane and I had trained for the flight like an athlete. And now, as I lay in bed, fully awake, I could still hear the quiet voice of the man from the Air Ministry intoning, like the voice of a dispassionate court clerk: ' ... the weather for tonight and tomorrow ... will be about the best you can expect.' I should have liked to discuss the flight once more with Tom before I took off, but he was on a special job up north. I got out of bed and bathed and put on my flying clothes and took some cold chicken packed in a cardboard box and flew over to the military field at Abingdon, where the Vega Gull waited for me under the care of the R.A.F. I remember that the weather was clear and still.

Jim Mollison lent me his watch. He said: 'This is not a gift. I wouldn't part with it for anything. It got me across the North Atlantic and the South Atlantic too. Don't lose it — and, for God's sake, don't get it wet. Salt water would ruin the works.'

Brian Lewis gave me a life-saving jacket. Brian owned the plane I had been using between Elstree and Gravesend, and he had thought a long time about a farewell gift. What could be more practical than a pneumatic jacket that could be inflated through a rubber tube?

'You could float around in it for days,' said Brian. But I had to decide between the life-saver and warm clothes. I

281

couldn't have both, because of their bulk, and I hate the cold, so I left the jacket.

And Jock Cameron, Brian's mechanic, gave me a sprig of heather. If it had been a whole bush of heather, complete with roots growing in an earthen jar, I think I should have taken it, bulky or not. The blessing of Scotland, bestowed by a Scotsman, is not to be dismissed. Nor is the well-wishing of a ground mechanic to be taken lightly, for these men are the pilot's contact with reality.

It is too much that with all those pedestrian centuries behind us we should, in a few decades, have learned to fly; it is too heady a thought, too proud a boast. Only the dirt on a mechanic's hands, the straining vise, the splintered bolt of steel underfoot on the hangar floor — only these and such anxiety as the face of a Jock Cameron can hold for a pilot and his plane before a flight, serve to remind us that, not unlike the heather, we too are earthbound. We fly, but we have not 'conquered' the air. Nature presides in all her dignity, permitting us the study and the use of such of her forces as we may understand. It is when we presume to intimacy, having been granted only tolerance, that the harsh stick falls across our impudent knuckles and we rub the pain, staring upward, startled by our ignorance.

'Here is a sprig of heather,' said Jock, and I took it and pinned it into a pocket of my flying jacket.

There were press cars parked outside the field at Abingdon, and several press planes and photographers, but the R.A.F. kept everyone away from the grounds except technicians and a few of my friends.

The Carberrys had sailed for New York a month ago to wait for me there. Tom was still out of reach with no knowledge of my decision to leave, but that didn't matter so much, I thought. It didn't matter because Tom was unchanging —

neither a fairweather pilot nor a fairweather friend. If for a month, or a year, or two years we sometimes had not seen each other, it still hadn't mattered. Nor did this. Tom would never say, 'You should have let me know.' He assumed that I had learned all that he had tried to teach me, and for my part, I thought of him, even then, as the merest student must think of his mentor. I could sit in a cabin overcrowded with petrol tanks and set my course for North America, but the knowledge of my hands on the controls would be Tom's knowledge. His words of caution and words of guidance, spoken so long ago, so many times, on bright mornings over the veldt or over a forest, or with a far mountain visible at the tip of our wing, would be spoken again, if I asked.

So it didn't matter, I thought. It was silly to think about.

You can live a lifetime and, at the end of it, know more about other people than you know about yourself. You learn to watch other people, but you never watch yourself because you strive against loneliness. If you read a book, or shuffle a deck of cards, or care for a dog, you are avoiding yourself. The abhorrence of loneliness is as natural as wanting to live at all. If it were otherwise, men would never have bothered to make an alphabet, nor to have fashioned words out of what were only animal sounds, nor to have crossed continents — each man to see what the other looked like.

Being alone in an aeroplane for even so short a time as a night and a day, irrevocably alone, with nothing to observe but your instruments and your own hands in semi-darkness, nothing to contemplate but the size of your small courage, nothing to wonder about but the beliefs, the faces, and the hopes rooted in your mind — such an experience can be as startling as the first awareness of a stranger walking by your side at night. You are the stranger.

It is dark already and I am over the south of Ireland. There are the lights of Cork and the lights are wet; they are drenched in Irish rain, and I am above them and dry. I am above them and the plane roars in a sobbing world, but it imparts no sadness to me. I feel the security of solitude, the exhilaration of escape. So long as I can see the lights and imagine the people walking under them, I feel selfishly triumphant, as if I have eluded care and left even the small sorrow of rain in other hands.

It is a little over an hour now since I left Abingdon. England, Wales, and the Irish Sea are behind me like so much time used up. On a long flight distance and time are the same. But there had been a moment when Time stopped — and Distance too. It was the moment I lifted the blue-and-silver Gull from the aerodrome, the moment the photographers aimed their cameras, the moment I felt the craft refuse its burden and strain toward the earth in sullen rebellion, only to listen at last to the persuasion of stick and elevators, the dogmatic argument of blueprints that said she *had* to fly because the figures proved it.

So she had flown, and once airborne, once she had yielded to the sophistry of a draughtsman's board, she had said, 'There: I have lifted the weight. Now, where are we bound?' — and the question had frightened me.

'We are bound for a place thirty-six hundred miles from here — two thousand miles of it unbroken ocean. Most of the way it will be night. We are flying west with the night.'

So there behind me is Cork; and ahead of me is Berehaven Lighthouse. It is the last light, standing on the last land. I watch it, counting the frequency of its flashes — so many to the minute. Then I pass it and fly out to sea.

The fear is gone now — not overcome nor reasoned away. It is gone because something else has taken its place; the confidence and the trust, the inherent belief in the security of land underfoot — now this faith is transferred to my plane, because the land has vanished and there is no other tangible thing to fix faith upon. Flight is but momentary escape from the eternal custody of earth.

Rain continues to fall, and outside the cabin it is totally dark. My altimeter says that the Atlantic is two thousand feet below me, my Sperry Artificial Horizon says that I am flying level. I judge my drift at three degrees more than my weather chart suggests, and fly accordingly. I am flying blind. A beam to follow would help. So would a radio — but then, so would clear weather. The voice of the man at the Air Ministry had not promised storm.

I feel the wind rising and the rain falls hard. The smell of petrol in the cabin is so strong and the roar of the plane so loud that my senses are almost deadened. Gradually it becomes unthinkable that existence was ever otherwise.

At ten o'clock P.M. I am flying along the Great Circle Course for Harbour Grace, Newfoundland, into a forty-mile headwind at a speed of one hundred and thirty miles an hour. Because of the weather, I cannot be sure of how many more hours I have to fly, but I think it must be between sixteen and eighteen.

At ten-thirty I am still flying on the large cabin tank of petrol, hoping to use it up and put an end to the liquid swirl that has rocked the plane since my take-off. The tank has no gauge, but written on its side is the assurance: 'This tank is good for four hours.'

There is nothing ambiguous about such a guaranty. I believe it, but at twenty-five minutes to eleven, my motor coughs and dies, and the Gull is powerless above the sea.

I realize that the heavy drone of the plane has been, until this moment, complete and comforting silence. It is the actual silence following the last splutter of the engine that stuns me.

I can't feel any fear; I can't feel anything. I can only observe with a kind of stupid disinterest that my hands are violently active and know that, while they move, I am being hypnotized by the needle of my altimeter.

I suppose that the denial of natural impulse is what is meant by 'keeping calm,' but impulse has reason in it. If it is night and you are sitting in an aeroplane with a stalled motor, and there are two thousand feet between you and the sea, nothing can be more reasonable than the impulse to pull back your stick in the hope of adding to that two thousand, if only by a little. The thought, the knowledge, the law that tells you that your hope lies not in this, but in a contrary act — the act of directing your impotent craft toward the water — seems a terrifying abandonment, not only of reason, but of sanity. Your mind and your heart reject it. It is your hands — your stranger's hands — that follow with unfeeling precision the letter of the law.

I sit there and watch my hands push forward on the stick and feel the Gull respond and begin its dive to the sea. Of course it is a simple thing; surely the cabin tank has run dry too soon. I need only to turn another petcock . . .

But it is dark in the cabin. It is easy to see the luminous dial of the altimeter and to note that my height is now eleven hundred feet, but it is not easy to see a petcock that is somewhere near the floor of the plane. A hand gropes and reappears with an electric torch, and fingers, moving with agonizing composure, find the petcock and turn it; and I wait.

At three hundred feet the motor is still dead, and I am conscious that the needle of my altimeter seems to whirl like the spoke of a spindle winding up the remaining distance between the plane and the water. There is some lightning, but the quick flash only serves to emphasize the darkness. How high can waves reach — twenty feet, perhaps? Thirty?

It is impossible to avoid the thought that this is the end of my flight, but my reactions are not orthodox; the various incidents of my entire life do not run through my mind like a motion-picture film gone mad. I only feel that all this has happened before — and it has. It has all happened a hundred times in my mind, in my sleep, so that now I am not really caught in terror; I recognize a familiar scene, a familiar story with its climax dulled by too much telling.

I do not know how close to the waves I am when the motor explodes to life again. But the sound is almost meaningless. I see my hand easing back on the stick, and I feel the Gull climb up into the storm, and I see the altimeter whirl like a spindle again, paying out the distance between myself and the sea.

The storm is strong. It is comforting. It is like a friend shaking me and saying, 'Wake up! You were only dreaming.'

But soon I am thinking. By simple calculation I find that my motor had been silent for perhaps an instant more than thirty seconds.

I ought to thank God — and I do, though indirectly. I thank Geoffrey De Havilland who designed the indomitable Gipsy, and who, after all, must have been designed by God in the first place.

A lighted ship — the daybreak — some steep cliffs standing in the sea. The meaning of these will never change for pilots. If one day an ocean can be flown within an hour, if men can build a plane that so masters time, the sight of land will be no less welcome to the steersman of that fantastic craft. He will have cheated laws that the cunning of science has taught him how to cheat, and he will feel his guilt and be eager for the sanctuary of the soil.

I saw the ship and the daybreak, and then I saw the cliffs of Newfoundland wound in ribbons of fog. I felt the elation I had so long imagined, and I felt the happy guilt of having circumvented the stern authority of the weather and the sea. But mine was a minor triumph; my swift Gull was not so swift as to have escaped unnoticed. The night and the storm had caught her and we had flown blind for nineteen hours.

I was tired now, and cold. Ice began to film the glass of the cabin windows and the fog played a magician's game with the land. But the land was there. I could not see it, but I had seen it. I could not afford to believe that it was any land but the land I wanted. I could not afford to believe that my navigation was at fault, because there was no time for doubt.

South to Cape Race, west to Sydney on Cape Breton Island. With my protractor, my map, and my compass, I set my new course, humming the ditty that Tom had taught me: 'Variation West — magnetic best. Variation East — magnetic least.' A silly rhyme, but it served to placate, for the moment, two warring poles — the magnetic and the true. I flew south and found the lighthouse of Cape Race protruding from the fog like a warning finger. I circled twice and went on over the Gulf of Saint Lawrence.

After a while there would be New Brunswick, and then Maine — and then New York. I could anticipate. I could almost say, 'Well, if you stay awake, you'll find it's only a matter of time now' — but there was no question of staying awake. I was tired and I had not moved an inch since that uncertain moment at Abingdon when the Gull had elected to rise with her load and fly, but I could not have closed my eyes. I could sit there in the cabin, walled in glass and petrol tanks, and be grateful for the sun and the light, and the fact that I could see the water under me. They were almost the last waves I had to pass. Four hundred miles of water, but then the land again — Cape Breton. I would stop at Sydney to refuel and go on. It was easy now. It would be like stopping at Kisumu and going on.

Success breeds confidence. But who has a right to confidence except the Gods? I had a following wind, my last tank of petrol was more than three-quarters full, and the world was as bright to me as if it were a new world, never touched. If I had been wiser, I might have known that such moments are, like innocence, short-lived. My engine began to shudder before I saw the land. It died, it spluttered, it started again and limped along. It coughed and spat black exhaust toward the sea.

There are words for everything. There was a word for this — airlock, I thought. This had to be an airlock because there was petrol enough. I thought I might clear it by turning on and turning off all the empty tanks, and so I did that. The handles of the petcocks were sharp little pins of metal, and when I had opened and closed them a dozen times, I saw that my hands were bleeding and that the blood was dropping on my maps and on my clothes, but the effort wasn't any good. I coasted along on a sick and halting engine. The oil pressure and the oil temperature gauges were normal, the magnetos working, and yet I lost altitude slowly while the realization of failure seeped into my heart. If I made the land, I should have been the first to fly the North Atlantic from England, but from my point of view, from a pilot's point of view, a forced landing was failure because New York was my goal. If only I could land and then take off, I would make it still . . . if only, if only . . .

The engine cuts again, and then catches, and each time it spurts to life I climb as high as I can get, and then it splutters and stops and I glide once more toward the water, to rise again and descend again, like a hunting sea bird.

I find the land. Visibility is perfect now and I see land forty or fifty miles ahead. If I am on my course, that will be Cape

Breton. Minute after minute goes by. The minutes almost materialize; they pass before my eyes like links in a long slow-moving chain, and each time the engine cuts, I see a broken link in the chain and catch my breath until it passes.

The land is under me. I snatch my map and stare at it to confirm my whereabouts. I am, even at my present crippled speed, only twelve minutes from Sydney Airport, where I can land for repairs and then go on.

The engine cuts once more and I begin to glide, but now I am not worried; she will start again, as she has done, and I will gain altitude and fly into Sydney.

But she doesn't start. This time she's dead as death; the Gull settles earthward and it isn't any earth I know. It is black earth stuck with boulders and I hang above it, on hope and on a motionless propeller. Only I cannot hang above it long. The earth hurries to meet me, I bank, turn, and side-slip to dodge the boulders, my wheels touch, and I feel them submerge. The nose of the plane is engulfed in mud, and I go forward striking my head on the glass of the cabin front, hearing it shatter, feeling blood pour over my face.

I stumble out of the plane and sink to my knees in muck and stand there foolishly staring, not at the lifeless land, but at my watch.

Twenty-one hours and twenty-five minutes.

Atlantic flight. Abingdon, England, to a nameless swamp — nonstop.

A Cape Breton Islander found me — a fisherman trudging over the bog saw the Gull with her tail in the air and her nose buried, and then he saw me floundering in the embracing soil of his native land. I had been wandering for an hour and the black mud had got up to my waist and the blood from the cut in my head had met the mud halfway.

290

From a distance, the fisherman directed me with his arms and with shouts toward the firm places in the bog, and for another hour I walked on them and came toward him like a citizen of Hades blinded by the sun, but it wasn't the sun; I hadn't slept for forty hours.

He took me to his hut on the edge of the coast and I found that built upon the rocks there was a little cubicle that housed an ancient telephone — put there in case of shipwrecks.

I telephoned to Sydney Airport to say that I was safe and to prevent a needless search being made. On the following morning I did step out of a plane at Floyd Bennett Field and there was a crowd of people still waiting there to greet me, but the plane I stepped from was not the Gull, and for days while I was in New York I kept thinking about that and wishing over and over again that it had been the Gull, until the wish lost its significance, and time moved on, overcoming many things it met on the way.

XXIV

The Sea Will Take Small Pride

LIKE all oceans, the Indian Ocean seems never to end, and the ships that sail on it are small and slow. They have no speed, nor any sense of urgency; they do not cross the water, they live on it until the land comes home.

I can't remember her name any more, but the little freighter I sailed on, from Australia to South Africa, appeared not to move for nearly a month, and during the voyage I sat on the deck and read books, or thought about past things, or talked with the few other dwellers in our bobbing cloister.

I was going back to Africa to see my father, after an interval too long, too crowded, and now complete; it was the end of a phase that I felt had grown and rounded out and tapered to its full design, inevitably, like a leaf. I might have started from any place on the earth, I thought, from whatever point — but in the end I should still have been there, on that toy boat, measuring the time.

I carried with me the paper treasure I had gathered — cablegrams about my Atlantic flight from everywhere, a few newspaper clippings culled out of many, a picture of the Vega Gull, nose down in the Nova Scotia bog — and some of the things that had been written about Tom.

Tom was dead. He had been killed at the controls of his plane, and I had got the news a long time ago in New York. It had been telephoned to me from London while I sat, still dazed, in the midst of ringing bells and telegrams and eager people telling me what a fine thing I had done to have almost made Floyd Bennett Field — and would I sign an autograph? There was even a letter in my file, purporting to have been written by a dog, signed 'Jojo.' I was deeply grateful for the warmth and unending kindness of America, but I had no complaint about the transitory nature of my fame.

Tom had been killed simply, and avoidably — on the ground. While he was taxi-ing to a take-off position on the Liverpool Aerodrome, an incoming plane had struck his plane, and that was all. No one else had been injured, but Tom had been killed. I suppose it was no more than chance that he had died with the blade of a propeller buried under his heart.

The Gull too was dead. I had been unable to buy her after my flight, and so J. C. had shipped her to Seramai and sold her to a wealthy Indian who might have understood many things, but not the beauty, nor the needs, of a plane. He left her exposed to the weather on the airport at Dar es Salaam until her engine rusted and her wings peeled and she was forgotten by everyone, I think, except myself. Perhaps, by now, some official with an eye for immaculacy, has had her skeleton dragged to the sea and buried in it, but the sea will take small pride in that. The Gull had not failed me. When she was checked, after my flight, it was learned that somewhere off the coast of Newfoundland ice had lodged in the air intake of the last petrol tank, partially choking fuel flow to the carburetor. I had wondered since how, so handicapped, the Gull had flown so long.

All this had happened, and if some of it was hard for me to believe, I had my logbooks and my pound of scraps and papers to prove it to myself — memory in ink. It was only needed that someone should say, 'You ought to write about it, you know. You really ought!'

And so the little freighter sat upon the sea, and, though Africa came closer day by day, the freighter never moved. She was old and weather-weary, and she had learned to let the world come round to her.